CONCEPTS IN ENTERPRISE RESOURCE PLANNING

Fourth Edition

CONCEPTS IN ENTERPRISE RESOURCE PLANNING

Fourth Edition

Ellen F. Monk
University of Delaware

Bret J. Wagner
Western Michigan University

COURSE TECHNOLOGY
CENGAGE Learning·

Australia • Brazil • Japan • Korea • Mexico • Singapore • Spain • United Kingdom • United States

COURSE TECHNOLOGY
CENGAGE Learning·

Concepts in Enterprise Resource Planning, Fourth Edition

Ellen F. Monk and Bret J. Wagner

Editor-in-Chief: Joe Sabatino

Senior Acquisitions Editor: Charles McCormick, Jr.

Senior Product Manager: Kate Mason

Development Editor: Mary Pat Shaffer

Senior Marketing Communications Manager: Libby Shipp

Marketing Coordinator: Eileen Corcoran

Design Direction, Production Management, and Composition: PreMediaGlobal

Media Editor: Chris Valentine

Cover Credit:

Woman holding tablet: Howard Kingsnorth/ The Image Bank/Getty Images

Grain plant: Copyright: ©John Foxx/Stockbyte/ Thinkstock

Bag of grain and hands: Copyright: ©Brand X Pictures/Thinkstock

Cutting the field with machinery, evening harvest: Copyright: ©iStockphoto/Thinkstock

Grain (soy) pouring from machine into bin: Copyright: ©iStockphoto/Thinkstock

Truck on bridge: Copyright: ©Hemera/Thinkstock

Girl Holding granola bar: ©iStockphoto.com/ Fine Collection

Manufacturing Coordinator: Julio Esperas

Library of Congress Control Number: 2012934925

Student Edition
ISBN-13: 978-1-111-82039-8
ISBN-10: 1-111-82039-2

Instructor Edition
ISBN-13: 978-1-111-82040-4
ISBN-10: 1-111-82040-6

Course Technology
20 Channel Center Street
Boston, MA 02210
USA

Printed in the United States of America
1 2 3 4 5 6 7 16 15 14 13 12

In memory of our colleague Majdi Najm.
His support and friendship are sorely missed.

BRIEF CONTENTS

TABLE OF CONTENTS

PREFACE

This is a book about Enterprise Resource Planning (ERP) systems; it is also about how a business works and how information systems fit into business operations. More specifically, it is about looking at the processes that make up a business enterprise and seeing how ERP software can improve the performance of these business processes. ERP software is complicated and expensive. Unless a company uses it to become more efficient and effective in delivering goods and services to its customers, an ERP system will only be a drain on company resources.

Our experience in teaching about ERP systems has revealed that undergraduate business students do not always understand how businesses operate, and advanced undergraduate students—and even many MBA students—do not truly grasp the problems inherent in unintegrated systems. These students also do not comprehend business processes and how different functional areas must work together to achieve company goals. As a result, many students do not understand how an information system should help business managers make decisions.

Consequently, we set out to write a book that does the following:

- Describes basic business functional areas and explains how they are related
- Illustrates how unintegrated information systems fail to support business functions and business processes that cut across functional area boundaries
- Demonstrates how integrated information systems can help a company prosper by improving business processes and by providing business managers with accurate, consistent, and current data

We have found that our focus on business processes has been well received.

The Approach of This Book

A key feature of our book is the use of the fictitious Fitter Snacker Company, a manufacturer of nutritious snack bars, as an illustrative example throughout the book. We show how Fitter Snacker's somewhat primitive and unintegrated information systems cause operational problems. We intentionally made the systems' problems easy to understand, so the student could readily comprehend them. Potential solutions for solving integration problems are illustrated using SAP's ERP software.

The fourth edition of *Concepts in Enterprise Resource Planning* reflects the current state of the ERP software market and other areas of the information technology market that affect ERP systems, while adding updated examples of how companies are using integrated systems to solve business problems and achieve greater success. The book has eight chapters:

- Chapter 1, "Business Functions and Business Processes," explains the purposes for, and information systems requirements of, **main business functional areas**—Marketing and Sales, Supply Chain Management, Accounting and

Finance, and Human Resources. This chapter also describes how a business process cuts across the activities within business functional areas and why managers need to think about making business processes work.

- Chapter 2, "The Development of Enterprise Resource Planning Systems," provides a short history of business computing and the **developments that led to today's ERP systems**. Chapter 2 concludes with an overview of ERP issues and an introduction to the SAP ERP software.

- Chapter 3, "Marketing Information Systems and the Sales Order Process," describes the **Marketing and Sales functional area**, and it highlights the problems that arise with unintegrated information systems. To make concepts easy to understand, the Fitter Snacker running example is introduced. After explaining Fitter Snacker's problems with its unintegrated systems, we show how an ERP system can help a company avoid these problems. Sample SAP ERP screens are used to illustrate the concepts. Because using ERP can naturally lead a company into ever-broadening systems' integration, a discussion of customer-relationship management (CRM) software concludes the chapter.

- Chapter 4, "Production and Supply Chain Management Information Systems," describes how ERP systems support Supply Chain Management—the coordinated activities of all the organizations involved in converting raw materials into consumer products on the retail shelf. As in Chapter 3, the problems caused by Fitter Snacker's unintegrated information system are explored, followed by a discussion of how ERP software could help solve these problems.

- Chapter 5, "Accounting in ERP Systems," describes accounting processes and how ERP systems support those processes. This chapter clearly distinguishes between financial accounting (FI) and managerial accounting (CO) issues. Included is an overview of the Enron collapse and the resulting Sarbanes-Oxley Act along with the act's impact on information systems, specifically management controls and audit capabilities. XBRL—and its relationship to ERP systems and financial reporting—is explored, along with the transition to the IFRS accounting standards.

- Chapter 6, "Human Resources Processes with ERP," covers human resource management. While the Human Resource software module is the least integrated component of all ERP systems, it includes numerous processes that are critical to a company's success, including strategic issues like succession planning.

- Chapter 7, "Process Modeling, Process Improvement, and ERP Implementation," first presents flowcharting basics, followed by the highly structured EPC process model. Implementation issues conclude the chapter. We believe that process improvement, not large-scale implementation, should be the focus in an introductory ERP course.

- Chapter 8, "RFID, Business Intelligence (BI), Mobile Computing, and the Cloud," covers current technologies that are impacting ERP systems. In this edition, the text covers radio frequency identification (RFID), business intelligence (BI) and in-memory computing, mobile computing, and the cloud. Because technology changes rapidly, this chapter provides an introduction to these current topics, rather than an exhaustive treatment of the subjects, and the instructor will likely want to provide current supplements.

How Can You Use This Book?

This fourth edition continues our goal of keeping the text at an introductory level. The book can be used in a number of ways:

- The book, or selected chapters, could be used for a three-week ERP treatment in undergraduate Management Information Systems, Accounting Information Systems, or Operations Management courses.
- Similarly, the book or selected chapters could be used in MBA courses, such as foundation Information Systems or Operations Management courses. Although the concepts presented here are basic, the astute instructor can build on them with more sophisticated material to challenge the advanced MBA student. Many of the exercises in the book require research for their solution, and the MBA student could do these in some depth.
- The book could serve as an introductory text in a course devoted wholly to ERP. It would provide the student with a basis in how ERP systems help companies to integrate different business functions. The instructor might use Chapter 8 as the starting point for teaching the higher-level strategic implications of ERP and related topics. The instructor can pursue these and related topics using his or her own resources, such as case studies and current articles.
- Because of the focus on fundamental business issues and business processes, the book can also be used in a sophomore-level Introduction to Business course.

Except for a computer literacy course, we assume no particular educational or business background. Chapters 1 and 2 lay out most of the needed business and computing groundwork, and the rest of the chapters build on that base.

Features of This Text

To bring ERP concepts to life (and down to earth) this book uses sales, manufacturing, purchasing, human resources, and accounting examples for the Fitter Snacker company. Thus, the student can see problems, not just at an abstract level, but within the context of a company's operations. We believe this approach makes business problems and the role ERP can play in solving them easier to understand.

The book's exercises have the student analyze aspects of Fitter Snacker's information systems in various ways. The exercises vary in their difficulty; some can be solved in a straightforward way, and others require some research. Not all exercises need to be assigned. This gives the instructor flexibility in choosing which concepts to emphasize and how to assess students' knowledge. Some exercises explore Fitter Snacker's problems, and some ask the student to go beyond what is taught in the book and to research a subject. A solution might require the student to generate a spreadsheet, perform calculations, document higher-level reasoning, present the results of research in writing, or participate in a debate.

The book includes an additional element designed to bring ERP concepts to life: Another Look features, which are short, detailed case studies that focus on problems faced by real-world companies.

We have illustrated ERP concepts and applications by showing how SAP ERP would handle the problems discussed in the book. Screen shots of key SAP ERP tools are shown throughout to illustrate ERP concepts. Many of the book's exercises ask the student to think about how a problem would be addressed using ERP software.

Instructor Materials

The following supplemental materials are available when this book is used in a classroom setting. All of the teaching tools available with this book are provided to the instructor on a single CD-ROM. Most can also be found online at www.course.com. Instructor materials are password-protected.

- **Electronic Instructor's Manual**—The Instructor's Manual assists in class preparation by providing suggestions and strategies for teaching the text, chapter outlines, technical notes, quick quizzes, discussion topics, and key terms.
- **Solutions**—Answers to end-of-chapter questions and exercises are provided.
- **Sample syllabi**—The sample syllabi and course outlines are provided as a foundation to begin planning and organizing your course.
- **ExamView Test Bank**—ExamView allows instructors to create and administer printed, computer (LAN-based), and Internet exams. The Test Bank includes hundreds of questions that correspond to the topics covered in this text, enabling students to generate detailed study guides that include page references for further review. The computer-based and Internet testing components allow students to take exams at their computers, and also save the instructor time by grading each exam automatically. The Test Bank is also available in Blackboard and WebCT versions posted online at www.course.com.
- **PowerPoint Presentations**—Microsoft PowerPoint slides for each chapter are included as a teaching aid for classroom presentation, to make available to students on the network for chapter review, or to be printed for classroom distribution. Instructors can add their own slides for additional topics they introduce to the class.
- **Distance learning**—Course Technology is proud to present online test banks in WebCT and Blackboard to provide the most complete and dynamic learning experience possible. Instructors are encouraged to make the most of the course, both online and offline. For more information on how to access the online test bank, contact your local Course Technology sales representative.
- **Figure files**—Figure and table files from each chapter are provided for your use in the classroom.
- **Hands-on SAP exercises**—Exercises are available for member institutions through the SAP University Alliance. These exercises use a database that was built for the fictitious Fitter Snacker company.

ACKNOWLEDGMENTS

Our thanks go out to our development editor, Mary Pat Shaffer, whose attention to detail made much more work for us, but resulted in a much-improved text for this edition. We are grateful for the support and guidance of the entire MIS team at Course Technology, particularly Kate Mason, Senior Product Manager, and Aimee Poirier, MIS Product Manager, for working with authors who frequently had problems meeting deadlines. We would not have been able to continue on our journey to understand ERP systems without the continued support of SAP America through its University Alliance program, especially Heather Czech Matthews, John Baxter, Gale Corbitt, and Alex McLeod, Jr. And finally, we thank our students, whose honesty and desire to learn have inspired us.

CHAPTER 1

BUSINESS FUNCTIONS AND BUSINESS PROCESSES

LEARNING OBJECTIVES

After completing this chapter, you will be able to:

- Name the main functional areas of operation used in business
- Differentiate between a business process and a business function
- Identify the kinds of data each main functional area produces
- Identify the kinds of data each main functional area needs
- Define integrated information systems, and explain why they are essential in today's globally competitive business environment

INTRODUCTION

Enterprise Resource Planning (ERP) systems are core software programs used by companies to integrate and coordinate information in every area of the business. ERP (pronounced "*E-R-P*") programs help organizations manage company-wide business processes, using a common database and shared management reporting tools. A **business process** is a collection of activities that takes one or more kinds of input and creates an output, such as a report or forecast, that is of value to the customer. ERP software supports the efficient operation of business processes by integrating tasks related to sales, marketing, manufacturing, logistics, accounting, and staffing—throughout a business. In addition to this cross-functional integration, which is at the heart of an ERP system, companies connect their ERP systems, using various methods, to coordinate business processes with their customers and suppliers. In later chapters, you will learn how successful businesspeople use ERP programs to improve how work is done within a company and between companies. Chapter 1 provides a background for learning about ERP software.

FUNCTIONAL AREAS AND BUSINESS PROCESSES

To understand ERP, you must first understand how a business works. Let's begin by looking at a typical business's areas of operation. These areas, called **functional areas of operation**, are broad categories of business activities.

Functional Areas of Operation

Most companies have four main functional areas of operation: Marketing and Sales (M/S), Supply Chain Management (SCM), Accounting and Finance (A/F), and Human Resources (HR). Each area is composed of a variety of narrower **business functions**, which are activities specific to that functional area of operation. Examples of the business functions of each area are shown in Figure 1-1.

Functional area of operation	Marketing and Sales	Supply Chain Management	Accounting and Finance	Human Resources
Business functions	Marketing a product	Purchasing goods and raw materials	Financial accounting of payments from customers and to suppliers	Recruiting and hiring
	Taking sales orders	Receiving goods and raw materials	Cost allocation and control	Training
	Customer support	Transportation and logistics	Planning and budgeting	Payroll
	Customer relationship management	Scheduling production runs	Cash-flow management	Benefits
	Sales forecasting	Manufacturing goods		Government compliance
	Advertising	Plant maintenance		

Source Line: Course Technology/Cengage Learning.

FIGURE 1-1   Examples of functional areas of operation and their business functions

Historically, businesses have had organizational structures that separated the functional areas. Business schools have been similarly organized, so each functional area has been taught as a separate course. In a company separating functional areas in this way, Marketing and Sales might be completely isolated from Supply Chain Management, even though the Marketing and Sales staff sell what the employees in Supply Chain Management procure and produce. Thus, you might conclude that what happens in one functional area is not closely related to what happens in others. As you will learn in this chapter, however, functional areas are interdependent, each requiring data from the others. The better a company can integrate the activities of each functional area, the more successful it will be in today's highly competitive environment. The Association to Advance Collegiate Schools of Business (AACSB)—the accreditation board of university business schools—is now promoting integration between functional areas of business for higher education.

Integration also contributes to improvements in communication and workflow. Each area's information system depends on data from other functional areas. An **information system (IS)** includes the people, procedures, software, and computers that store, organize, analyze, and deliver information. This chapter illustrates the need for information sharing between functional areas and the effects on the business if this information is not integrated. In later sections, you will also see some examples of typical business processes and how these processes routinely cross functional areas.

Business Processes

More managers are now thinking in terms of business processes rather than business functions. Recall that a business process is a collection of activities that takes one or more kinds of input and creates an output that is of value to the customer. The customer for a business process may be a traditional external customer (the person who buys the finished product), or it may be an internal customer (such as a colleague in another department). For example, what is sold through Marketing and Sales is linked to what is procured and produced by Supply Chain Management. This concept is illustrated in Figure 1-2.

Input	Functional area responsible for input	Process	Output
Request to purchase smartphone	Marketing and Sales	Sales order	Order is generated
Financial help for purchase	Accounting and Finance	Arranging financing in-house	Customer finances through the smartphone company
Fulfillment of order	Supply Chain Management	Shipping and delivery	Customer receives smartphone
Technical support	Marketing and Sales	24-hour help line available	Customer's technical query is resolved

Source Line: Course Technology/Cengage Learning.

FIGURE 1-2   Sample business processes related to the sale of a smartphone

Thinking in terms of business processes helps managers look at their organization from the customer's perspective. Consider the example illustrated in Figure 1-2 of a customer who wants to purchase a new smartphone. The customer wants information about the company's products so she can select a smartphone and various high-tech accessories for the phone. She wants to place her order quickly and easily, and perhaps even arrange for financing through the company. She expects quick delivery of the correct model of smartphone, and she wants 24-hour customer support for any problems. The customer is not concerned about how the smartphone was marketed, how its components were purchased, how it was built, or how the delivery truck will find the best route to her house. The customer wants the satisfaction of having the latest in mobile phone technology at a reasonable price.

Businesses must always consider the customer's viewpoint in any transaction. What is the difference between a business function and a business process from the customer's point of view? Suppose the customer's mobile phone is damaged during shipment. Because only one functional area is involved in accepting the return of the damaged item, receipt of the return is a *business function*—specifically, it is part of the customer relationship management function of Marketing and Sales. Because several functional areas are involved in the repair and return of the mobile phone back to the customer, the handling of the repair is a *business process*. Thus, in this example, the customer is dealing with many of the company's functional areas in the process of buying and obtaining a smartphone.

A successful customer interaction is one in which the customer (either internal or external) is not required to interact separately with each business function involved in the process. If companies are not coordinating their business functions, a customer could receive conflicting information and likely would quickly become dissatisfied. Successful business managers view their business operations from the perspective of a satisfied customer and strive to present one consistent (and positive) "face" to the customer.

For the mobile phone company to satisfy its customers, it must make sure its functional areas of operation are integrated. Mobile phone technology changes rapidly, and the devices the phone company sells change frequently. To provide customers with accurate information, people performing the sales function must have up-to-date information about the latest mobile phones available for sale; otherwise, a customer might order a smartphone that the company's manufacturing plant no longer produces. People performing the manufacturing function need to receive the details of a customer's smartphone order quickly and accurately from the employee (or online ordering system) performing the sales function, so the right phone can be packaged and shipped on time to the customer. If the customer is financing the smartphone through the mobile phone company, the employees performing the sales order function must gather information about the customer and process it quickly, so financing can be approved in time to support shipping the phone.

Sharing data effectively and efficiently between and within functional areas leads to more efficient business processes. Information systems that are designed so functional areas share data are called **integrated information systems**. Working through this textbook will help you understand the benefits of integrated information systems and the problems that can occur when information systems are not integrated. Research has shown that integrated information systems can help managers better control their organizations. With enhanced information flow, communication between parts of the company improves, productivity increases, and costs decrease. In effect, integrating the information systems can make for a more effective overall organization—hence, more efficient business processes. Figure 1-3 illustrates the process view of business operations.

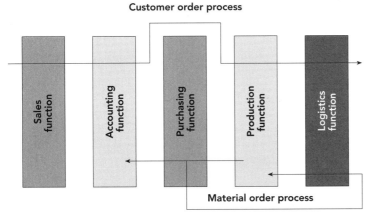

Source Line: Course Technology/Cengage Learning.

FIGURE 1-3 A process view of business operations

   Businesses take inputs (resources) in the form of material, people, and equipment, and transform these inputs into goods and services for customers. Effectively managing these inputs and business processes requires accurate and up-to-date information. For example, the sales staff takes a customer's order, and production employees schedule the manufacturing of the product. Logistics employees schedule and carry out the delivery of the product. If raw materials are needed to make the product, production prompts purchasing staff to arrange for their purchase and delivery. Logistics will receive the raw material, verify its receipt to accounting so the vendor can be paid, and deliver the goods to production. Throughout, accounting keeps appropriate transaction records.

ANOTHER LOOK

Integrated Information Systems

The world today is information driven. Getting the right information to the right person can make a huge difference in terms of a company's bottom line. But are some systems just too complicated to be fully integrated? Although the financial services industry spends more on information technology than any other industry ($500 billion worldwide in 2009), many financial institutions do not have fully integrated information systems.

   Why is this so? The reasons are many. Banks were the first organizations to adopt information systems, so many of their systems are legacy (old) systems that would be difficult and expensive to update. In addition, many banks have gone through multiple phases of acquisition, which in itself results in duplicate information systems. Government regulations on financial institutions have also brought about additional

(continued)

systems. And many financial organizations write their own proprietary systems for market trading, thinking that gives them a leg up on their competition. Some of the more sophisticated financial products, such as hedge funds and derivatives, are generated via complex programs. In addition, a great deal of financial tracking is performed on spreadsheets, which may not be connected to any integrated system.

The end result of these unintegrated systems is a lack of consistent data across systems, which can lead to an inaccurate assessment of risk. Most financial systems written today are honed for rapid trading, not for regulation or for tracking anomalies that could lead to problems. Some IT experts claim that the global financial networks are now unstable and that the fast quantitative trading programs in place could lead rapidly to potentially disastrous outcomes.

Question:

1. Do you think some of the problems associated with the financial crisis of 2008 could have been avoided if financial firms had more integrated information? If so, how, or if not, why not?

FUNCTIONAL AREAS AND BUSINESS PROCESSES OF A VERY SMALL BUSINESS

Next, we will look at the way business processes involve more than one functional area, using a fictitious small business as an example—a coffee shop that you own. We will examine the business processes of the coffee shop and see why coordination of the functional areas helps achieve efficient and effective business processes. You will see the role that information plays in this coordination and how integration of the information system improves your business.

Even though just a few people can run a small coffee shop, the operation of the business requires a number of processes. Coordinating the activities within different functional areas requires accurate and timely information.

Marketing and Sales

Marketing and Sales (M/S) functions include developing products, determining pricing, promoting products to customers, and taking customers' orders. Marketing and Sales also helps create a sales forecast to ensure the successful operation of the coffee shop.

For the most part, this is a cash business, but you still need to keep track of your customers so you can send flyers or occasional thank-you notes to repeat customers. Thus, your records must not only show the amount of sales, but also identify repeat customers.

Product development can be done informally in such a simple business; you gather information about who buys which kind of coffee and note what customers say about each product. You also analyze historical sales records to spot trends that are not obvious. Deciding whether to sell a product also depends on how much it costs to produce the product. For example, some customers might be asking for a fair-trade decaffeinated coffee or a chai tea. To determine whether the new product could be profitably produced and sold, you could analyze data from Supply Chain Management, including production information (such as the cost of purchasing an extra coffee machine to make the special fair-trade decaffeinated brew) and materials management data (the cost of decaffeinated coffee beans and chai tea).

This is a very small coffee shop, and you know most of your clientele. Therefore, although you run a cash business, good repeat customers are allowed to run up a tab—up to a point. Thus, your records must show how much each customer owes as well as his or her available credit. It is very important that the data be available and accurate at the time of a customer's credit request. Since Accounting and Finance records must be accessed as a part of the selling process, the accounting function has a critical role to play in the sales process.

Supply Chain Management

The functions within **Supply Chain Management (SCM)** include developing production plans, ordering raw materials from suppliers, receiving the raw material into the facility, manufacturing products, maintaining facilities, and shipping products to customers. In our coffee shop example, Supply Chain Management functions involve making the coffee (manufacturing/production) and buying raw materials (purchasing). Production is planned so that, as much as possible, coffee is available when needed, without excess that must be disposed of. This planning requires sales forecasts from the Marketing and Sales functional area. **Sales forecasts** are estimates of future product demand, which is the amount of a product customers will want to buy. A forecast's accuracy will be improved if it is based on historical sales figures (for example, factors such as cold weather or local downtown social events would impact the forecast for a given time period). Thus, forecasts from Marketing and Sales play an important role in the production planning process.

Production plans are also used to develop requirements for raw materials (coffee beans, tea bags, sweeteners, cream, and milk) and packaging (cups, stirrers, straws, plates, and napkins). You must generate raw material and packaging orders from these requirements. If the forecasts are accurate, you will not lose sales because of material shortages, nor will you have excessive inventory that might spoil.

Supply Chain Management and Marketing and Sales must choose a recipe for each beverage product sold, such as the quantity of coffee beans used to brew each pot of coffee. The standard recipe is a key input for deciding how much to order of each raw material, which is a purchasing function. Access to this recipe is also necessary for keeping good manufacturing records, allowing managers within the Supply Chain Management functional area (working with those in Accounting and Finance) to break down the costs to a per-cup cost. Managers can then compare how much it actually costs to make a cup of coffee, versus how much the recipe *should* have cost.

Accounting and Finance

Accounting and Finance (A/F) performs financial accounting to provide summaries of operational data in managerial reports, and it is also responsible for tasks such as controlling accounts, planning and budgeting, and cash-flow management. Accounting and Finance functions include recording raw data about sales transactions, raw material purchases, payroll, and receipt of cash from customers. **Raw data** are simply numbers collected from sales, manufacturing, and other operations—without any manipulation, calculation, or arrangement for presentation. Those data are then summarized in meaningful ways to determine the profitability of the coffee shop and to support decision making.

Note that data from Accounting and Finance are used by Marketing and Sales as well as by Supply Chain Management. The sales records are an important component of the sales forecast, which is used in making staffing decisions and in production planning. The records from accounts receivable, which you use to determine whether to grant credit to a particular customer, are also used to monitor the overall credit-granting policy of the coffee shop. You need to be sure you have enough cash on hand to purchase raw materials, as well as to finance the purchase of new equipment, such as an additional coffee machine for the fair-trade decaffeinated coffee.

Human Resources

Even a simple business needs employees to support the Marketing and Sales and Supply Chain Management functional areas, which means the business must recruit, train, evaluate, and compensate employees. These are the functions of **Human Resources (HR)**.

At the coffee shop, the number of employees needed and the timing of hiring depend on the level of coffee and tea sales. Human Resources uses sales forecasts to plan personnel needs. A part-time helper might be needed at forecasted peak hours or days, but how much should a part-time helper be paid? That depends on prevailing job market conditions and state laws, and it is Human Resources' job to monitor those conditions.

Would increased sales justify hiring a part-time worker at the prevailing wage? Or, should you think about acquiring more automated ways of making coffee, so a person working alone could run the shop? Resolving these questions requires input from Marketing and Sales, Supply Chain Management, and Accounting and Finance.

The coffee shop, while a relatively simple business, has many of the processes needed in larger organizations, and these processes involve activities in more than one functional area. In fact, it is impossible to discuss the processes in one functional area without discussing the links to other functional areas—connections that invariably require the sharing of data. Systems that are integrated using ERP software provide the data sharing that is necessary between functional areas.

FUNCTIONAL AREA INFORMATION SYSTEMS

This section will describe potential inputs and outputs for each functional area of a business (refer back to Figure 1-2 to review sample inputs and outputs related to the sale of a smartphone). Note the kinds of data needed by each area and how people use the data. Also note that the information systems maintain relationships between all functional areas and processes.

Marketing and Sales

As shown in Figure 1-4, the Marketing and Sales (M/S) area needs information from all other functional areas to effectively complete the business activities for which it is responsible.

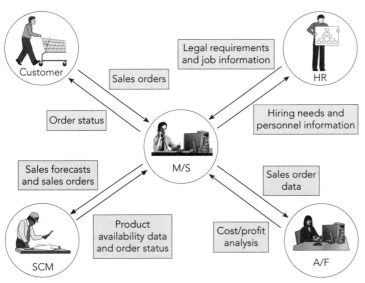

Source Line: Course Technology/Cengage Learning.

FIGURE 1-4   The Marketing and Sales functional area exchanges data with customers and with the Human Resources, Accounting and Finance, and Supply Chain Management functional areas

Customers communicate their orders to sales staff in person or by telephone, email, fax, the Web, and so on. In the case of Web-based systems, customer and order data are stored automatically in the information system; otherwise, data must be entered manually, by typing data into a computer keyboard or point-of-sale system, or by using a bar-code reader or similar device. Sales orders must be passed to Supply Chain Management for planning purposes and to Accounting and Finance for billing. Sales order data are also valuable for analyzing sales trends for business decision making. For example, Marketing and Sales management might use a report showing the trend of a product's sales to evaluate marketing efforts and to determine strategies for the sales force.

Marketing and Sales also has a role in determining product prices, which requires an understanding of the market competition and the costs of manufacturing the product. Pricing might be determined based on a product's unit cost, plus some percentage markup. For example, if a product costs $5 per unit to make, and management wants a 40 percent markup, the selling price must be $7 per unit. Where does the per-unit cost data come from? Determining the cost of manufacturing a product requires information from Accounting and Finance, which, in turn, relies on Supply Chain Management data.

People are a valuable asset to the firm, and Marketing and Sales needs to interact with Human Resources to exchange information on hiring needs, legal requirements, and other matters. For example, when Marketing and Sales has an opening for a junior salesperson, Human Resources will do the advertising for the job vacancy. Human Resources might also communicate information about expense reimbursement policies to salespeople whose jobs require travel.

To summarize, inputs for Marketing and Sales could include the following:

- Customer data
- Order data
- Sales trend data
- Per-unit cost
- Company travel expense policy

Outputs for Marketing and Sales could include the following:

- Sales strategies
- Product pricing
- Employment needs

Supply Chain Management

Supply Chain Management (SCM) also needs information from the various functional areas, as shown in Figure 1-5.

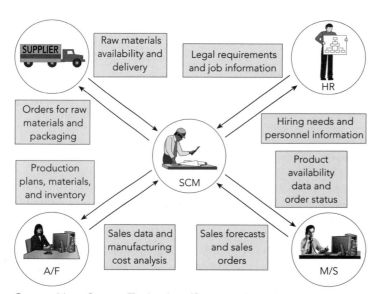

Source Line: Course Technology/Cengage Learning.

FIGURE 1-5   The Supply Chain Management functional area exchanges data with suppliers and with the Human Resources, Marketing and Sales, and Accounting and Finance functional areas

Manufacturing firms often develop production plans of varying length and detail, such as short-range, medium-range, and long-range plans. Plans could be developed for expanding manufacturing capacity (based on sales forecasts), hiring new workers, and paying extra overtime for existing workers.

Production plans are based on information about product sales (actual and projected), which comes from Marketing and Sales. The purchasing function bases its orders of raw materials on production plans, expected shipments, delivery lead times, and existing inventory levels. With accurate data about required production levels, raw material and packaging can be ordered as needed, and inventory levels can be kept low, saving money. On the other hand, if data are inaccurate or not current, manufacturing may run out of raw material or packaging; such a shortfall is called a **stockout**. Shortages of this type can shut down production and cause the company to miss delivery dates. To avoid stockouts, management might choose to carry extra raw material and packaging, known as **safety stock**, which can result in an overinvestment in inventory. If certain time-sensitive goods are held too long, they can spoil and will have to be destroyed rather than sold for profit. The accuracy of the forecast determines the amount of safety stock required to reduce the risk of a stockout to an acceptable level. The less accurate the forecast, the more safety stock is required. Accurate forecasting and production planning can reduce the need for extra inventory and manufacturing capacity. In addition, Supply Chain Management can share its planning information with the company's suppliers so they can plan their operations more efficiently, which should allow the suppliers to reduce the price they charge the company for their products.

Supply Chain Management records can provide the data needed by Accounting and Finance to determine how much of each resource (materials, labor, supplies, and overhead) was used to make completed products in inventory.

Supply Chain Management data can support the Marketing and Sales function by providing information about what has been produced and shipped. For example, online retailers such as Amazon provide detailed information on customer orders through their Web sites, and some send automated emails to notify customers when their orders have shipped. Shipping companies, such as UPS and FedEx, provide online shipment-tracking information. By entering a tracking number, the customer can see each step of the shipping process by noting where the package's bar code was scanned. Domino's Pizza allows customers who order through their Web site to track the progress of their pizza order— from preparation to baking to delivery. Thus, accurate and timely production information supports the sales process and can increase customer satisfaction. In fact, Amazon ranked number one in the Temkin Group's 2011 survey of customer experience. Two of the three survey components relate to business process: functional experience (how well the customer was able to do what they wanted to do) and accessiblility experience (how easy it was to interact with the company). Performing well in such a survey requires a smooth integration of the Marketing and Sales and Supply Chain Management processes.

Supply Chain Management also interacts with Human Resources. For instance, Supply Chain Management passes hiring information to Human Resources, and Human Resources informs Supply Chain Management of the company's layoff and recall policy, which might pertain to workers in the plant.

To summarize, inputs for Supply Chain Management could include the following:

- Product sales data
- Production plans
- Inventory levels
- Layoff and recall company policy

Outputs for Supply Chain Management could include the following:

- Raw material orders
- Packaging orders

- Resource expenditure data
- Production and inventory reports
- Hiring information

Accounting and Finance

Accounting and Finance (A/F) needs information from all the other functional areas to complete its tasks accurately, as shown in Figure 1-6.

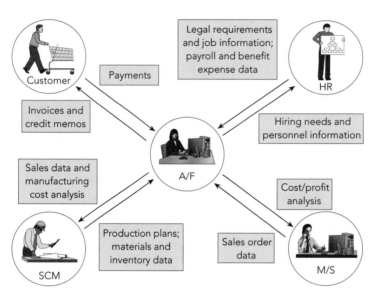

Source Line: Course Technology/Cengage Learning.

FIGURE 1-6   The Accounting and Finance functional area exchanges data with customers and with the Human Resources, Marketing and Sales, and Supply Chain Management functional areas

Accounting and Finance personnel record the company's transactions in the books of account (which often are computerized records). For example, they record accounts receivable when sales are made and cash receipts when customers send in payments. In addition, they record accounts payable when raw materials are purchased and cash outflows when they pay for materials. Finally, Accounting and Finance personnel summarize the transaction data to prepare reports about the company's financial position and profitability.

Employees in other functional areas provide data to Accounting and Finance: Marketing and Sales provides sales data, Supply Chain Management provides production and inventory data, and Human Resources provides payroll and benefit expense data. The accuracy and timeliness of Accounting and Finance data depend on the accuracy and timeliness of the data from the other functional areas.

Marketing and Sales personnel require data from Accounting and Finance to evaluate customer credit. If an order will cause a customer to exceed his or her credit limit, Marketing and Sales should see that the customer's accounts receivable balance (the amount owed to the company) is too high and hold new orders until the customer's balance is lowered. If Accounting and Finance is slow to record sales, the accounts receivable balances will be inaccurate, and Marketing and Sales might approve credit for customers who have already exceeded their credit limits and who might never pay off their accounts. If Accounting and Finance does not record customers' payments promptly, the company could deny credit to customers who actually owe less than their credit limit, potentially damaging the company's relationship with those customers.

To summarize, inputs for Accounting and Finance could include the following:

- Payments from customers
- Accounts receivable data
- Accounts payable data
- Sales data
- Production and inventory data
- Payroll and expense data

Outputs for Accounting and Finance could include the following:

- Payments to suppliers
- Financial reports
- Customer credit data

Human Resources

Like the other functional areas, Human Resources (HR) needs information from the other departments to efficiently complete its business activities, as shown in Figure 1-7.

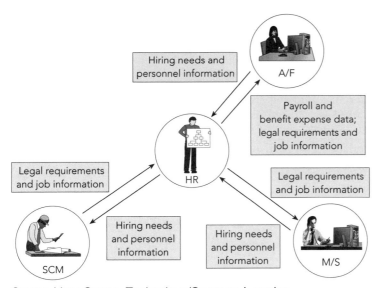

Source Line: Course Technology/Cengage Learning.

FIGURE 1-7   The Human Resources functional area exchanges data with the Accounting and Finance, Marketing and Sales, and Supply Chain Management functional areas

Tasks related to employee hiring, benefits, training, and government compliance are all the responsibilities of a human resources department. Human Resources staff need accurate forecasts of personnel needs from all functional units. In addition, Human Resources needs to know what skills are required to perform a particular job and how much the company can afford to pay employees. These data also come from all functional units.

State and federal laws require companies to observe many governmental regulations in recruiting, training, compensating, promoting, and terminating employees—and these regulations must be observed company-wide. Usually, it is also Human Resources' responsibility to ensure that employees receive training in a timely manner and that they get certified (and recertified) in key skills, such as materials handling and equipment operation. Human Resources must also disburse wages, salaries, raises, and bonuses. For these and other reasons, corporate Human Resources needs timely and accurate data from other areas.

Human Resources must create accurate and timely data and reports for management use. For example, Human Resources should maintain a database of skills required to do particular jobs as well as the prevailing pay rate for each position. When the company evaluates employees' performance and compensation, analysis of these data can help to prevent the loss of valued employees because of low pay.

To summarize, inputs for Human Resources could include the following:

- Personnel forecasts
- Skills data

Outputs for Human Resources could include the following:

- Regulation compliance
- Employee training and certification
- Skills database
- Employee evaluation and compensation

As shown in Figure 1-4 through Figure 1-7, a significant amount of data is maintained by and shared among the different functional areas. The timeliness and accuracy of these data are critical to each area's success and to the company's ability to make a profit and generate future growth. ERP software allows all the functional areas to share a common database so accurate, real-time information is available. In Chapter 2, we will trace the evolution of data management systems that led to ERP.

ANOTHER LOOK

Integrated Information Systems

Large organizations dealing with hundreds or thousands of suppliers have a difficult task in keeping information flowing to the right person at the right time. At one point, Lockheed Martin Aeronautics, with $13.2 billion in sales (2010) and over 29,000 employees, was running 75 legacy systems, some dating from the 1970s. To stay efficient while keeping customers happy and taking on more aircraft orders, the company decided to implement an Enterprise Resource Planning system.

Lockheed Martin's final system allows suppliers to handle more of their own transactions by accessing the new ERP system through an existing secure Web portal. For example, using the portal, a supplier can now track each step of an order. In addition, the supplier can see the production trends at Lockheed Martin, and plan its own production to satisfy Lockheed Martin's needs—in effect, anticipating orders. Through this integration of many systems into one large ERP system, Lockheed Martin was able to cut costs and connect suppliers worldwide into its system, enabling the company to become more efficient.

In another industry, Tumi, Inc., the luggage and travel products company, was running several legacy systems that were written "in-house," meaning they were programmed by company staff. The different systems covered processes such as taking an order, running the warehouse, and completing financial statements. None of the systems were linked; therefore, passing information from one system to another was a slow and cumbersome process. Tumi could not fill its orders on time, had excess inventory in the warehouse, and was frequently unable to meet customers' shipping deadlines. To address these issues—and to better support the company's expansion plans—Tumi made a conscious effort to make information technology a business driver, and the company brought in an ERP system to integrate the business functions.

With the new integrated ERP system, Tumi has been able to expand its business, decrease inventory by 30 percent, cut its warehouse space by 38 percent, and increase sales by 25 percent. Tumi's management believes that one of the company's primary strengths lies in its integrated systems. Manufacturing is now quick to react when demand increases, and forecasting is more accurate.

Question:

1. Using the Internet, research how many suppliers are typically used for manufacturing large commercial aircraft. List 10 such suppliers and what they do. How would an integrated ERP system, such as the one at Lockheed Martin, help manage all those suppliers?

Chapter Summary

- Companies that make and sell products have business processes that involve four main functional areas: Marketing and Sales (M/S), Supply Chain Management (SCM), Accounting and Finance (A/F), and Human Resources (HR). These areas of operation perform the following functions:

  - Marketing and Sales develops products, sets product prices, promotes products through advertising and marketing, takes customer orders, supports customers, and creates sales forecasts.

  - Supply Chain Management develops production plans, orders raw materials from suppliers, receives the raw material into the facility, manufactures products, maintains facilities, and ships products to customers.

  - Accounting and Finance performs financial accounting to provide summaries of operational data in managerial reports, and also is responsible for tasks such as controlling accounts, planning and budgeting, and cash-flow management.

  - Human Resources recruits, hires, trains, and compensates employees, ensures compliance with government regulations, and oversees the evaluation of employees.

- Each functional area is served by an information system. Information systems capture, process, and store data to provide information needed for decision making.

- Employees working in one functional area often need data from other functional areas. Ideally, functional area information systems are integrated, so shared data are accurate and timely.

- Today, business managers try to think in terms of business processes that integrate the functional areas, thus promoting efficiency and competitiveness. An important aspect of this integration is the need to share information between functional areas, and with business partners. ERP software provides this capability by means of a single common database.

Key Terms

Accounting and Finance (A/F)	integrated information system
business function	Marketing and Sales (M/S)
business process	raw data
Enterprise Resource Planning (ERP)	safety stock
functional areas of operation	sales forecast
Human Resources (HR)	stockout
information system (IS)	Supply Chain Management (SCM)

Exercises

1. Distinguish between a business function and a business process. Describe how a business process cuts across functional lines in an organization. How might a manager organize his or her staff in terms of business processes rather than functional departments? What benefits would there be with this type of organization? What challenges would it pose?

2. How could a university organize its business education around business processes rather than business functions? What would be the benefits to students?

3. Assume your uncle raises bees for honey on his farm. You help him package the honey and sell it on the Internet. Reproduce Figure 1-1 for this small business example. Add a one-sentence description for each function as it relates to selling this artisan honey online.

4. Go to the Amazon Web site (*http://www.amazon.com*), and step through the process of buying an item without actually purchasing the item. Based on this experience, describe the flows of information between Marketing and Sales, Accounting and Finance, and Supply Chain Management at Amazon. How easy is it to buy that item?

5. Using the Internet, research your state's regulations for employing teenagers—such as minimum age of employment. Do the same for a neighboring state. Are the two state regulations the same? Why would it be important for Human Resources to communicate this information to a hiring department?

6. Think of the last time you bought a high-tech electronic item. How does the process of buying that item cut across the store's various functional lines? What information from your receipt would need to be available to the business functions? Which business functions would need that information? How could your receipt help in the process of returning that item?

7. Assume you own and run a small ice cream shop located on the grounds of a private pool. You want to maximize sales and decide that allowing customers to buy on credit could be a big driver of sales since most people come to the pool without cash. What information do you need to keep track of to make sure a given customer doesn't go over their $20 credit limit. What problems might occur?

For Further Study and Research

Amrani, Radouane E., Frantz Rowe, and Bénédicte Geffroy-Maronnat. "The Effects of Enterprise Resource Planning Implementation Strategy on Cross-Functionality." *Information Systems Journal* 16, no. 1 (January 2006): 79.

Aurand, Timothy W., Carol DeMoranville, and Geoffrey L. Gordon. "Cross-Functional Business Programs: Critical Design and Development Considerations." *Mid-American Journal of Business* 16, no. 2 (Fall 2001): 21–30.

Economist. "Silo But Deadly." December 5, 2009. http://www.economist.com/node/15016132.

Hannon, David. "Lockheed Martin Aeronautics Revolutionizes Its Supply Chain." *InsiderPROFILES* 2, no. 2 (April 2011). http://insiderprofiles.wispubs.com/article.aspx?iArticleId=5706.

Hannon, David. "How TUMI, Inc. Cut Inventory by 30% and Increased Sales by 25%." *InsiderPROFILES* 2, no. 1 (January 2011). http://insiderprofiles.wispubs.com/article.aspx?iArticleId=5600.

Temkin Group. "2011 Temkin Experience Ratings." March 29, 2011. http://www.temkingroup.com/news/2011-temkin-experience-ratings.

CHAPTER **2**

THE DEVELOPMENT OF ENTERPRISE RESOURCE PLANNING SYSTEMS

LEARNING OBJECTIVES

After completing this chapter, you will be able to:

- Identify the factors that led to the development of Enterprise Resource Planning (ERP) systems
- Describe the distinguishing modular characteristics of ERP software
- Discuss the pros and cons of implementing an ERP system
- Summarize ongoing developments in ERP

INTRODUCTION

In today's competitive business environment, companies try to provide customers with goods and services faster and less expensively than their competition. How do they do that? Often, the key is an efficient, integrated information system. Increasing the efficiency of information systems results in more efficient management of business processes. When companies have efficient business processes, they can be more competitive in the marketplace.

An Enterprise Resource Planning (ERP) system can help a company integrate its operations by serving as a company-wide computing environment that includes a shared database—delivering consistent data across all business functions in real time. (The term *real time* refers to data and processes that are always current).

This chapter will help you to understand how and why ERP systems came into being and what the future might hold for business information systems. The chapter follows this sequence:

- Review of the evolution of information systems and related causes for the recent development of ERP systems

- Discussion of the few ERP software vendors that dominate the market; the current industry leader, German software maker SAP AG's industry-leading software product, SAP ERP, is discussed as an example of an ERP system.

- Review of the factors influencing a company's decision to purchase an ERP system

- Description of ERP's benefits

- Overview of frequently asked questions related to ERP systems

- Discussion of the future of ERP software, including the emphasis being placed on mobile applications and accessibility of data

THE EVOLUTION OF INFORMATION SYSTEMS

Until recently, most companies had unintegrated information systems that supported only the activities of individual business functional areas. Thus, a company would have a marketing information system, a production information system, and so on—each with its own hardware, software, and methods of processing data and information. Information systems configured in this way are known as a **silos** because each department has its own stack, or silo, of information that is unconnected to the next silo; silos are also known as stovepipes.

Such unintegrated systems might work well within each individual functional area, but to be competitive, a company must share data among all the functional areas. When a company's information systems are not integrated, costly inefficiencies can result. For example, suppose two functional areas have separate, unintegrated information systems. To share data, a clerk in one functional area needs to print out data from another area and then enter the data into her area's information system. Not only does this data input take twice the time, it also significantly increases the chance for data entry errors. Alternatively, this process might be automated by having one information system write data to a file to be read by another information system. This would reduce the probability of errors, but it could only be done periodically (usually overnight or on a weekend) to minimize the disruption to normal business transactions. Because of the time lag in updating the system, the transferred data would rarely be up to date. In addition, data can be defined differently in different data systems; for instance, products might be referred to by different part numbers in different systems. This variance can create further problems in timely and accurate information sharing between functional areas.

It seems obvious today that a business should have integrated software to manage all functional areas. An integrated ERP system, however, is an incredibly complex hardware and software system that was not feasible until the 1990s. Current ERP systems evolved as a result of three things: (1) the advancement of the hardware and software technology (computing power, memory, and communications) needed to support the system, (2) the development of a vision of integrated information systems, and (3) the reengineering of companies to shift from a functional focus to a business-process focus.

Computer Hardware and Software Development

Computer hardware and software developed rapidly in the 1960s and 1970s. The first practical business computers were the mainframe computers of the 1960s. Although these computers began to change the way business was conducted, they were not powerful enough to provide integrated, real-time data for business decision making. Over time, computers got faster, smaller, and cheaper—leading to today's proliferation of mobile devices. The rapid development of computer hardware capabilities has been accurately described by Moore's Law. In 1965, Intel employee Gordon Moore observed that the number of transistors that could be built into a computer chip doubled every 24 months. This meant that in the 1960s and 1970s the capabilities of computer hardware were doubling every 24 months, and this trend has continued, as shown in Figure 2-1.

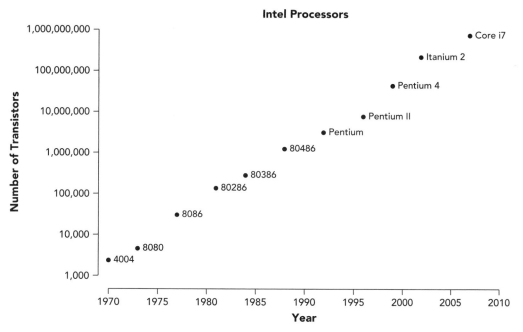

Source Line: "The Evolution of a Revolution," ftp://download.intel.com/pressroom/kits/Intel ProcessorHistory.pdf," Intel.

FIGURE 2-1 The actual increase in transistors on a chip approximates Moore's Law

During this time, computer software was also advancing to take advantage of the increasing capabilities of computer hardware. In the 1970s, relational database software was developed, providing businesses with the ability to store, retrieve, and analyze large volumes of data. Spreadsheet software, a fundamental business tool today, became popular in the 1980s. With spreadsheets, managers could perform complex business analyses without having to rely on a computer programmer to develop custom programs.

The computer hardware and software developments of the 1960s, 1970s, and 1980s paved the way for the development of ERP systems.

Early Attempts to Share Resources

As PCs gained popularity in business in the 1980s, it became clear that users needed a way to share peripheral equipment (such as printers and hard disks, which were fairly expensive in the early 1980s) and, more importantly, data. At that point, important business information was being stored on individual PCs, but there was no easy way to share the information electronically.

By the mid-1980s, telecommunications developments allowed users to share data and peripherals on local networks. Usually, these networks were groups of computers connected to one another within a single physical location. This meant that workers could download data from a central computer to their desktop PCs and work with the data at their desks.

This central computer–local computer arrangement is now called a **client-server architecture**. Servers (central computers) became more powerful and less expensive and provided scalability. **Scalability** means that the capacity of a piece of equipment can be increased by adding new hardware. In the case of a client-server network, the ability to add servers makes the network scalable—thus extending the life of the hardware investment. Scalability is a characteristic of client-server networks, but usually not of mainframe-based systems.

By the end of the 1980s, much of the hardware and software needed to support the development of ERP systems was in place: fast computers, networked access, and advanced database technology. Recall from Chapter 1 that ERP programs help organizations manage company-wide business processes using a common database, which holds a very large amount of data. The software that holds that data in an organized fashion, and that allows for the easy retrieval of data, is the **database management system (DBMS)**. By the mid-1980s, the DBMS required to manage the development of complex ERP software existed. The final element required for the development of ERP software was understanding and acceptance from the business community. Many businesspeople did not yet recognize the benefits of integrated information systems nor were they willing to commit the resources to develop ERP software.

The Manufacturing Roots of ERP

The concept of an integrated information system took shape on the factory floor. Manufacturing software advanced during the 1960s and 1970s, evolving from simple inventory-tracking systems to **material requirements planning (MRP)** software. MRP is a production-scheduling methodology that determines the timing and quantity of production runs and purchase-order releases to meet a master production schedule. MRP software allowed a plant manager to plan production and raw materials requirements by working backward from the sales forecast, the prediction of future sales. The plant manager first looked at Marketing and Sales' forecast of customer demand, then looked at the production schedule needed to meet that demand, calculated the raw materials needed to meet the required production levels, and finally, projected the cost of those raw materials. For a company with many products, raw materials, and shared production resources, this kind of projection was impossible without a computer to keep track of various inputs.

The basic functions of MRP could be handled by mainframe computers; however, the advent of **electronic data interchange (EDI)**—the direct computer-to-computer exchange of standard business documents—allowed companies to handle the purchasing process electronically, avoiding the cost and delays resulting from paper purchase order and invoice systems. The functional area now known as Supply Chain Management (SCM) began with the sharing of long-range production schedules between manufacturers and their suppliers.

Management's Impetus to Adopt ERP

The hard economic times of the late 1980s and early 1990s caused many companies to downsize and reorganize. These company overhauls were one stimulus for ERP development. Companies needed to find some way to avoid the following kind of situation (which they had tolerated for a long time):

> Imagine you are the CEO of Mountaineering, Inc., an outdoor outfitter catering to the young and trendy sportsperson. Mountaineering, Inc. is profitable and keeping pace with the competition, but the company's information systems are unintegrated and inefficient (as are the systems of your competitors). The Marketing and Sales Department creates a time-consuming and unwieldy paper trail when negotiating and closing sales with retailers. To schedule factory production, however, the manager of the Manufacturing Department needs accurate, timely information about actual and projected sales orders from the Marketing and Sales manager. Without such information, the Manufacturing manager must make a guess about which products to produce—and how many—in order to keep goods moving through the production line. Sometimes a guess overestimates demand, and sometimes it underestimates demand.
>
> Overproduction of a certain product might mean your company is stuck with a product for which there is a diminishing market due to style changes or changes in seasonal demand. When your company stores product—such as hiking boots—as it waits for a buyer, you incur warehouse expense. On the other hand, underproduction of a certain style of boot might result in product not being ready for a promised delivery date, leading to unhappy customers and, possibly, canceled orders. If you try to catch up on orders, you'll have to pay factory workers overtime or resort to the extra expense of rapid-delivery shipments.

Eventually, the management of large companies decided they could no longer afford the type of inefficiencies illustrated by the Mountaineering example—inefficiencies caused by the functional model of business organization. This model had deep roots in U.S. business, starting with the General Motors organizational model developed by Alfred P. Sloan in the 1930s. The functional business model shown in Figure 2-2 illustrates the concept of silos of information, which limit the exchange of information between the lower operating levels. Instead, the exchange of information between operating groups is handled by top management, which might not be knowledgeable about an individual functional area.

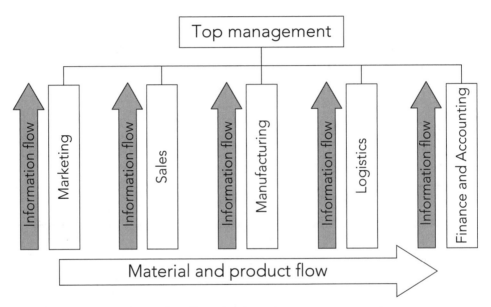

Source Line: Course Technology/Cengage Learning.

FIGURE 2-2   Information and material flows in a functional business model

The functional model was very useful for decades, and it was successful in the United States where there was limited competition and where flexibility and rapid decision making were not requirements for success. In the quickly changing markets of the 1990s, however, the functional model led to top-heavy and overstaffed organizations incapable of reacting quickly to change. The time was right to view a business as a set of cross-functional processes, as illustrated in Figure 2-3. In this organizational model, the functional business model, with its separate silos of information, is gone. Now information flows between the operating groups without top management's involvement.

In a process-oriented company, the flow of information and management activity is "horizontal" across functions, in line with the flow of materials and products. This

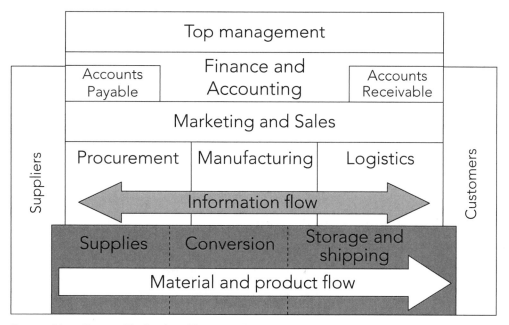

Source Line: Course Technology/Cengage Learning.

FIGURE 2-3   Information and material flows in a process business model

horizontal flow promotes flexibility and rapid decision making. Michael Hammer's 1993 landmark book, *Reengineering the Corporation: A Manifesto for Business Revolution,* stimulated managers to see the importance of managing business processes. Books like Hammer's, along with the difficult economic times of the late 1980s, led to a climate in which managers began to view ERP software as a solution to business problems.

In recent years, further impetus for adopting ERP systems has come from companies' efforts to be in compliance with the Sarbanes-Oxley Act of 2002, a federal law passed in response to the accounting fraud discovered at large companies such as Enron and WorldCom, among others. The law, which is covered in more detail in Chapter 5, requires companies to substantiate internal controls on all information.

In the next section, you will learn about the development of the first ERP software. SAP was the first company to develop software for ERP systems and is the current market leader in ERP software sales. As of 2011, SAP has over 109,000 customers, 53,000 employees, and sales of $12.5 billion annually.

ERP SOFTWARE EMERGES: SAP AND R/3

In 1972, five former IBM systems analysts in Mannheim, Germany—Dietmar Hopp, Claus Wellenreuther, Hasso Plattner, Klaus Tschira, and Hans-Werner Hector—formed *Systemanalyse und Programmentwicklung* (Systems Analysis and Program Development), or SAP—pronounced "S-A-P". Later, the acronym was changed to *Systeme, Anwendungen und Produkte in der Datenverarbeitung* (Systems, Applications and

Products in Data Processing.) The computer industry of the time was quite different from that of today. IBM controlled the computer market with its 360 mainframe computer, which had only 512K of main memory. In this mainframe computer environment, the SAP founders recognized that all companies developing computer software faced the same basic business problems, and each developed unique, but similar, solutions for their needs in payroll processing, accounting, materials management, and other functional areas of business. SAP's goal was to develop a standard software product that could be configured to meet the needs of each company. According to founder Dietmar Hopp, SAP's concept from the beginning was to set standards in information technology. In addition, the founders wanted data available in real time, and they wanted users to work on a computer screen rather than with voluminous printed output. These goals were lofty and forward-looking for 1972, and it took almost 20 years to achieve them.

SAP Begins Developing Software Modules

Before leaving IBM, Plattner and Hopp had worked on an order-processing system for the German chemical company ICI. The order-processing system was so successful that ICI managers also wanted a materials and logistics management system—a system for handling the purchase, receiving, and storage of materials—that could be integrated into the new order-processing system. In the course of their work for ICI, Plattner and Hopp had already developed the idea of modular software development. Software **modules** are individual programs that can be purchased, installed, and run separately, but all of the modules extract data from a common database.

In the course of their work together, Plattner and Hopp began to consider the idea of leaving IBM to form their own company so they would be free to pursue their own approach to software development. They also asked Claus Wellenreuther, an expert in financial accounting who had just left IBM, to join them, and on April 1, 1972, SAP was founded. At the time Plattner, Hopp, and Wellenreuther established the company, they could not even afford to purchase their own computer. Their first contract, with ICI, to develop the follow-on materials and logistics management system, included access to ICI's mainframe computer at night—a practice they repeated with other clients until they acquired their first computer in 1980. At ICI, the SAP founders developed their first software package, variously called System R, System RF (for real-time financial accounting), and R/1.

To keep up with the ongoing development of mainframe computer technology, in 1978 SAP began developing a more integrated version of its software products, called the R/2 system. In 1982, after four years of development, SAP released its R/2 mainframe ERP software package.

Sales grew rapidly in the 1980s, and SAP extended its software's capabilities and expanded into international markets. This was no small task, because the software had to be able to accommodate different languages, currencies, accounting practices, and tax laws.

By 1988, SAP had established subsidiaries in numerous foreign countries, launched a joint venture with consulting company Arthur Andersen, and sold its 1,000th system. SAP also became SAP AG, a publicly traded company.

SAP R/3

In 1988, SAP realized the potential of client-server hardware architecture and began development of its **R/3** system to take advantage of client-server technology. The first version of SAP R/3 was released in 1992. Each subsequent release of the SAP R/3 software contained new features and capabilities. The client-server architecture used by SAP allowed R/3 to run on a variety of computer platforms, including UNIX and Windows NT. The SAP R/3 system was also designed using an open architecture approach. In **open architecture**, third-party software companies are encouraged to develop add-on software products that can be integrated with existing software. The open architecture also makes it easy for companies to integrate their hardware products, such as bar-code scanners, personal digital assistants (PDAs), cell phones, and global information systems with the SAP system.

New Directions in ERP

In the late 1990s, the year 2000, or Y2K, problem motivated many companies to move to ERP systems. As it became clear that the date turnover from December 31, 1999, to January 1, 2000, could wreak havoc on some information systems, companies searched for ways to consolidate data, and ERP systems provided one solution.

The Y2K problem originated from programming shortcuts made by programmers in the preceding decades. With memory and storage space a small fraction of what it is today, early programmers developed software that used as few computer resources as possible. To save memory, programmers in the 1970s and 1980s typically wrote programs that only used two digits to identify a year. For example, if an invoice was posted on October 29, 1975, the programmer could just store the date as 10/29/75, rather than 10/29/1975. While this may not seem like a big storage savings, for companies with millions of transactions that needed to be stored and manipulated, it added up. These programmers never imagined that software written in the 1970s would still be running major companies and financial institutions in 1999. These old systems were known as **legacy systems**. Many companies were faced with a choice: pay programmers millions of dollars to correct the Y2K problem in their old, already outdated software—or invest in an ERP system that would not only solve the Y2K problem, but potentially provide better management of their business processes as well. Thus, the Y2K problem led to a dramatic increase in business for ERP vendors in the late 1990s. However, the rapid growth of the 1990s was followed by an ERP slump starting in 1999. By 1999, many companies were in the final stages of either an ERP implementation or modification of their existing software. Many companies that had not yet decided to move to a Y2K-compliant ERP system waited until after the new millennium to upgrade their information systems.

By 2000, SAP AG had 22,000 employees in 50 countries and 10 million users at 30,000 installations around the world. By that time, SAP also had competition in the ERP market, namely from Oracle and PeopleSoft.

PeopleSoft

PeopleSoft was founded by David Duffield, a former IBM employee who, like SAP's founders, faced opposition to his ideas from IBM management. PeopleSoft started out offering software for human resources and payroll accounting, and it achieved considerable success, even with companies that already were using SAP for accounting and production. In fact, PeopleSoft's success caused SAP to make significant modifications to its Human Resources module. In 2003, PeopleSoft strengthened its offerings in the supply chain area with its acquisition of ERP software vendor JD Edwards. Then, in late 2004, Oracle succeeded in its bid to take over PeopleSoft. Today, PeopleSoft, under

Oracle, is a popular software choice for managing human resources and financial activities at universities. Currently Oracle offers PeopleSoft's ERP solution under the PeopleSoft Enterprise Applications name; it offers JD Edwards ERP solutions as JD Edwards EnterpriseOne and JD Edwards World.

Oracle

Oracle is now SAP's biggest competitor. Oracle began in 1977 as Software Development Laboratories (SDL). Its founders, Larry Ellison, Bob Miner, and Ed Oates, won a contract from the Central Intelligence Agency (CIA) to develop a system, called Oracle, to manage large volumes of data and extract information quickly. Although the Oracle project was canceled before a successful product was developed, the three founders of SDL saw the commercial potential of a relational database system. In 1979, SDL became Relational Software, Inc., and released its first commercial database product. The company changed its name again, to Oracle, and in 1986 released the client-server Oracle relational database. The company continued to improve its database product, and in 1988 released Oracle Financials, a set of financial applications. The financial applications suite of modules included Oracle Financials, Oracle Supply Chain Management, Oracle Manufacturing, Oracle Project Systems, Oracle Human Resources, and Oracle Market Management. Oracle Financials was the foundation for what would become Oracle's ERP product.

Much of Oracle's recent growth in ERP applications has been through acquisition. In addition to PeopleSoft and JD Edwards, in 2005 Oracle acquired Siebel, a major customer relationship management (CRM) software company. (CRM is discussed in more detail in Chapter 3.) In 2010, Oracle completed its acquisition of Sun Microsystems, a major manufacturer of computer hardware and software that developed the Java software development platform. According to Oracle CEO Larry Ellison, with this latest acquisition, "Oracle will be the only company that can engineer an integrated system—applications to disk—where all the pieces fit and work together so customers do not have to do it themselves. Our customers benefit as their systems integration costs go down while system performance, reliability, and security go up."

In 2010, in an effort to consolidate its customer base on a single software platform, Oracle released Fusion Applications, which is a software suite designed to give its PeopleSoft, JD Edwards, and Siebel customers a modular and flexible upgrade path to a single Oracle ERP solution.

The concepts of an Enterprise Resource Planning system are similar for the large ERP vendors, such as SAP and Oracle, and for the many smaller vendors of ERP software. Because of SAP's leadership in the ERP industry, this textbook focuses primarily on SAP's ERP software products as an example of an Enterprise Resource Planning system. Keep in mind that most other ERP software vendors provide similar functionality, with some having strengths in certain areas.

SAP ERP

SAP ERP software (previous versions were known as R/3, and later, mySAP ERP) has changed over the years, owing to product evolution—and for marketing purposes. The latest versions of ERP systems by SAP and other companies allow all business areas to access the same database, as shown in Figure 2-4, eliminating redundant data and communications lags.

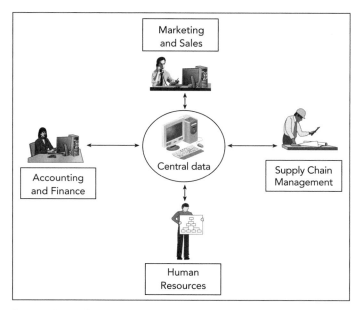

Source Line: Course Technology/Cengage Learning.

FIGURE 2-4 Data flow within an integrated information system

Perhaps most importantly, an ERP system allows data to be entered once, and then used throughout the organization. In information systems, errors most frequently occur where human beings interact with the system. ERP systems ensure that data are entered only once, where they are most likely to be accurate. For example, with access to real-time stock data, a salesperson taking an order can confirm the availability of the desired material. When the salesperson enters the sales order into the system, the order data are immediately available to Supply Chain Management, so Manufacturing can update production plans, and Materials Management can plan the delivery of the order. If the sales order data are entered correctly by the salesperson, then Supply Chain Management personnel are working with the same, correct data. The same sales data are also available to Accounting for invoice preparation.

Earlier in this chapter, you learned how software modules work. Figure 2-5 shows the major functional modules in the current SAP ERP system, also known as SAP ECC 6.0 (Enterprise Central Component 6.0), and depicts how the modules provide integration.

The basic functions of each of the modules are as follows:

- The **Sales and Distribution (SD) module** records sales orders and scheduled deliveries. Information about the customer (pricing, address and shipping instructions, billing details, and so on) is maintained and accessed from this module.
- The **Materials Management (MM) module** manages the acquisition of raw materials from suppliers (purchasing) and the subsequent handling of raw materials inventory, from storage to work-in-progress goods to shipping of finished goods to the customer.
- The **Production Planning (PP) module** maintains production information. Here production is planned and scheduled, and actual production activities are recorded.

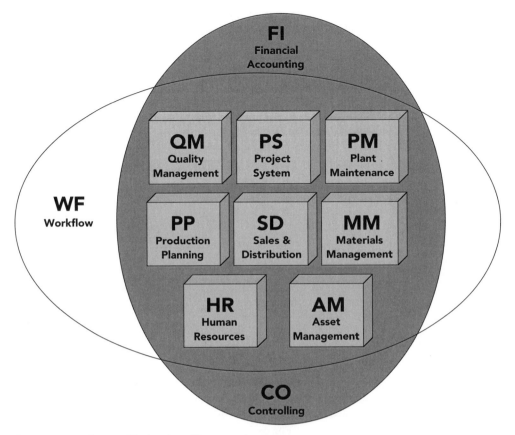

FIGURE 2-5   Modules within the SAP ERP integrated information systems environment

- The **Quality Management (QM) module** plans and records quality control activities, such as product inspections and material certifications.
- The **Plant Maintenance (PM) module** manages maintenance resources and planning for preventive maintenance of plant machinery in order to minimize equipment breakdowns.
- The **Asset Management (AM) module** helps the company manage fixed-asset purchases (plant and machinery) and related depreciation.
- The **Human Resources (HR) module** facilitates employee recruiting, hiring, and training. This module also includes payroll and benefits.
- The **Project System (PS) module** facilitates the planning for and control over new research and development (R&D), construction, and marketing projects. This module allows for costs to be collected against a project, and it is frequently used to manage the implementation of the SAP ERP system. PS manages build-to-order items, which are low-volume, highly complex products such as ships and aircrafts.

Two financial modules, Financial Accounting (FI) and Controlling (CO), are shown in Figure 2-5 as encompassing the modules described above. That is because nearly every activity in the company has an impact on the financial position of the company:

- The **Financial Accounting (FI) module** records transactions in the general ledger accounts. This module generates financial statements for external reporting purposes.
- The **Controlling (CO) module** serves internal management purposes, assigning manufacturing costs to products and to cost centers so the profitability of the company's activities can be analyzed. The CO module supports managerial decision making.

The **Workflow (WF) module** is not a module that automates a specific business function. Rather, it is a set of tools that can be used to automate any of the activities in SAP ERP. It can perform task-flow analysis and prompt employees (by email) if they need to take action. The Workflow module works well for business processes that are not daily activities but that occur frequently enough to be worth the effort to implement the workflow module—such as preparing customer invoices.

In summary, ERP integrates business functional areas with one another. Before ERP, each functional area operated independently, using its own information systems and methods for recording transactions. ERP software also makes management reporting and decision making faster and more uniform throughout an organization. In addition, ERP promotes thinking about corporate goals, as opposed to focusing only on the goals of a single department or functional area. When top management is queried on the reasons for implementing ERP systems, the overriding answer is *control*. With the capability to see integrated data on their entire company's operation, managers use ERP systems for the control they provide, allowing managers to set corporate goals correctly.

SAP ERP Software Implementation

A truly integrated information system requires integrating all functional areas, but for various reasons, not all companies that adopt SAP software use all of the SAP ERP modules. For example, a company without factories wouldn't select the manufacturing-related modules. Another company might consider its Human Resources Department's operations to be so separate from its other operations that it would decide not integrate its Human Resources functional area. And another company might believe that its internally developed production and logistics software gives it a competitive advantage. So it might implement the SAP ERP Financial Accounting and Human Resources modules, and then integrate its internally developed production and logistics system into the SAP ERP system.

Generally, a company's level of data integration is highest when the company uses one vendor to supply all its ERP modules. When a company uses modules from different vendors, additional software must be created to get the modules to work together. Frequently, companies integrate different systems using batch data transfer processes that are performed periodically. In those cases, however, the company no longer has accurate data available in real time across the enterprise. Thus, a company must be sure the decision to use multiple vendors—or to maintain a legacy system—is based on sound business analysis, not on a resistance to change. Software upgrades of nonintegrated systems are made more problematic because further work must be done to get software from different vendors to interact. SAP's NetWeaver development platform (discussed in Chapter 8) eases the integration of SAP ERP with other software products.

Any large software implementation is challenging—and ERP systems are no exception. There are countless examples of large implementations failing, and it is easy to understand why. Many different departments are involved, as are the many users of the system, programmers, systems analysts, and other personnel. Without top management commitment, large projects are doomed to fail. More implementation issues are discussed in Chapter 7.

After a company chooses its major modules, it must make an incredible number of decisions on how to configure the system. These configuration options allow the company to customize the modules it has chosen to fit its needs. For example, in the Financial Accounting (FI) module, a business might need to define limits on the dollar value of business transactions that certain employees can process. This is an important consideration in minimizing the risk of fraud and abuse, and is just one example of the many decisions facing a company at the start of a major ERP implementation.

ANOTHER LOOK

Tolerance Groups

In configuring the SAP system, a company can define **tolerance groups**, which are specific ranges that define transaction limits. An example of a tolerance group is shown in Figure 2-6. As part of the configuration process, a company can define any number of tolerance groups with a range of limits, and can then assign employees to these tolerance groups.

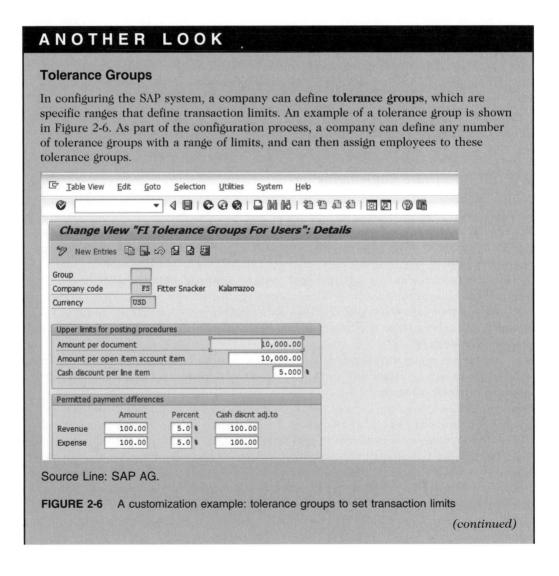

Source Line: SAP AG.

FIGURE 2-6   A customization example: tolerance groups to set transaction limits

(continued)

While SAP has defined the tolerance group methodology as its method for placing limits on an employee, configuration allows a company the flexibility to further tailor this methodology for other uses. Assume a sporting goods company places an order in January for 1,000 life jackets. The company receives only 995 in the shipment from the manufacturer, which arrives in March. This delivery, although it is short five life jackets, is close enough to the original order that it is accepted as complete. The difference of the five life jackets represents the tolerance. By defining the tolerance group to accept a variance of a small percentage of the shipment, the company has determined that it is not worth pursuing the five extra life jackets. Tolerance could indicate a shortage, as in this example, or an overabundance in an order. Thus, an order of 1,005 life jackets would also be within the tolerance. Tolerance groups should be defined and documented, in part to deal with fraud issues. The sporting goods company should know the reason for a short order: is it because the order is within the tolerance range, or is it because a worker on the loading dock stole five life jackets?

Question:

1. Can you think of other areas within a company that would need to have some limits set on variances or payments? Why would it be beneficial to set those tolerance groups?

Features of SAP ERP

Not only was SAP ERP the first software to deliver real-time ERP integration, it has other features worthy of note. Its most significant characteristics are its suitability for large companies, high cost, automation of data updates, and applicability of best practices—all of which are described below.

The original SAP ERP system targeted very large companies. Prior to the development of ERP systems, it was assumed that these giants could never have integrated systems because of the sheer amount of computing power required to integrate them. Increased computing speeds, however, meant that large companies in a variety of industries, including manufacturing, gas and oil, airlines, and consulting, could have integrated information systems.

Acquiring an SAP ERP software system is very expensive. In addition to the cost of the software, many companies find they must buy new hardware to accommodate such powerful programs. For a *Fortune* 500 company, software, hardware, and consulting costs can easily exceed $100 million. Large companies can also spend $50 million to $100 million when it is time to upgrade to a newer version of their ERP software. Full implementation of all modules can take years. In fact, most companies view ERP implementations as an ongoing process, not a one-off project. As implementations are completed in one area of a company, other areas may begin an implementation or upgrade a previous implementation.

The modular design of SAP ERP is based on business processes, such as sales order handling, materials requirement handling, and employee recruiting. When data are entered into the system, data in all related files in the central database are automatically updated. No further human input is required to make the changes.

Before the development of SAP ERP, companies often sought vendors to write software to fit their business processes. As SAP accumulated experience developing information systems, however, the company began to develop models of how certain industries' business processes should be managed. Thus, SAP ERP's design incorporates best practices for a wide variety of processes. A **best practice** is the best, most efficient way of handling a certain business process. If a company's business practices do not follow one of the best practices incorporated in the SAP ERP design, then the business must redesign its practices so it can use the software. Although some customization is possible during implementation, many companies find they must still change some of the ways they work to fit the software.

ERP FOR MIDSIZED AND SMALLER COMPANIES

By 1998, most of the *Fortune* 500 companies had already installed ERP systems, so ERP vendors refocused their marketing efforts on midsized companies (those with fewer than 1,000 employees). Small and midsized companies represented a ripe, profitable market. For example, in 2001, small and midsized companies in the United States increased their IT expenditure by more than 4 percent over the previous year. To appeal to this new market, SAP developed SAP Business All-in-One, a single package containing specific, preconfigured bundles of SAP ERP tailored for particular industries, such as automotive, banking, chemicals, and oil and gas. Because it is tailored to specific industries, SAP Business All-in-One can be installed more quickly than the standard ERP product.

To address the needs of smaller companies, such as those with less than 500 employees, SAP purchased the ERP system of Israeli-based TopManage Financial Systems in 2002, and renamed this package SAP Business One. The capabilities of SAP Business One have increased over the years through both internal development at SAP and the acquisition of other software companies such as iLytix Systems AS, which added new reporting capabilities to SAP Business One. In July 2011, SAP announced that SAP Business One would be available in a new subscription-based, hosted offering through SAP partners.

In addition, SAP has developed its BusinessByDesign product, which is an ERP product hosted by SAP and accessed through a Web browser. It is an example of the software-as-a-service (SaaS) approach that eliminates the need for a company to buy and maintain the software and hardware to run an ERP application. SaaS does not eliminate the need to configure the software to manage a company's processes or the need to train users of the system, but it does reduce the need for IT support staff to operate the ERP system. SaaS is discussed more fully in Chapter 8.

SAP and Oracle have significant competition for small-business customers from a number of smaller ERP software companies such as Sage Business Solutions, Exact, Infor, and Epicor. In 2000, software giant Microsoft acquired Great Plains, a provider of ERP software, as an entry into the small-business ERP market. Microsoft currently has five ERP products offered under the Microsoft Dynamics label.

Responses of the Software to the Changing Market

In the mid-1990s, many companies complained about the difficulty of implementing the SAP R/3 system. SAP faced a canceled implementation by Dell Computers, a lengthy implementation at Owens Corning, and a lawsuit by the now-defunct FoxMeyer drug company. Cadbury experienced a well-publicized surplus of chocolate bars at the end of 2005, due, in part, to a troubled SAP ERP implementation. In response to these and other implementation challenges, SAP developed the Accelerated SAP (ASAP) implementation methodology, a framework for implementing systems, to ease the implementation process. SAP has continued developing implementation methodology; the latest version, Solution Manager, is designed to greatly speed the implementation process.

SAP continues to extend the capabilities of SAP ERP with additional, separate products that run on separate hardware and that extract data from the SAP ERP system. In many cases, these products provide more flexible and powerful versions of tools available in the SAP ERP system. SAP's Business Warehouse (BW) product is an example of one such solution. Customers needing more capability and flexibility to analyze data beyond the standard tools and reports in the SD, PP, and FI modules can add Business Warehouse (BW). The BW software runs on a separate server and lets the user define unique reporting and analysis methods and integrate information from other systems.

The tools used to analyze data in the BW system are known as business intelligence (BI). As an example of the use of the business intelligence that can be gained through using SAP's Business Warehouse module, SAP has recently announced its in-memory data analysis tool, SAP HANA (High-performance ANalytical Appliance), a technology which will likely revolutionize Business Intelligence. Rather than storing data on hard disk drives, SAP's HANA system stores data in memory for dramatically quicker access. SAP HANA will allow companies to analyze business operations and large volumes of transactional and analytical data in real time.

The SAP ERP system provides some tools to manage customer interactions and analyze the success of promotional campaigns, but SAP also sells a separate application called Customer Relationship Management (CRM), which has extended customer service capabilities. SAP's CRM product is designed to compete with CRM systems from competitors, such as Oracle's Siebel CRM application.

SAP addressed the issue of Internet-based data exchange with its NetWeaver integration platform, which provides a unified means to connect SAP systems to other systems and to the Internet.

Like all technology, ERP software and related products are constantly changing. Thus, the challenge for a company is not only to evaluate an ERP vendor's current product offerings, but also to assess its development strategies and product plans.

CHOOSING CONSULTANTS AND VENDORS

Because ERP software packages are so large and complex, one person cannot fully understand a single ERP system; it is also impossible for an individual to adequately compare various systems. So, before choosing a software vendor, most companies study their needs and then hire an external team of software consultants to help choose the right software vendor(s) and the best approach to implementing ERP. Working as a team with the customer, the consultants apply their expertise to selecting an ERP vendor (or vendors) that will best meet their customer's needs.

After recommending a vendor, the consultants will typically recommend the software modules best suited to the company's operations, along with the configurations within those modules that are most appropriate. This preplanning should involve not only the consultants and a company's IT department, but the management of all functional business areas as well.

THE SIGNIFICANCE AND BENEFITS OF ERP SOFTWARE AND SYSTEMS

The significance of ERP lies in its many benefits. Recall that integrated information systems can lead to more efficient business processes that cost less than those in unintegrated systems. In addition, ERP systems offer the following benefits:

- ERP allows easier global integration. Barriers of currency exchange rates, language, and culture can be bridged automatically, so data can be integrated across international borders.
- ERP integrates people and data while eliminating the need to update and repair many separate computer systems. For example, at one point, Boeing had 450 data systems that fed data into its production process; the company now has a single system for recording production data.
- ERP allows management to actually manage operations, not just monitor them. For example, without ERP, getting an answer to "How are we doing?" requires getting data from each business unit and then analyzing that data for a comprehensive, integrated picture. The ERP system already has all the data, allowing the manager to focus on improving processes. This focus enhances management of the company as a whole, and makes the organization more adaptable when change is required.

An ERP system can dramatically reduce costs and improve operational efficiency. For example, EZ-FLO International, Inc., a family-run plumbing products manufacturer and distributor, had been experiencing double-digit growth and needed a scalable business platform to support its global growth. The company selected SAP Business All-in-One customized for wholesale distribution. As a result of the integrated process capabilities, EZ-FLO has been able to greatly improve its inventory management processes and has eliminated its annual inventory count, which used to take 100 employees two days to complete. In addition, the company has reduced manufacturing lead times in its domestic plants by two weeks. These process improvements led to improved customer service, and a 20 percent increase in the number of new customers—with a 12 percent growth in sales per customer.

Welch Foods, Inc., is the processing and marketing subsidiary of the National Grape Cooperative, an organization of 1,200 U.S. and Canadian grape growers. In 2004, Welch's decided to implement Oracle's E-Business Suite to make better decisions regarding product mix, production, and marketing. For Welch's, a key advantage of the ERP system is that it provides a "single source of truth" on production costs and on customer and product profitability, allowing Welch's management team to make better business decisions.

QUESTIONS ABOUT ERP

How Much Does an ERP System Cost?

The total cost of an ERP system implementation includes several factors, including the following:

- The scale of the ERP software, which corresponds to the size of the company it serves
- The need for new hardware capable of running complex ERP software
- Consultants' and analysts' fees

- Length of time required for implementation (which causes disruption of business)
- Training (which costs both time and money)

A large company, one with well over 1,000 employees, will likely spend $100 million to $500 million for an ERP system with operations involving multiple countries, currencies, languages, and tax laws. Such an installation might cost as much as $30 million in software license fees, $200 million in consulting fees, additional millions to purchase new hardware, and even more millions to train managers and employees—and full implementation of the new system could take four to six years.

A midsized company (one with fewer than 1,000 employees) might spend $10 million to $20 million in total implementation costs and have its ERP system up and running in about two years.

A smaller company, one with less than $50 million in annual revenue, could expect to pay about $300,000 for an ERP implementation, and one with revenue of $100–250 million could spend around $1.4 million. For these smaller companies, implementations usually take about 10 months.

Should Every Business Buy an ERP Package?

ERP packages imply, by their design, a certain way of doing business, and they require users to follow that way of doing business. For a particular business, some of its operations—or certain segments of its operations—might not be a good match with the constraints inherent in ERP. Therefore, it is imperative for a business to analyze its own business strategy, organization, culture, and operation *before* choosing an ERP approach.

A 1998 article in the *Harvard Business Review* provides examples that show the value of planning before trying to implement an ERP system: "Applied Materials gave up on its system when it found itself overwhelmed by the organization changes involved. Dow Chemical spent seven years and close to half a billion dollars implementing a mainframe-based enterprise system; now it has decided to start over again on a client-server version." In another example, Kmart in 2002 wrote off $130 million because of a failed ERP supply chain project. At the time, Kmart was not happy with its existing supply chain software, and it attempted to implement another product too quickly.

For years, the giant U.S. retailer Walmart chose not to purchase an ERP system, but rather to write all its software in-house. Walmart's philosophy was that the global strategic business process should drive the technology. The company's IT personnel were encouraged to consider the merchandising aspect of a process first and foremost, and then let the technology follow. However, in 2007, Walmart changed its course and decided to implement SAP Financials. The CIO of Walmart is reported to have said that implementing SAP's financial package would enable the company to grow in many countries, including China.

ERP systems are popping up in some unlikely industries. The government of Singapore is implementing an ERP project that will link 20 different healthcare providers together under one system, which is estimated to be 20 percent more efficient and will eliminate a tremendous amount of duplicate information. Along with the normal modules that an ERP system contains, such as financials and human resource management, this enterprise healthcare system will include electronic medical records and clinical management modules.

Sometimes, a company is not ready for ERP. In many cases, ERP implementation difficulties arise when management does not fully understand its current business processes and cannot make implementation decisions in a timely manner. An advantage of an ERP system is that it can reduce costs by streamlining business processes. If a company is not prepared to change its business processes to make them more efficient, then it will find itself with a large bill for software and consulting fees, with no improvement in organizational performance.

ANOTHER LOOK

Sustainability and ERP

ERP systems are helping companies track their energy consumption. SAP and Walmart are not only teaming up for the implementation of the retail giant's financial software, but they are also promoting a unified front on sustainability—focusing on reducing pollution while increasing profits—through the use of ERP software. Many SAP customers have cut energy usage; for example, 7-Eleven reduced its cooling energy usage by 12 percent, Dannon cut its fuel costs by 22 percent with better management of its transportation system, and Kendall-Jackson wine makers cut their lighting bill by 40 percent—all through the use of enhanced information from their ERP system.

Companies can use the software to track and report on their energy consumption; however, in order to make changes, a company must determine the baseline of its energy consumption. For instance, Walmart was surprised to find that only 8 percent of its carbon footprint was under the direct control of the company, the remaining 92 percent was in the company's supply chain. Since 85 percent of Walmart's suppliers run SAP, Walmart saw an opportunity to encourage energy savings on the part of the companies that supply the Walmart stores. SAP sustainability software application allows Walmart and its suppliers to track their energy usage, emissions, and consumption of other natural resources.

Question:

1. How important is sustainability to a company's bottom line? How about it its image?

Is ERP Software Inflexible?

Although many people claim that ERP systems (especially the SAP ERP system) are rigid, SAP ERP does offer numerous configuration options that help businesses customize the software to fit their unique needs. In addition, programmers can write specific routines for special applications in SAP's internal programming language, called **Advanced Business Application Programming (ABAP)**. The integration platform, NetWeaver, offers further flexibility in adding both SAP and non-SAP components to a company's IT infrastructure. Companies need to be careful about how much custom programming they include in their implementations, or they could find they have simply re-created their existing information systems in a new software package instead of gaining the benefits of improved, integrated business processes. In its implementation of PeopleSoft, FedEx Corporation installed the systems for Financial and Human Resources functions with little or no modification.

Once an ERP system is in place, trying to reconfigure it while retaining data integrity is expensive and time consuming. That is why thorough pre-implementation planning is so important. It is much easier to customize an ERP program during system configuration, before any data have been stored.

What Return Can a Company Expect from Its ERP Investment?

The financial benefits provided by an ERP system can be difficult to calculate because sometimes ERP increases revenue and decreases expenses in ways that are difficult to measure. In addition, some changes take place over such a long period of time that they are difficult to track. Finally, the old information system may not be able to provide good data on the performance of the company before the ERP implementation, making comparison difficult. Still, the return on an ERP investment can be measured and interpreted in many ways:

- Because ERP eliminates redundant effort and duplicated data, it can generate savings in operations expense. And because an ERP system can help a company produce goods and services more quickly, more sales can be generated every month.
- In some instances, a company that does not implement an ERP system might be forced out of business by competitors that have an ERP system—how do you calculate the monetary advantage of remaining in business?
- A smoothly running ERP system can save a company's personnel, suppliers, distributors, and customers much frustration—a benefit that is real, but difficult to quantify.
- Because both cost savings and increased revenue occur over many years, it is difficult to put an exact dollar figure to the amount accrued from the original ERP investment.
- Because ERP implementations take time, there may be other business factors affecting the company's costs and profitability, making it difficult to isolate the impact of the ERP system alone.
- ERP systems provide real-time data, allowing companies to improve external customer communications, which can improve customer relationships and increase sales.

How Long Does It Take to See a Return on an ERP Investment?

A **return on investment (ROI)** is an assessment of an investment project's value, calculated by dividing the value of the project's benefits by the project's costs. An ERP system's ROI can be difficult to calculate because of the many intangible costs and benefits previously mentioned. Some companies do not even try to make the calculation, on the grounds that the package is as necessary as having electricity (which is not justified as an investment project). Companies that do make the ROI calculation have seen widely varying results. Some ERP consulting firms refuse to do ERP implementations unless their client company performs an ROI. Peerstone Research reported on over 200 companies using SAP or Oracle ERP systems and found that 38 percent of survey respondents do not perform formal ROI evaluations.

In the Peerstone Research study, 63 percent of companies that did perform the calculation reported a positive ROI for ERP. Manufacturing firms are more likely to see a positive ROI than government or educational organizations. However, most companies reported that nonfinancial goals were the primary motivation for their ERP installations. Seventy-one percent of those companies surveyed said that the goal behind the ERP installation was improved management vision. Although Nestlé USA had problems with its ERP implementation, it estimated a cost savings of $325 million, after spending six years and over $200 million on the implementation.

Toro, a wholesale lawnmower manufacturer, spent $25 million and four years to implement an ERP system. At first, ROI was difficult for Toro to quantify. Then, the emergence of an expanded customer base of national retailers, such as Sears and Home Depot, made it easier to quantify benefits. With this larger pool of customers, Toro's ERP system allowed it to save $10 million in inventory costs annually—the result of better production, warehousing, and distribution methods.

A recent survey of small and midsized companies showed that only 48 percent always do an ROI evaluation, and only 25 percent always repeat the calculation after implementation. These small and midsized business owners feel they just need an ERP to support their business, even if the ROI calculation is not performed.

Why Do Some Companies Have More Success with ERP Than Others?

Early ERP implementation reports indicated that only a small percentage of companies experienced a smooth rollout of their new ERP systems *and* immediately began receiving the benefits they anticipated. However, it is important to put such reports into perspective. *All* kinds of software implementations can suffer from delays, cost overruns, and performance problems—not just ERP projects. Such delays have been a major problem for the IS industry since the early days of business computing. Nevertheless, it is worth thinking specifically about why ERP installation problems can occur.

You can find numerous cases of implementation woes in the news. W. L. Gore, the maker of GoreTex fabric, had problems implementing its PeopleSoft system for personnel, payroll, and benefits. The manufacturer sued PeopleSoft, Deloitte & Touche LLP, and Deloitte Consulting for incompetence. W. L. Gore blamed the consultants for not understanding the system and leaving its Personnel department in a mess. PeopleSoft consultants were brought in to resolve the problems after implementation, but the fix cost W. L. Gore additional hundreds of thousands of dollars.

Hershey Foods (now The Hershey Company) had a rough rollout of its ERP system in 1999, due to its use of what experts call the "Big Bang" approach to implementation, in which huge pieces of the system are implemented all at once. Companies rarely use this approach because it is so risky. Hershey's order-processing and shipping departments had glitches that were being fixed as late as September. Because of that, Hershey lost a large share of the Halloween candy market that year.

Usually, a bumpy rollout and low ROI are caused by *people* problems and misguided expectations, not computer malfunctions:

- Some executives blindly hope that new software will cure fundamental business problems that are not curable by any software. The root of a problem may lie in flawed core business processes. Unless the company changes its business processes, it will just be computerizing an ineffective way of doing business.
- Some executives and IT managers don't take enough time for a proper analysis during the planning and implementation phase.
- Some executives and IT managers skimp on employee education and training.
- Some companies do not place the ownership or accountability for the implementation project on the personnel who will operate the system. This lack of ownership can lead to a situation in which the implementation becomes an IT project rather than a company-wide project.

- Unless a large project such as an ERP installation is promoted from the top down, it is doomed to fail; top executives must be behind a project 100 percent if it is going to be successful.
- A recent academic study attempting to identify the critical success factors of ERP implementations showed that a good project manager was critical and central to success of a project. In addition, training was crucial—along with a project champion, that is, someone who might not be in the CEO role but who brings enthusiasm and leadership to a project.
- ERP implementation brings a tremendous amount of change for users of the system. Managers need to effectively manage that change in order to ensure a smooth implementation.

Many ERP implementation experts emphasize the importance of proper education and training for both employees and managers. Most people will naturally resist changing the way they do their jobs. Many analysts have noted that active top management support is crucial for successful acceptance and implementation of such company-wide changes.

Some companies willingly part with funds for software and new hardware, but they do not properly budget for employee training. ERP software is complex and can be intimidating at first. This fact alone supports the case for adequate training. Gartner Research recommends allocating 17 percent of a project's budget to training. Those companies spending less than 13 percent on training are three times more likely to have problems with their ERP implementations. The cost includes training employees on how to use the software to do their job, employees' nonproductive downtime during training, and—very importantly—educating employees about how the data they control affect the entire business operation.

Nestlé learned many lessons from its implementation of an ERP system. Its six-year, $210 million project was initially headed for failure because Nestlé didn't include on the implementation team any employees from the operating groups affected. Employees left the company, morale was down, and help desk calls were up. After three years, the ERP implementation was temporarily stopped. Nestlé USA's vice president and CIO at that time, Jeri Dunn, learned that major software implementation projects are not really about the software, rather they are about change management. "When you move to SAP, you are changing the way people work.... You are challenging their principles, their beliefs, and the way they have done things for many, many years," said Dunn. After addressing the initial problems, Nestlé ultimately reaped benefits from its ERP installation.

For many companies, it takes years before they can take full advantage of the wide variety of capabilities of their ERP systems. Most ERP installations do generate returns, and news coverage now focuses on how companies gain value from their existing systems or are upgrading and adding functionality to their existing ERP systems. Del Monte Foods needed to meet Walmart's and Target's requirements for package tracking using radio frequency identification devices (RFIDs), so approximately a year after its ERP system installation, the company tied its RFID applications into its existing SAP platform and is working to make its supply chain more efficient.

The Continuing Evolution of ERP

Understanding the social and business implications of new technologies is not easy. Howard H. Aiken, the pioneering computer engineer behind the first large-scale digital computer, the Harvard Mark I, predicted in 1947 that only six electronic digital computers would be needed to satisfy the computing needs of the entire United States. Hewlett-Packard passed up the opportunity to market the computer created by Steve Wozniak that became the Apple I. And Microsoft founder Bill Gates did not appreciate the importance of the Internet until 1995, by which time Netscape controlled the bulk of the Internet browser market. (Gates, however, did dramatically reshape Microsoft around an Internet strategy by the late 1990s. Its Internet Explorer browser is now more commonly used than any other.) Thus, even people who are most knowledgeable about a new technology do not always fully understand its capabilities or how it will change business and society.

ERP systems have been in common use only since the mid-1990s. As this young technology continues to mature, ERP vendors are working to solve the adaptability problems that plague customers. The growth in the computing power of mobile devices such as smartphones and tablets will create more opportunities for ERP companies to develop applications that provide customers with instantaneous data while improving their efficiency.

ANOTHER LOOK

ERP Allows for Bakery Chain Expansion

Au Bon Pain, the bakery and café chain based in Boston, operates 200 outlets in the United States and Asia. Over the last three years, *Health* magazine has named Au Bon Pain one of America's top five healthiest fast-food restaurant chains. The company had an interest in expanding, and Tim Oliveri, the company's chief financial officer, wanted Au Bon Pain to be able to react to market changes more rapidly while also reducing its costs. The company's existing legacy information systems were holding it back, but the company's decision to implement an SAP ERP system is now helping it achieve these goals.

The new ERP system replaced disparate systems, some of which were in paper format. This integrated enterprise system brings the storefront to the back office through a number of different module implementations. With the single system, the company is able to reduce its financial reporting cycle from weeks to days, and the system allows better management of Au Bon Pain's workforce through a Web-based portal. In addition, the new system facilitates greater compliance with financial regulations and better sales management, along with the electronic purchasing of all raw materials.

One impetus for installing this ERP system was for management to be able to digest information on market conditions, and react quickly to open new stores or renovate existing stores. For example, cafés in New York City have recently undergone major renovations, resulting in double-digit sales increases. More cafes are planned to open soon.

Question:

1. Assume you own and run a small local coffee shop. You do all your ordering of ingredients for your coffee shop by hand—using pencil, paper, mail, and telephone. All your sales are recorded by hand in a book, and transcribed for filing of small-business taxes. How could a small ERP system help your business become more efficient? What would an ERP system allow you to do?

ANOTHER LOOK

Buyer Beware: Check that Contract

The history of the ERP software industry is fraught with failed implementations. One of the latest lawsuits is by Montclair State University in New Jersey, which is suing Oracle for a failed implementation. Originally, the school contracted with Oracle (PeopleSoft) to buy an ERP package for $4.3 million, with an additional $15.75 million for the implementation. The following year, after some delays, Oracle sought an additional $8 million to complete the project. Montclair University refused the additional fee, and Oracle left the project. Now Montclair is estimating that it will take it a further $20 million to complete the implementation.

Experts agree that lawsuits such as these are not productive; no one really wins. It is essential that customers pay close inspection to the legal contract drawn up between themselves and the software vendor. ERP software is extremely complex, and it is often difficult to ask the right questions when negotiating the contracts. Most importantly, the customer should understand its own business processes and be able to relay them to the software vendor. The customer must also accept that their business processes will need to change to fit the software. To top it off, the pricing of many ERP packages is very complex, with a variety of different licensing models to choose from. The bottom line is: Understand the contract you are signing.

Question:

1. Research the topic of ERP contracts on the Internet. How could ERP vendors make it easier for customers to understand their licensing models? What could customers do to ensure a contract contains all possible eventualities?

Chapter Summary

- Several developments in business and technology allowed ERP systems to evolve to their current form:

  - The speed and power of computing hardware increased exponentially, while cost and size decreased.

  - Early client-server architecture provided the conceptual framework for multiple users sharing common data.

  - Increasingly sophisticated software facilitated integration, especially in two areas: Accounting and Finance and material requirements planning.

  - As businesses grew in size, and the business environment became more complex and competitive, business managers began to demand more efficient and competitive information systems.

  - SAP AG produced a complex, modular ERP program called R/3. The software could integrate a company's entire business by using a common database that linked all operations, allowing real-time data sharing and streamlined operations.

  - SAP R/3, now called SAP ERP, is modular software offering modules for Sales and Distribution, Materials Management, Production Planning, Quality Management, and other areas.

  - ERP software is expensive to purchase and time consuming to implement, and it requires significant employee training—but the payoffs can be spectacular. For some companies, however, the ROI may not be immediate or even calculable.

  - Experts anticipate that ERP's future focus will be on applications for mobile devices and providing instant access to large volumes of data.

Key Terms

Advanced Business Application
  Programming (ABAP)

Asset Management (AM) module

best practice

client-server architecture

Controlling (CO) module

database management system (DBMS)

electronic data interchange (EDI)

Financial Accounting (FI) module

Human Resources (HR) module

legacy system

material requirements planning (MRP)

Materials Management (MM) module

module

open architecture

Plant Maintenance (PM) module

Production Planning (PP) module

Project System (PS) module

Quality Management (QM) module

R/3

return on investment (ROI)

Sales and Distribution (SD) module

SAP ERP

Scalability

silo

tolerance group

Workflow (WF) module

Exercises

1. Moore's Law is said to be more of a trend, rather than a representation of the actual number of transistors on a silicon chip. What is the current status of Moore's Law? If it is not exactly holding true, what does this mean for the future of the computing industry?

2. What are the main characteristics of an ERP system? What are some newly developed features of ERP systems?

3. Imagine that your uncle owns and operates a construction company. The company owns a number of very expensive pieces of machinery, such as backhoes, for building houses and apartment buildings. Up until now, your aunt has "taken care of the books" by keeping financial records by hand. However, business is picking up, and she has gotten far behind in filing taxes, paying bills, and so on. Write a persuasive essay to your uncle about why he needs an ERP system and how it would help with not only the burden of billing, payroll, and filing taxes, but also with keeping track of the company's expensive machinery. Use the Internet for research.

4. Much has been written in the news media about ERP systems, both in print and online. Using library resources or the Internet, report on one company's positive experience with implementing an ERP system, and on another company's disappointing experience.

5. Some of examples shown in this chapter are from a traditional ERP system, SAP. Consider some smaller ERP systems. Look on the Internet at Business One by SAP, and an additional smaller system, such as Pronto software or Exact software. Compare two of the systems, and list the similarities between the module-type offerings. Are there any clear differences between them?

6. Visit *CIO* magazine's Web site, www.cio.com, and conduct a search on ERP. Based on the search results, choose an example of an ERP implementation, and write a memo to your instructor describing the implementation. Discuss ways in which you think the company adopting the ERP system could have improved its implementation.

7. [Challenge Exercise] From your university's electronic library, obtain a copy of the article, "Management Based Critical Success Factors in the Implementation of Enterprise Resource Planning Systems," by Joseph Bradley (*International Journal of Accounting Information Systems*, Volume 9, no. 3, pages 175-200, September 2008). Write a three-page paper on the findings of this study concerning factors critical to the success of an ERP implementation. Choose five factors you think are most important, and focus your writing on those five.

For Further Study and Research

Allesch, Adolf. "Thriving or Surviving? How to Take Your SAP NetWeaver Pulse." *insiderProfiles* 3, no. 3 (Summer 2007). http://insiderprofiles.wispubs.com/article.aspx?iArticleId=4672.

Au Bon Pain. "Au Bon Pain Launches Cafe Remodel Program as Part of National Expansion Strategy; Transforms New York City Cafes." *PR Newswire*, June 8, 2011. www.aubonpain.com/releases/Au%20Bon%20Pain%20Launches%20Cafe%20Remodel%20Program.pdf.

Barlas, Demir. "Wal-Mart's Confused SAP Strategy." *IT Knowledge Exchange*, May 27 2008. http://itknowledgeexchange.techtarget.com/sap-watch/wal-marts-confused-sap-strategy.

Blau, John. "SAP Arrives at Home Depot." *InfoWorld*, June 1, 2005. www.infoworld.com/article/05/06/01/HNsaphomedepot_1.html?SUPPLY%20CHAIN%20MANAGEMENT.

Blau, John. "Whirlpool Whirls into Web Services." *InfoWorld*, May 23, 2006. www.infoworld.com/article/06/05/23/78591_HNwhirlpoolwebservices_1.html?WEB%20SERVICES%20DEVELOPMENT.

Bradley, Joseph. "Management-Based Critical Success Factors in the Implementation of Enterprise Resource Planning Systems." *International Journal of Accounting Information Systems* 9, no. 3 (September 2008): 175–200.

Burleson, Donald. "Four Factors that Shape the Cost of ERP." *TechRepublic*, August 16, 2001. http://search.techrepublic.com.com/index.php?q=Four+factors+that+shape+the+cost+of+ERP&t=11&go=Search.

Business Wire. "U.S. Small and Midsize Business IT Spending Continues to Bounce Back from Recession's Low Point, According to IDC." June 1, 2011. www.businesswire.com/news/home/20110601005379/en/U.S.-Small-Midsize-Business-Spending-Continues-Bounce.

Chemical Week. "Connecting the Chemical Industry." September 25, 2002.

Davenport, Thomas H. "Putting the Enterprise into the Enterprise System." *Harvard Business Review*, (July–August 1998): 121–31.

Dignan, Larry. "Oracle Officially Launches its Fusion Apps." *CNET*, September 20, 2010. http://news.cnet.com/8301-1001_3-20016932-92.html.

Few, Stephen. "The Information Cannot Speak for Itself." *IntelligentEnterprise.com*, July 10, 2004. www.intelligententerprise.com/showArticle.jhtml;jsessionid=0VWVEUEXBJOASQSNDLPCKH0CJUNN2JVN?articleID=22102226.

Foroohar, Rana. "Software Savior?" *Newsweek*, January 29, 2007. www.thedailybeast.com/newsweek/2007/01/28/software-savior.html.

Forbes. "SAP Sees Orders From Mid-Sized Businesses Climbing to 45% From 30% by 2010." April 13, 2007. www.forbes.com/afxnewslimited/feeds/afx/2007/04/13/afx3609185.html.

Greenbaum, Joshua. "The Ecosystem Advantage: It's Not Nice to Fool Mother Nature." *insiderProfiles* 3, no. 3 (Summer 2007). http://insiderprofiles.wispubs.com/article.aspx?iArticleId=4680.

Hammer, Michael, and James Champy. *Reengineering the Corporation*. New York: Harper Business, 1993.

Hamerman, Paul, and R. Wang. "ERP: Still a Challenge After All These Years." *InformationWeek*, July 11, 2005. www.informationweek.com/showArticle.jhtml?articleID=165600651.

Henschen, Doug. "Wal-Mart, SAP Set Sights on Sustainability." *InformationWeek*, January 12, 2010. www.informationweek.com/news/global-cio/roi/222301155.

Ho, Victoria. "One ERP for S'pore Non-Profit Healthcare." *ZDNet Asia*, November 29, 2007. www.pulsesync.com/news/MediaCoverage/ZDNet%20IngoT%20Coverage_30112007.pdf.

Kanaracus, Chris. "SAP Business One Gets New Hosted, Subscription Model." *InfoWorld*, July 5, 2011. www.infoworld.com/d/applications/sap-business-one-gets-new-hosted-subscription-model-102

Kanaracus, Chris. "SAP's HANA In-Memory Analytics Engine Now Available." *Computerworld*, June 20, 2011. www.computerworld.com/s/article/9217779/SAP_s_HANA_in_memory_analytics_engine_now_available.

Kirkpatrick, David. "The E-Ware War." *Fortune*, December 7, 1998, 102–112.

Kumar, Kuldeep, and Jos van Hillegersberg. "ERP Experiences and Evolution." *Communications of the ACM* 43, no. 4 (April 2000): 23–26.

MacDonald, Elizabeth. "W. L. Gore Alleges PeopleSoft, Deloitte Botched a Costly Software Installation." *Wall Street Journal*, November 2, 1999.

McCue, Andy. "Too Much Candy: IT Glitch Costs Cadbury." *BusinessWeek*, June 8, 2006. www.businessweek.com/globalbiz/content/jun2006/gb20060608_252289.htm?chan=search.

Meissner, Gerd. *SAP: Inside the Secret Software Power*. New York: McGraw-Hill, 2000.

Montgomery, Nigel. "European Retailers Divided Over ERP Versus Best of Breed." *Tech Update*, April 18, 2003. http://techupdate.zdnet.com/techupdate/stories/main/0%2C14179%2C2913405%2C00.html.

Nadeau, Michael. "5 Keys to McKesson's Rapid BI Transformation." *SAP NetWeaver Magazine* 1, 2005. www.sap.com/belux/platform/netweaver/pdf/CS_NW_Magazine_McKesson.pdf.

Nelson, Emily, and Evan Ramstad. "Hershey's Biggest Dud Is Its New Computer System." *Wall Street Journal*, November 4, 1999.

Nolan, Sean. "By the Numbers: November 2003." *Baseline.com*, November 1, 2003. www.baselinemag.com/article2/0,1540,1374440,00.asp.

Oracle. "Oracle Customer Snapshot, Welch Foods Inc." 2010. www.oracle.com/us/corporate/customers/welch-foods-demantra-snapshot-150658.pdf.

Oracle. "Press Release: Oracle Completes Acquisition of Sun." January 27, 2010. www.oracle.com/us/corporate/press/044428.

Oracle, "Press Release: Oracle Buys Sun." April 20, 2009. www.oracle.com/us/corporate/press/018363.

Osterland, Andrew. "Blaming ERP." *CFO.com*, January 1, 2000. www.cfo.com/article.cfm/2987370.

Peerstone Research. "ERP ROI: Myth and Reality." *InformationWeek*, March 29, 2004. www.informationweek.com/reports/showReport.jhtml;jsessionid=5WZPDA3FLJXX0QSNDLQSKHSCJUNN2JVN?articleID=18600087&_requestid=16698.

PeopleSoft. "PeopleSoft Case Studies." 2002. www.peoplesoft-hp.com/tools/successstories/%5Bfiles%5D/Enterprise/Automotive/Toyota%20Motor%20Manufacturing%20NA%20Drives%20Real-Time%20Productivity%20with%20PeopleSoft%208%20HRMS%20and%20Enterprise%20Portal.pdf.

Preston, Rob, "Down to Business: No One Wins an ERP Lawsuit." *InformationWeek*, June 3, 2011. www.informationweek.com/news/global-cio/interviews/229900060?queryText=erp.

Richard, Kenneth J. "When It Comes to Enterprise Software, It's the Contract Stupid." *InformationWeek*, March 26, 2011. www.informationweek.com/news/global-cio/interviews/229400394?pgno=1.

SAP AG. "SAP 2011 Curriculum Congress: Run Better with SAP University Alliances." March 11, 2011. www.sdn.sap.com/irj/uac/index?rid=/webcontent/uuid/30262b82-87d8-2d10-fa86-86ca8a9751dc.

SAP AG. "EZ-Flo International: Growing Family-Run Business Goes Global With SAP® Software." 2008.

SAP AG. "Retail Café Chain Au Bon Pain Takes Fresh Approach with SAP." September 19, 2006. www.sap.com/corporate-en/press.epx?pressid=6747.

SAP AG. "Welcome to the 24th Annual SAP Annual General Meeting of Shareholders." May 25, 2011. www.sap.com/corporate-en/investors/governance/meetings/pdf/2011-05-25-ShareholderMeeting-e-presentation.pdf.

Schneider, Polly. "Human Touch Sorely Needed in ERP." *CIO*, March 2, 1999. www.cnn.com/TECH/computing/9903/02/erpeople.ent.idg/index.html.

Slater, Derek. "How to Choose the Right ERP Software Package." *CNN*, February 16, 1999. www.cnn.com/TECH/computing/9902/16/erppkg.ent.idg/index.html.

Sliwa, Carol. "IT Difficulties Help Take Kmart Down." *Computerworld*, January 28, 2002. www.computerworld.com/s/article/67749/IT_difficulties_help_take_Kmart_down.

Stein, Tom. "Making ERP Add Up." *InformationWeek*, May 24, 1999. www.informationweek.com/735/erp.htm.

Steinert-Threlkeld, Tom. "Home Depot Hopes SAP Can Help Boost Sales." *Baseline*, May 18, 2005. www.baselinemag.com/article2/0,1397,1817341,00.asp.

Sullivan, Laurie. "ERPzilla." *InformationWeek*, July 11, 2005. www.informationweek.com/story/showArticle.jhtml?articleID=165700832.

van Everdingen, Yvonne, Jos van Hillegersberg, and Eric Waarts. "ERP Adoption by European Midsize Companies." *Communications of the ACM* 43, no. 4 (April 2000): 27–31.

Wailgum, Thomas. "SMB ERP Projects: Don't Forget the ROI." *CIO*, April 01, 2009. www.cio.com/article/487794/SMB_ERP_Projects_Don_t_Forget_the_ROI, cio.com.

Wailgum, Thomas. "University ERP: Big Mess on Campus." *CIO*, May 1, 2005. www.cio.com/article/107706/University_ERP_Big_Mess_on_Campus.

Westervelt, Robert. "U.S. Software Sales Boost SAP earnings, Says CEO." *SearchSAP.com*, April 22, 2004. http://searchsap.techtarget.com/originalContent/0,289142, sid21_gci961032,00.html.

Wheatley, Malcolm. "ERP Training Stinks." *CIO*, June 1, 2000. www.cio.com/article/148900/ERP_Training_Stinks.

White, Joseph B., Don Clark, and Silvia Ascarelli. "Program of Pain." *Wall Street Journal*, March 14, 1997.

Whiting, Rick. "At SAP, R/3 Is a Distant Memory." *InformationWeek*, July 24, 2006. www.informationweek.com/story/showArticle.jhtml?articleID=190900725.

Whiting, Rick. "Home Depot Looks to SAP As It Modernizes." *InformationWeek*, May 23, 2005. www.informationweek.com/story/showArticle.jhtml?articleID=163106241.

Worthen, Ben. "Extreme ERP Makeover: How to Determine If a Single-Instance ERP Implementation Is Right for You." *CIO*, November 15, 2003. www.cio.com/article/31964/How_to_Determine_If_a_Single_Instance_ERP_Implementation_is_Right_for_You.

Worthen, Ben. "Nestlé's Enterprise Resource Planning (ERP) Odyssey." *CIO*, May 15, 2002. www.cio.com/article/31066/Nestle_s_Enterprise_Resource_Planning_ERP_Odyssey.

MARKETING INFORMATION SYSTEMS AND THE SALES ORDER PROCESS

LEARNING OBJECTIVES

After completing this chapter, you will be able to:

- Describe the unintegrated sales processes of the fictitious Fitter Snacker company
- Explain why unintegrated Marketing and Sales information systems lead to company-wide inefficiency, higher costs, lost profits, and customer dissatisfaction
- Discuss sales and distribution in the SAP ERP system, and explain how integrated data sharing increases company-wide efficiency
- Describe how SAP ERP processes a standard sales order
- Describe the benefits of customer relationship management (CRM) software

INTRODUCTION

In this chapter, you will begin learning about the operations of Fitter Snacker (FS), a fictitious company that makes healthy snack bars. As you will see, the company's current information systems are not integrated, which causes problems in all of the functional areas. Throughout the remainder of this book, we will use Fitter Snacker to illustrate information systems concepts in general and ERP concepts in particular.

As with many companies, Marketing and Sales is the focal point of many of Fitter's activities. Why? Because Marketing and Sales is responsible for selling the company's product, and those sales are the company's only source of revenue. That means marketing personnel often guide the company's key strategies and tactics by making decisions regarding such critical questions as:

- What products should we produce?

- How much of each product should we produce?

- How can we best promote and advertise our products?

- How should we distribute our products for maximum customer satisfaction?

- What price should we charge for our products?

On a day-to-day basis, Marketing and Sales is involved in generating key transaction data (including data for recording sales), creating customers' invoices, and allocating credit to customers. As you learned in previous chapters, the availability of a common database is one of the advantages of having an integrated information system, because the data in the system are consistent across the different modules. Integration can lead to problems, however. If the data are not correct, the error will carry over into all modules.

As noted above, Fitter's Marketing and Sales information systems are currently not well integrated with the company's other information systems. Because of this, company-wide use of transaction data is inefficient, as you will see later in this chapter. You will also learn how Fitter's Marketing and Sales information systems could be improved by using ERP software. We begin by looking at an overview of the company's operations.

OVERVIEW OF FITTER SNACKER

Fitter Snacker manufactures and sells two types of nutritious snack bars: NRG-A and NRG-B. The NRG-A bar touts "advanced energy," and NRG-B boasts "body-building proteins." Each bar contains a mix of the following ingredients:

- Dry base mixture: oats, wheat germ, protein powder, and spices

- Wet base mixture: honey and canola oil
- Vitamins and minerals

Each type of bar contains additional unique ingredients: NRG-A contains carob chips and raisins, and NRG-B contains hazelnuts and dates.

Fitter's sales force is organized into two groups: the Wholesale Division and the Direct Sales Division. The Wholesale Division sells to intermediaries that distribute the bars to small shops, vending machine operators, and health food stores. The Direct Sales Division sells directly to large grocery stores, sporting goods stores, and other large chain stores. The two divisions operate separately from one another, in effect breaking the Marketing and Sales functional area into two pieces. Each division has an organizational structure that interacts with Fitter's other functional areas, such as Accounting and Finance and Supply Chain Management.

The two sales divisions differ primarily in terms of order volume and pricing terms. The Direct Sales Division offers customers volume discounts to encourage larger sales orders, which are more efficient to process. The Wholesale Division charges customers a lower fixed price because the orders are usually large. Each order—regardless of size—generates costs related to the paperwork, shipping, and handling of the order. Thus, an order of 500 cases of snack bars incurs the same handling costs as an order of 10 cases. However, the large order might generate $5,000 in profit, while the small order might generate only $100. Both divisions send their customers invoices requesting the total balance within 30 days and offering a 2 percent discount if the customer pays within 10 days (2–10/net 30).

In addition to selling snack bars under the Fitter Snacker brand name, the company also packages the bars in store-brand wrappers for some chain stores.

PROBLEMS WITH FITTER SNACKER'S SALES PROCESS

Many of Fitter's sales orders have some sort of problem, such as incorrect pricing, excessive calls to the customer for information, order-processing delays, missed delivery dates, and so on. These problems occur because Fitter has three separate information systems: the sales order system, the warehouse system, and the accounting system. Information from each system is shared either electronically through periodic file transfers (sales order system to accounting system) or manually by paper printout (credit status from the Accounting Department to sales clerks). The high number of manual transactions creates many opportunities for data entry errors. Further, not all the information stored in the three systems is available in real time, resulting in incorrect prices and credit information.

In each sales division, Fitter has four salespeople who work on the road, plus two clerks who work in the sales office. Salespeople work on commission and have some leeway in offering customers "discretionary discounts" to make a sale. The entire sales process involves a series of steps that require coordination between Sales, Warehouse, Accounting, and Receiving, as shown in Figure 3-1. (Notice that Production is not directly involved in the sales process because Fitter plans production using a make-to-stock strategy, with product shipped to customers from warehouse inventory rather than being manufactured for specific orders.)

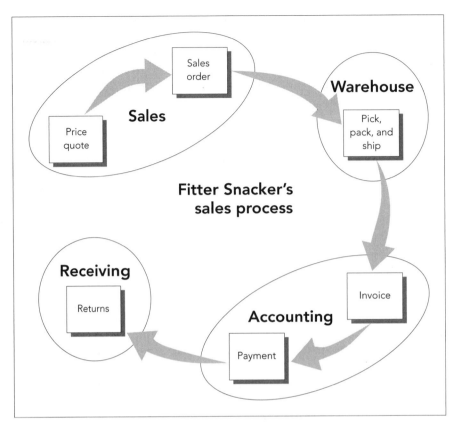

Source Line: Course Technology/Cengage Learning.

FIGURE 3-1   The sales process at Fitter Snacker

Sales Quotations and Orders

Giving a customer a price quotation and then taking the customer's order should be a straightforward process, but at Fitter it is not. For a new customer, the sales process begins with a sales call, which might be over the telephone or in person. At the end of the sales call, the salesperson prepares a handwritten quotation on a form that generates two copies. The original quotation goes to the customer, and the middle copy is first faxed and then mailed to the sales office; the salesperson keeps the bottom copy for his or her records. On the quotation form is a toll-free number that the customer can call to place an order.

A number of problems can occur with this process, including the following:

- The salesperson might make an error in the sales quotation. For example, a salesperson in the Direct Sales Division might offer both a quantity discount and a discretionary discount. If the salesperson is not careful, the two discounts combined might be so deep that the company makes little or no profit on the order.
- Salespeople fax a copy of their sales quotations to the sales office, but sometimes a customer calls to place an order before the fax is transmitted.

In such cases, the sales clerk has no knowledge of the terms of the sale (which are outlined on the quotation) and must ask the customer to repeat the information. On the other hand, even if the quotation has been faxed, the data might not have been entered into the customer database, so the customer might still need to repeat the order information. This situation can also lead to a duplicate order.

- The fax received by the sales office is a copy of a handwritten form, and might not be legible.

When customers place an order, they usually inquire about the delivery date. To get a shipping date, the sales clerk must contact the warehouse supervisor and ask whether the customer's order can be immediately shipped from inventory, or whether shipping will be delayed until a future production run is delivered to the warehouse. However, because the warehouse supervisor is generally too busy to get an updated inventory count, total all the orders waiting to be filled, and find out how many other orders are in process in the sales office, she can only estimate the shipping date.

Once the sales clerk has the warehouse supervisor's estimated shipping date, she determines the shipping method and how long delivery will take. Next, the clerk checks the customer's credit status. For new customers, the clerk fills out a paper credit-check form that includes basic customer data and the amount of the order. The form goes to Accounting, where accountants perform the credit check and then return the credit-check form showing the customer's credit limit. If the order is from an existing customer, the clerk checks a paper report from Accounting that shows the customer's current balance, credit limit, and available balance. However, because the report is generated weekly, it might not reflect a customer's most recent payments or orders. If a customer's available credit is less than the amount of the current order, assuming there are no other orders outstanding, the clerk calls the customer to determine what action the customer wants to take (reduce the amount of the order, prepay, or dispute the amount of credit granted).

Once the order details have been finalized, the sales clerk enters the order into the order-entry system. The computer program performs four important tasks. First, it stores the customer's order data, which are used later to analyze sales performance at the division level. Second, it prints out a packing list and shipping labels for the warehouse to use to pick, pack, and ship the customer's order. Third, it produces a data file of all current transactions for the Accounting Department to use for preparing invoices (this file is also used for financial, tax, and managerial accounting, which is discussed in Chapter 5). And fourth, the data file is copied to a USB key each evening for uploading into the company's PC-based accounting system.

Order Filling

Fitter's process for filling an order is no more efficient than its sales order process. Packing lists and shipping labels are printed in the sales department twice a day—at noon and at the end of the day. These are carried by hand to the warehouse, where they are manually sorted into small orders and large orders.

The Production Department produces and wraps the snack bars and packs them in display boxes, 24 bars to a box. The display boxes have promotional printing and are designed to serve as a display case. Fitter packs 12 display boxes together to form a standard shipping case. The warehouse stores both individual display boxes and shipping cases, organized by label type (Fitter brand and store brand), so depending on the inventory levels in the warehouse, Production personnel might transfer individual display boxes directly to the warehouse, or they might first pack the display boxes into shipping cases.

For small orders (less than a full shipping case), the order picker goes to the warehouse with a handcart and pulls the number of display boxes listed on the packing list. If there are not enough individual display boxes in the warehouse to fill the order, the picker might break open a shipping case to get the required number of display boxes. If he does this, he is supposed to advise the warehouse supervisor so she can update the inventory records—but sometimes this step is overlooked.

The picker then brings the display boxes back to the small-order packing area, where they are packed into a labeled box—with the packing list enclosed—and prepared for shipping by a small package shipper.

For large orders (one or more shipping cases), the picker uses a forklift to move the appropriate number of shipping cases to the large-order packing area. Workers label them for shipping, load them on a pallet, and attach them to the pallet with shrink-wrap plastic for protection. These pallets are shipped either by one of Fitter's two delivery trucks or by a less-than-truckload (LTL) common carrier.

Fitter uses a PC database program to manage inventory levels in the warehouse. The program adjusts inventory level figures on a daily basis, using data from production records (showing what has been added to the warehouse), packing lists (showing what has been shipped from the warehouse), and any additional sources of data (such as shipping cases that have been opened to pull display boxes). Each month the warehouse staff conducts a physical inventory count to compare the actual inventory on hand with what the inventory records in the database show. Fitter's monthly inventory counts show that inventory records are more than 95 percent accurate. Although 95 percent accuracy may not sound too bad, having 5 percent errors means that Fitter regularly has problems filling orders.

Because snack bars are somewhat perishable, Fitter keeps inventory levels fairly low. Inventory levels change rapidly during the day, and Fitter's current system does not provide a good method for checking inventory availability. As a result, a picker might go to the shelves to pick an order and discover that there are not enough snack bars to fill the order. In this case, there are several possible outcomes:

- There might be more of that type of bar in the production area—ready to be transferred to the warehouse—in which case the picker could wait until the inventory is received into the warehouse to finish picking the order.
- For an important customer that purchases store-branded snack bars, production might change the wrappers and display box labels currently on the production line to the customer's brand to produce enough bars to complete the order.
- In other situations, the customer may be willing to take a partial shipment consisting of whatever is on hand, with the rest shipped when it becomes available—which is known as a backorder.
- Or, the customer might prefer to take the goods on hand, cancel the balance of the order, and place a new order later.
- If the customer's company has enough inventory on hand, the customer may prefer to wait until the whole order can be shipped, thus saving on delivery charges.

To determine what to do in this situation, the order picker might have conversations with the warehouse supervisor, production supervisor, and sales clerks. Whatever the final decision, the warehouse supervisor has to contact the sales clerk so she can notify the customer (which does not always happen when things are busy) and the Accounting Department so they can change the invoice.

Accounting and Invoicing

Invoicing the customer is problematic as well. First, the data from the current order-entry system is only loaded into the accounting system at the end of each day, so the Accounting Department does not have information on new sales orders until the following day. In addition, clerks must manually make adjustments in both the order-entry system and the accounting system for partial shipments and for any other changes that have occurred during the order-fulfillment process. Many times these corrections are not made in both systems, causing discrepancies that must be corrected at the end of the month, at which point it is more difficult for the parties involved to remember what happened. Delayed order corrections also sometimes result in late or inaccurate invoices. If the completed invoice is waiting to be mailed when the warehouse notifies Accounting of a partial shipment, then a new invoice must be prepared. In any case, an invoice is eventually sent to the customer, separate from the shipment.

Payment and Returns

Fitter's procedure for processing payments often yields frustrating results for customers. Almost all customers pay the invoice within 10 days to receive the 2 percent discount. If any errors have occurred in the sales or order-fulfillment process—from the original quotation to entering the order into the sales order program to filling the order in the warehouse—the customer will receive an incorrect invoice. Even though Fitter provides customers with two invoice copies, many customers do not return a copy of the invoice with their payment, as instructed. Errors sometimes result in the incorrect customer's account being credited.

Fitter's returns processing is also flawed. Because Fitter's snack bars contain no preservatives, they have a relatively short shelf life. Thus, the company has a policy of crediting customer accounts for returned snack bars that have exceeded their "sell by" date (this is a generous policy, because it is impossible to know who—Fitter or the customer—is responsible for the bars not selling before they expire). Fitter also gives credit for damaged or defective cases returned by customers. Customers are supposed to call Fitter to get a returned material authorization (RMA) number to simplify the crediting process. When cases are returned to Fitter, the Receiving Department completes a handwritten returned material sheet, listing the returning customer's name, the materials returned, and the RMA number. However, many customers do not call for the RMA number, or fail to include it with their returned material, which makes it more difficult for the Accounting Department to credit the appropriate account. Poor penmanship on the returned material sheet also creates problems for Accounting.

When an account becomes past due, Fitter sends a dunning letter, which is the term for a letter notifying a customer that their account is past due and requesting payment if payment has not already been sent. As the account gets more delinquent, the dunning letters usually get more direct and threatening. If a customer's account has not been properly credited, however, the customer may receive a dunning letter in error, or may receive a call about exceeding their credit limit after placing a new order. Such situations damage goodwill with both new and repeat customers.

In the following sections, you will learn how an ERP system could improve the sales process for Fitter Snacker.

SALES AND DISTRIBUTION IN ERP

An ERP system can improve a company's sales order process in several ways. Because an ERP system uses a common database, it can minimize data entry errors and provide accurate information in real time to all users. An ERP system can also track all transaction data (such as invoices, packing lists, RMA numbers, and payments) involved in the sales order process.

We will look at how one ERP system, SAP ERP—in particular, its Sales and Distribution module—manages the sales order process. (Other ERP software handles the process in a similar fashion.) In SAP ERP, important transactions and events are assigned a number for record-keeping purposes. The electronic evidence of a transaction in SAP ERP is called a "document."

The SAP ERP Sales and Distribution module treats the sales order process as a cycle of events. SAP ERP defines up to six events for any sale:

- Presales activities
- Sales order processing
- Inventory sourcing
- Delivery
- Billing
- Payment

Presales Activities

The first step in the SAP ERP sales and distribution process is presales activities. At this phase, customers can get pricing information about the company's products, either through an inquiry or a sales quotation. The difference between an inquiry and a quotation is that a quotation is a written, binding document; the seller guarantees the buyer that, for some specified period of time, he can buy the product at the quoted price. An inquiry is simply a statement of prices, with no guarantee implied. In either case, the event is recorded in the central database.

Presales activities also include marketing activities such as tracking customer contacts—including sales calls, visits, and mailings. A company can maintain customer data in the ERP system and generate mailing lists based on specific customer characteristics, which enhances targeted marketing efforts.

Sales Order Processing

In the SAP ERP system, sales order processing is the series of activities that must take place to record a sales order. The sales order can start from a quotation or inquiry generated in the presales step. Any information that was collected from the customer to support the quotation (contact name, address, phone number) is immediately included in the sales order.

Critical sales order processing steps include recording the items to be purchased, determining the selling price, and recording the order quantities. Users can define various pricing alternatives in the SAP ERP system. For example, a company can use product-specific pricing, such as establishing quantity discounts for a particular item, or it can define discounts that depend on both the product and a particular customer. Configuring a complex pricing scheme requires a significant amount of programming work, but once the system is in place, it will automatically calculate the correct price for each customer, eliminating many of the problems that Fitter currently experiences.

During sales order processing, the SAP ERP system checks the accounts receivable tables in the SAP ERP database to confirm the customer's available credit. SAP ERP adds the value of the order to the customer's credit balance, and then compares the result to the customer's credit limit (also available in the database). If the customer has sufficient credit available, the order is completed. If not, the SAP ERP system prompts sales personnel to reject the order, call the customer to check on recent payments, or contact Accounting to discuss any extenuating circumstances.

Inventory Sourcing

When recording an order, the SAP ERP system checks the company's inventory records and the production planning records to see whether the requested material is available and can be delivered on the date the customer desires. This available-to-promise (ATP) check includes the expected shipping time, taking into account weekends and holidays. In the SAP ERP system, availability is automatically checked, and the system can recommend an increase in planned production if a shortfall is expected. SAP also keeps a record of all open orders, so even if product for a particular order is still in the warehouse, the system will not allow it to be sold to another customer.

Delivery

In the SAP ERP system, creating a **delivery** means releasing the documents that the warehouse uses to pick, pack, and ship orders—rather than the traditional definition of transferring goods. The process allows deliveries to be created so the warehouse and shipping activities are carried out efficiently (for example, combining similar orders for picking, or grouping orders based on shipping method and destination).

Once the system has created the documents for picking, packing, and shipping, the documents are transferred to the Materials Management module, where the warehouse activities of picking, packing, and shipping are carried out.

Billing

Next, the SAP ERP system creates an invoice by copying the sales order data into the invoice document. Accounting can print this document and mail it, fax it, or transmit it electronically to the customer. Accounting records are also updated at this point. To record the sale, SAP ERP debits (increases) accounts receivable and credits sales, thus updating the accounting records automatically.

Payment

When the customer sends in a payment, this payment must be recorded in the SAP system. If the payment is made electronically, it can be automatically processed by the SAP ERP system, which records the payment as an electronic sales order document, debits the cash account, and credits (reduces) the customer's account balance. If the customer sends a check, a clerk must manually enter the payment information, at which point the system updates all information related to the sale. The timely recording of this transaction has an effect on the timeliness and accuracy of any subsequent credit checks for the customer. With its current systems, Fitter has had a problem with getting accurate credit checks, frequently blocking orders for customers that are within their credit limit, while granting credit to other companies beyond what is advisable.

A STANDARD ORDER IN SAP ERP

Now we will examine how Fitter's sales order process would work with an SAP ERP system in place. You will learn how this ERP system can make Fitter's sales order process more accurate and efficient. Notice that ERP allows business processes to cut across functional area lines.

Taking an Order in SAP ERP

Figure 3-2 shows an order-entry screen in SAP ERP's Enterprise Central Component 6.0 system. The important fields in this screen are summarized in Figure 3-3.

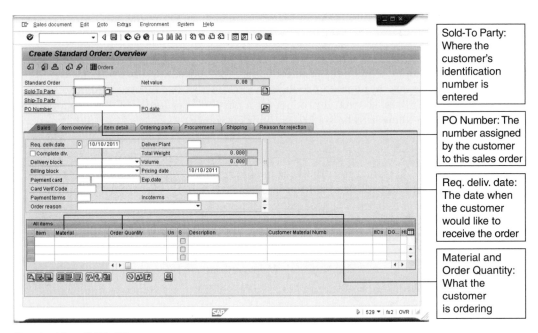

Source Line: SAP AG.

FIGURE 3-2   SAP ERP order-entry screen

Data entry field	Explanation
Sold-To Party	Identification number assigned to customer
PO Number	The number assigned by the customer to the sales transaction; this is different from the sales order number assigned by the seller (using SAP ERP) to the sales transaction. In a paper process, the purchase order number is usually a sequential number preprinted on the purchase order form
Req. deliv. date	The delivery date for the order requested by the customer; the SAP ERP system will evaluate the ability to meet this date and suggest alternatives, if necessary
Material	The identification number assigned in the SAP ERP system to the item requested by the customer
Order Quantity	The number of units of the material the customer is requesting

Source Line: Course Technology/Cengage Learning.

FIGURE 3-3   Data entry fields in the order-entry screen

In SAP ERP, a sales order clerk must enter code numbers for customers' names and the product sold, rather than using customer and product item names. Because more than one customer might have the same name, a unique number is assigned by the company to each customer in the database. This number acts as the primary identifier for the customer. The same logic applies to distinguishing one inventory item from another. In database terminology, such codes are called *key fields*. For most data entry fields, the SAP ERP system determines whether an entry is valid. Figure 3-4 shows how SAP ERP lists the system's 34 predefined sales order document types. The sales order clerk can choose the correct type from among these.

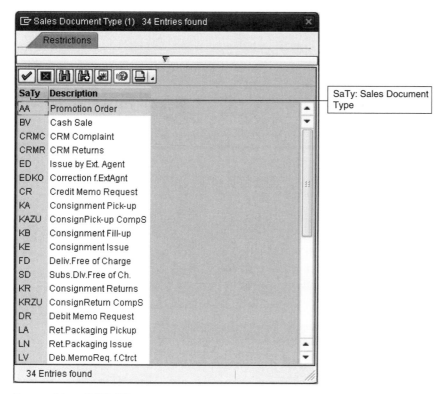

Source Line: SAP AG.

FIGURE 3-4   Some of the sales order document types predefined in SAP ERP

While it might sound as if a sales order clerk must remember a lot of code numbers to use the SAP ERP system, this is not the case. For instance, when a sales order clerk has to find a customer in the SAP ERP system, he or she can click in the Sold-To Party field to display a search icon and then click the search icon to open the search window shown in Figure 3-5.

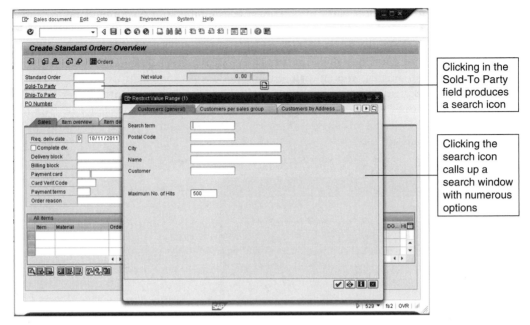

Clicking in the Sold-To Party field produces a search icon

Clicking the search icon calls up a search window with numerous options

Source Line: SAP AG.

FIGURE 3-5 Search screen for customers

Using the different tabs in this search window, the clerk can search for a customer using different criteria (for example, part of the customer's address, such as the city) to narrow the list produced by the search. Conducting a search using the criteria of Distribution Channel (specifying direct distribution) and Division (specifying snack bar sales division) produces a list of customers (shown in Figure 3-6) from which the clerk can pick the correct customer.

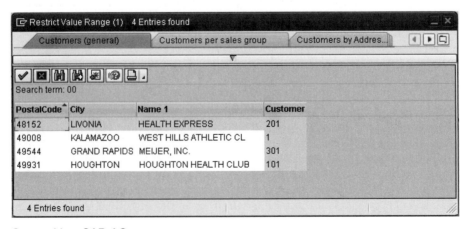

Source Line: SAP AG.

FIGURE 3-6 Results of customer search

In the SAP ERP system, a range of information is stored about each customer in multiple tables. These data are referred to as **customer master data**. Master data are data that remain fairly stable, such as customer name and address. Master data are maintained in the central database, and are available to all SAP ERP modules, including SD (Sales and Distribution), FI (Financial), and CO (Controlling).

Information about materials is in tables—collectively called **material master data**—which are used by the MM (Materials Management) and PP (Production Planning) modules in addition to the Sales and Distribution module.

The SAP ERP system allows a company to define various ways to group its customers and salespeople. These groupings are called **organizational structures**. One important organizational structure for Fitter Snacker is the Distribution Channel. With SAP ERP, the Distribution Channel allows the user to define different ways for materials to be sold and distributed to the customer. The Distribution Channel structure also allows for different types of relationships with different customers, and it lets the company specify aspects of the relationship, such as pricing, delivery method, and minimum order quantities. Defining a Wholesale Distribution Channel and a Direct Sales Distribution Channel for Fitter would help to ensure that customers' orders are correctly priced. Figure 3-7 shows a completed sales order screen for an order from West Hills Athletic Club for 10 cases of NRG-A bars and 10 cases of NRG-B bars.

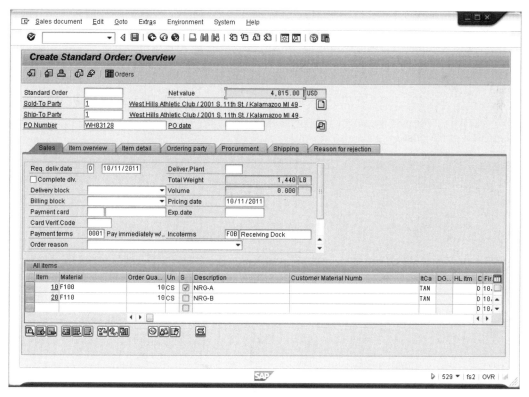

Source Line: SAP AG.

FIGURE 3-7   Order screen with complete data

West Hills's purchase order (PO) number for this sales transaction is WH83128. This is a unique number provided by the customer (West Hills) that allows it to track orders with its suppliers. If the customer has a question about an order, it will likely reference that PO number in its inquiry. Because the SAP ERP system records the customer's PO number, a Fitter employee can look up the status of the order using the customer's PO number. Alternatively, the order can be located using the sales order number that SAP assigns to this transaction.

Notice also that the order screen shows the name of the customer (West Hills Athletic Club) and the names of the products (NRG-A and NRG-B), even though they were not entered directly during the order process. How did they get on the screen at this point? Once the company or product code is entered, the clerk can easily request the SAP ERP system to search the database and access all the information needed to complete the order. Thus, the SAP ERP system simplifies the data entry tasks, reducing data entry time and the possibility of error.

When the SAP ERP system is instructed to save a sales order, it performs inventory sourcing—that is, it carries out checks to ensure that the customer's sales order can be delivered on the requested delivery date. Remember that previously when a customer wanted to know when an order could be delivered, the sales clerk had to make a series of phone calls. In the SAP ERP system, this process is handled automatically. The system performs a check on both inventory and production, and it takes into account the time required for shipping. When the requested delivery date cannot be met, the SAP ERP system automatically proposes alternatives to the sales order clerk. For example, Figure 3-8 shows what the sales order clerk will see if only five cases of NRG-A bars will be available by the requested delivery date. The SAP ERP system provides the sales order clerk with three alternatives:

1. Reduce the order quantity of NRG-A cases to five, which can be delivered by the requested delivery date.
2. Delay shipment of the NRG-A bars for three days, when 10 cases will be available.
3. Ship five cases by the requested delivery date, and ship five cases at the later date.

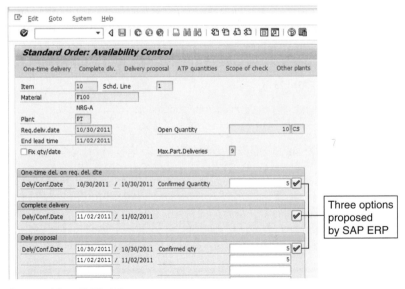

Source Line: SAP AG.

FIGURE 3-8   Order proposals

The best situation would be that the company could meet the customer's request, but when that is not possible, the integrated SAP ERP system can provide the clerk with accurate information about the ability to meet the customer's requirements. With Fitter's unintegrated systems, it could take days for the customer to find out that its requested delivery date could not be met.

When a sales order is saved, the SAP ERP system assigns a document number to the sales order transaction. In the SAP ERP system, a document is an electronic record of a business transaction, and a document number is created for each business transaction. When the sales order is ready to be processed by the warehouse, a delivery document will be created with its own unique document number, which the system will link to the sales order document. Finally, when the bill (invoice) is prepared for the customer, the bill's unique number (called the invoice number) will be created and linked to all the other numbers associated with the sales order.

The SAP ERP system has a mechanism for keeping track of the document numbers associated with each sales order so employees can track the status of an order while it is in process or research it after shipping. The linked set of document numbers related to a sales order, also known as the **audit trail**, is called the **document flow** in SAP ERP. Figure 3-9 shows the document flow for a completed order.

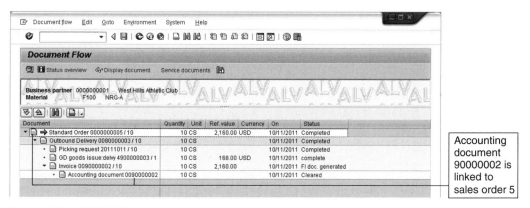

Source Line: SAP AG.

FIGURE 3-9   The Document Flow tool, which links sales order documents

If an order includes partial shipments, partial payments, and returned material credits, the document flow can become quite complex. Without an integrated information system, the audit trail can be hard to establish, especially if many paper documents are involved. With an integrated system such as SAP ERP, document numbers are all linked together electronically. Not only does the document flow show all documents related to a sales order, but the user can look at the details of each document simply by double-clicking a line in the document flow. For example, if West Hills Athletic Club chose to take delivery of five cases of NRG-A bars on its requested delivery date and five cases when they became available, a sales order clerk can easily check on the status of the five delayed cases using document flow. He or she can search the SAP system to find the original sales order by a number of methods (open orders for West Hills, the PO number that West Hills used, the sales order number assigned by the SAP ERP system, and so on) and then review the delivery document for the delayed cases. As another example, a customer may have a question about an invoice it has received. The clerk can search the SAP ERP system for the invoice, and the document flow will show all activity that led to the invoice. With an unintegrated information system, researching the invoice would require checking more than one information system and perhaps searching paper records as well.

Discount Pricing in SAP ERP

When a company installs an ERP system, it can configure it for a number of pricing strategies. For example, various kinds of discounts can be allowed (based on item number or for all items, based on unit price or total order value, with or without shipping charges and taxes, by individual customer, by a class of customer, and so on). As a safeguard, the system can enforce limits on the size of discounts to keep salespeople from offering unprofitable or unapproved discounts.

Suppose a salesperson wants to give a certain customer a 10 percent discretionary discount on NRG-A bars. But is the salesperson allowed to discount those bars? Is that discount appropriate for that customer? If so, will the discount be so deep that the sale will be unprofitable for Fitter? An ERP system automatically answers these questions.

Pricing, the process of determining how much to charge a particular customer, can be very complex. To accommodate the various ways that companies offer price discounts, SAP has developed a control mechanism it calls the **condition technique**. While detailed discussion of the condition technique is beyond the scope of this text, Figure 3-10 shows how a discount is automatically applied in the SAP ERP system.

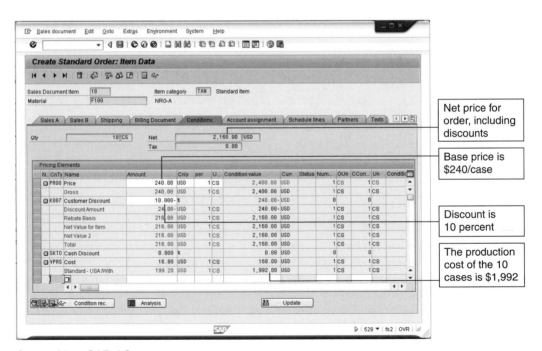

Source Line: SAP AG.

FIGURE 3-10 Pricing conditions for sales order

The screen shows the price that Fitter is offering to West Hills Athletic Club for 10 cases of NRG-A bars. The base price is $240/case, and West Hills is being given a 10 percent discount automatically.

The screen in Figure 3-11 shows that the SAP ERP system has been configured to give West Hills Athletic Club a 5 percent discount for ordering over $1,000 worth of a particular type of snack bar, and a 10 percent discount if the order for a particular type of snack bar is over $1,500 in value.

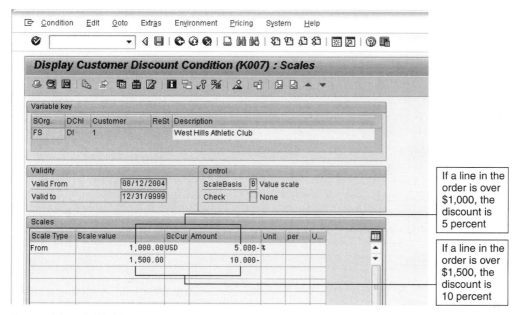

Source Line: SAP AG.

FIGURE 3-11   West Hills Athletic Club price discount

If you look again at Figure 3-10, you can see the SAP ERP system automatically applied the 10 percent discount (since the total amount of the order was over $1,500), so the net price for 10 cases of NRG-A bars is $2,160. Figure 3-10 also shows that Fitter will still make a profit on this order, because the cost to produce 10 cases of NRG-A bars is $1,992.

Integration of Sales and Accounting

In Fitter's old system, sales records were not integrated with the company's accounting records, so Accounting often did not have the most up-to-date information. By contrast, ERP systems integrate Accounting with all business processes, so when a sales order is recorded, the related accounting data are updated automatically.

In the document flow shown in Figure 3-9, Accounting document 90000002 is part of the sales order process. The clerk can select this line, and then click the Display document button to get the accounting detail shown in Figure 3-12.

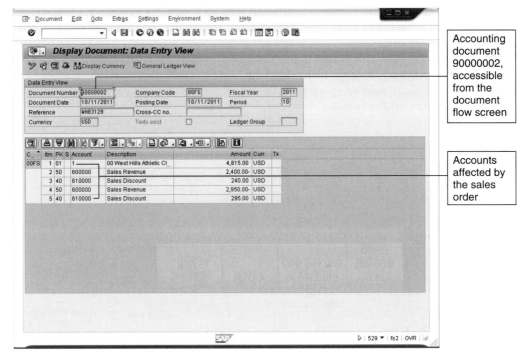

Accounting document 90000002, accessible from the document flow screen

Accounts affected by the sales order

Source Line: SAP AG.

FIGURE 3-12   Accounting detail for the West Hills sales order

This document shows that, as a result of this sales order, West Hills Athletic Club has paid Fitter $4,815. The Sales Revenue account (account number 600000) records sales revenue of $5,350 dollars, which is broken down into the revenue for the NRG-A bars ($2,400) and the revenue for the NRG-B bars ($2,950). These amounts represent the list prices of the snack bars on the order. The 10 percent discount is applied to the NRG-A bars ($240) and NRG-B bars ($295) dollars and is recorded in the Sales Discount account (account number 610000). Because the accounting documents are created automatically with the sales order, the Accounting Department is using the same data as the Sales Department, which results in up-to-date and accurate information. If Marketing needs a report on the size of discounts currently being offered, the system can easily generate a report of that data, and it will be up to date and accurate as well.

Now that you have looked at how an ERP system can help a company's sales order process, we will examine how data obtained during that process might be further used to help Fitter build long-term business relationships with its customers and improve business performance.

CUSTOMER RELATIONSHIP MANAGEMENT (CRM)

Companies without a good connection between their workers and their customers run the risk of losing business. Take Fitter Snacker, for example. Say a salesperson calls on a good customer, Health Express. The salesperson offers Health Express deep discounts for buying a certain number of NRG bars. At the same time, the Marketing Department is running a sale on NRG bars. Marketing sends Health Express a flyer advertising the discounted price, which is less than what the salesperson just offered in person. Meanwhile, the vice president of Fitter plays golf with the CEO of Health Express and offers yet another discount. The connection or relationship with the customer is confused because the customer is receiving inconsistent information. **Customer relationship management (CRM) software** can help companies streamline their interactions with customers to ensure a consistent message.

An ERP system offers a company an added benefit beyond systems integration: vast and complete quantities of data available for analysis. By adding other software tools to its ERP system, a company can extend the capabilities of the system, thus increasing its value. Many ERP vendors—and non-ERP software companies—provide CRM software. In 2011, the CRM software market was worth $12 billion and was forecasted to grow to $25 billion by 2018. SAP was the market leader in CRM software in 2011 with 21 percent of the CRM market, but SAP has been facing significant challenges from growing interest in on-demand CRM solutions provided by companies such as Salesforce.com. (With **on-demand CRM**, the software and computer equipment reside with the CRM provider; it is not installed in-house.) In 2006, SAP responded to competition from on-demand providers with CRM OnDemand. This product was essentially a hosted version of its CRM software with a few minor changes. In 2011, SAP introduced Sales OnDemand, based on its BusinessByDesign platform, which is a CRM product with a focus on sales.

With the goal of providing "a single face to the customer," the basic principle behind CRM is that any employee in contact with the customer should have access to all information about the company's past interactions with the customer. In a traditional sales organization, information might only be available to one individual, who might not share it with the organization. If that individual leaves the company, the information is lost.

Core CRM Activities

In general, CRM software supports the following activities and tools:

- *One-to-one marketing*—Once a customer is categorized, for example, based on the products they buy and the volume in which they buy those products, the company can tailor products, promotions, and pricing accordingly. Customers can be offered products related to what they are now buying (cross-selling), or the company could choose to promote higher-margin products in the same lines (up-selling) to those customers.
- *Sales force automation (SFA)*—Using the CRM software, occurrences of customer contacts are logged in the company's database. The SFA feature of CRM software can automatically route certain customers who contact the company to a particular sales representative. Companies can also use SFA tools to forecast customer needs, based on the customer's history and transactions, and to alert sales representatives accordingly. Sometimes this software is called "lead management software" because a transaction can be tracked from the initial lead to post-sale follow-up.
- *Sales campaign management*—This software feature lets a company organize a marketing campaign and compile its results automatically.
- *Marketing encyclopedias*—This feature serves as a database of promotional literature about products. The material can be routed to sales representatives or customers as needed.

- *Call center automation*—When customers call a company to get assistance with a company's products, representatives can query a knowledge management database containing information about the product. Some knowledge management software accepts queries in natural language. If the company must develop a new solution in response to a unique customer query, that information can be added to the knowledge base, which thus becomes "smarter."

SAP's CRM Software

A number of tools that provide CRM functionality exist within the SAP ERP system. For example, to make sure that information about sales contacts is available throughout the organization, the SAP ERP system provides a contact management tool, shown in Figure 3-13. This tool is essentially a database of personal contact information.

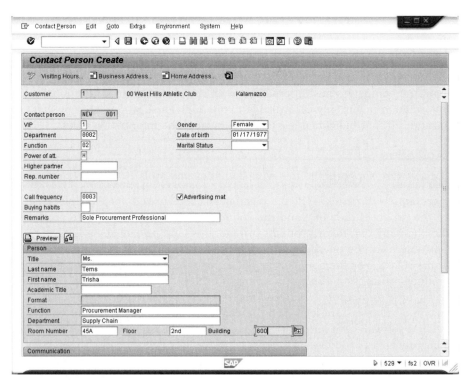

Source Line: SAP AG.

FIGURE 3-13 SAP ERP contact manager

Another CRM tool in the SAP ERP system is the sales activity manager; an example shown in Figure 3-14 shows what the company wants to accomplish with a particular sales call. This tool supports a strategic and organized approach to sales activity

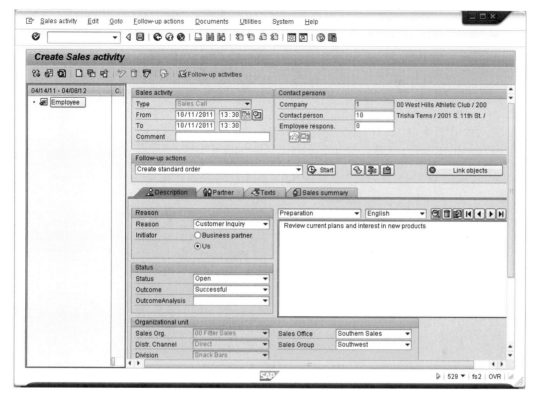

Source Line: SAP AG.

FIGURE 3-14   SAP ERP sales activity manager

While the CRM tools in the SAP ERP system, if employed properly, can help manage customer relationships, firms embracing the CRM concept often employ a separate CRM system that communicates with the ERP system. An advantage of this approach is that the planning and analysis performed in the CRM system do not interfere with the performance of the ERP system, which primarily processes large volumes of business transactions.

Figure 3-15 shows how SAP CRM relates to the SAP ERP system as well as SAP's Business Warehouse (BW) and Advanced Planner and Optimizer (APO) modules. The SAP CRM system communicates with the SAP ERP, BW, and APO systems in developing and executing its plans, thereby allowing SAP CRM to not only facilitate a company's interactions with its customers, but to also enable the company to analyze the customer data and best serve the customer.

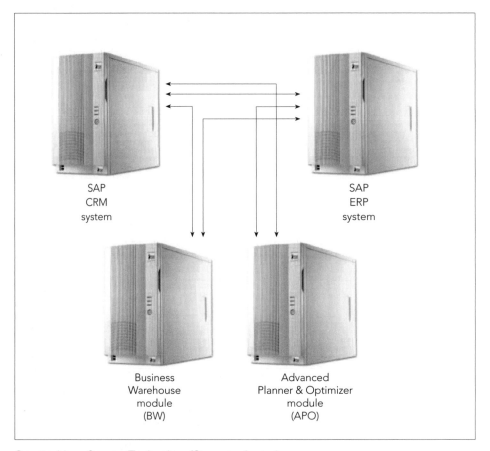

Source Line: Course Technology/Cengage Learning.

FIGURE 3-15   SAP CRM system landscape

As described previously, the SAP ERP system processes business transactions and provides much of the raw data for CRM. SAP's Business Warehouse (BW) is a flexible system for the reporting and analysis of transactional data that makes use of data mining techniques. **Data mining** is the statistical and logical analysis of large sets of transaction data, looking for patterns that can aid decision making and improve customer sales and service. By analyzing sales transactions using data mining, firms can discover trends and patterns to use in planning marketing activities.

The Advanced Planner and Optimizer (APO) is a component of SAP's Supply Chain Management (SCM) system that supports efficient planning of the supply chain. APO's role in the CRM process is to provide higher levels of customer support through its global available-to-promise (ATP) capabilities. In the standard SAP ERP system, the ATP capabilities function on a location-by-location basis. If the product or material a customer wants is not available in the location that usually serves the customer, then the sales order clerk can check for the material in other facilities, but this must be done on a facility-by-facility basis. With global ATP, the system automatically checks all facilities and determines the most cost-efficient facility to use to meet the customer's request.

SAP's approach to CRM is to provide a set of tools to manage the three basic task areas, or jobs, related to customers: marketing, sales, and service. These task areas contribute to the cultivation of the customer relationship. This cultivation goes through four phases, as defined by SAP: prospecting, acquiring, servicing, and retaining.

In prospecting, a potential new customer (or potential new business opportunity with an existing customer) is evaluated, and development activities (emails, sales calls, mailings, etc.) are planned to develop the prospective business. Marketing tasks predominate in this phase.

In acquiring, salespeople develop business prospects into customers. Marketing is still the critical task, but the sales tasks (processing inquiries, quotes, and eventually sales orders) become increasingly important in this phase.

Once sales are established with the customer, the business becomes one of servicing the account. In the servicing phase, sales tasks are still important, but service tasks (including technical support, warranty work, product returns, fixing quality problems, and complaint handling) are critical to maintaining customer satisfaction.

The rate at which prospects become customers is quite low; thus, a critical part of the process is retaining customers. It is much easier to retain a good customer than to find a new one, so the focus of the retaining phase is making sure that current customers are satisfied by timely delivery of quality products and services at a fair price. Sales and service tasks are still critical, but marketing tasks are again important in terms of anticipating changes in customers' requirements.

In SAP CRM, the customer development cycle (prospecting, acquiring, servicing, and retaining) is supported by contact channels, the methods the company uses to communicate with its customers. An interaction center provides contact through a variety of media (phone, fax, and email). Mobile technologies and the Internet are providing an increasingly large percentage of customer contacts. For example, the Contact Channels might aid a customer service agent on the telephone and prompt her to ask the customer various questions relating to the account.

Another set of tools in SAP CRM is Marketing and Campaign Management. Companies invest significant sums of money in marketing campaigns, which are promotional activities that publicize the product and the company. Successful planning, execution, and evaluation are critical to gain maximum effect from these efforts. Figure 3-16 shows how SAP CRM supports marketing and campaign management. The top half of this diagram represents planning activities, while the bottom half represents execution and evaluation activities. These activities are supported by most CRM software products.

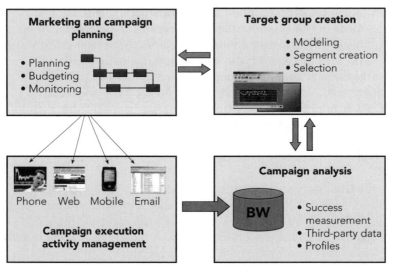

Source Line: Course Technology/Cengage Learning.

FIGURE 3-16   Marketing and campaign planning

Marketing and campaign planning includes task scheduling, resource allocation, and budgeting. These planning tasks are executed in conjunction with target group creation tasks, which use data from the SAP ERP system (perhaps using SAP BW) to categorize the company's customers, offering them more individual product and service promotions.

Campaign Execution Activity Management is a set of tools within SAP CRM to help manage the execution of the marketing campaign, which can include handling sales calls, mailings, personalized emails, and Web-based promotional activities directed to the targeted group of customers. These activities can be monitored throughout the campaign to make sure they are completed. For example, the status of a planned customer phone call will remain open until the call is completed.

The campaign analysis tool in SAP CRM allows the company to evaluate the success of the campaign so it can incorporate improvements in the next marketing campaign. Marketing employees can use a number of measures to determine the success of the campaign, including tracking lead generation and response rates. Staff can use SAP BW tools, by running queries, to support this analysis.

The Benefits of CRM

CRM software can provide companies with the following benefits:

- *Lower costs*—CRM can lead to operational efficiencies, such as better response times in call center operations and better use of sales force time, which lower costs.
- *Higher revenue*—Segmenting customers leads to better selling opportunities and revenue increases.
- *Improved strategy and performance measurement*—Installing and operating an ERP system requires management and staff to think of the company as a

whole. This attitude carries over into CRM work. With a CRM system in place, management can think about different performance measures; for example, should salespeople be rewarded for exceeding sales quotas, and marketing people rewarded for finding new customers—or, should both receive rewards that are based on some measure of customer satisfaction? The former approach, typical in days before CRM and ERP, can lead to unintegrated functional thinking. The latter approach—now feasible with CRM and ERP—can lead all personnel to think in terms of a company-wide effort to satisfy customers.

ANOTHER LOOK

CRM and Social Media

Customer relationship management tools now also include social media channels that consist of not only the more prominent ones—such as Facebook and Twitter—but also blogs, wikis, YouTube, and other purpose-built Web sites. For example, Salesforce.com, a company that provides CRM software via the Internet, has a product that searches for specific products and brands being mentioned on social networks—important information for companies either selling those brands or competing with those brands. Companies interested in making the most of these new CRM tools need a dedicated group of personnel to manage these new channels, which must be connected with other CRM channels. Social media channels cannot stand alone, and they cannot replace the other more traditional marketing channels.

The rise in popularity of social media means that companies must find ways to address these new avenues of communication with their customers. A company needs to make the most of any chance to connect with its customers, but these new opportunities can be challenging. Any response to a Facebook post or a tweet must be immediate; customers expect no less. Customer expectations have risen for response time; however, investments in the social media CRM processes and procedures are lagging. In addition, companies have yet to calculate the return on investment for investments in social media CRM tools.

Gartner research has shown that 30 percent of major businesses will implement some sort of social media with CRM over the next two years in order to improve customer service. Both SAP and Salesforce.com have social media tools embedded in their CRM software. Salesforce.com recently announced a new product called Data.com, which populates CRM with social media contact information, in effect, making every address for every contact up to date. They also have a new component of their CRM called Chatter, which is a Twitter-type system for rapid internal company communications.

Question:

1. Companies are losing their grip on maintaining their own public relations because of social media and the Internet. What challenges face companies with the advent of these new avenues of communication?

Chapter Summary

- Fitter Snacker's unintegrated information systems are at the root of an inefficient and costly sales order process. Because information is not shared in real time, customers are often asked to repeat initial sales order information. As an order is processed, errors in pricing, credit checks, and invoicing frequently occur, presenting a poor company image to customers. Integrated ERP software would help Fitter avoid errors by storing all customer data in a central database that is shared in real time by all company employees.

- An ERP system such as SAP ERP treats a sale as a sequence of related functions, including taking orders, setting prices, checking product availability, checking the customer's credit line, arranging for delivery, billing the customer, and collecting payment. In SAP ERP, all these transactions, or documents, are electronically linked, so tracking an order's status (partial shipments, returns, partial payments, and so forth) is easily accomplished.

- Installing an ERP system means making various configuration decisions, which reflect management's view of how transactions should be recorded and later used for decision making. For example, the system can be configured to limit selling price discounts, thus avoiding unprofitable pricing.

- An ERP system's central database contains tables of master data—relatively permanent data about customers, suppliers, material, and inventory—as well as transaction data tables, which store relatively temporary data such as sales orders and invoices.

- Customer relationship management (CRM) systems build on the organizational value ERP provides; specifically, they increase the flexibility of the company's common database regarding customer service. Various kinds of CRM software are available, some from ERP vendors (including SAP) and some from third-party software companies. CRM software can lead to operational savings, but most companies buy it because they believe that creating better customer relationships will result in higher revenue. Uses of CRM have evolved since the software was initially launched; what began as a customer contact repository has extended its capabilities to include sophisticated business intelligence. CRM can be installed in-house or on-demand.

Key Terms

audit trail	delivery
condition technique	document flow
customer master data	material master data
customer relationship management (CRM) software	on-demand CRM
	organizational structure
data mining	

Exercises

1. Assume you are Fitter Snacker's new marketing manager, hired to clean up some of the company's problems, as outlined in the beginning of this chapter. You just started this job, and you are getting to know your sales team and the company's processes. Describe all the problems you observe about the way Fitter's sales force currently takes and fills an order. Now convince upper management of the need to improve the existing system and put an ERP system in place.

2. If Fitter installs an ERP system, how could they reorganize their sales division to be more efficient? Be specific about how you would rearrange divisions, or consolidate them.

3. Fitter's current sales order accounting processes involves recording sales in each division and then periodically sending certain sales data to Accounting for invoicing and financial reporting. Complete sales order data are retained in each sales division for business analysis purposes.

   Assume that different divisions of the Yummy Foods Company buy NRG-A and NRG-B bars from each of Fitter's sales divisions. To complicate matters, some divisions of Yummy buy store-brand bars from Fitter. (Yummy owns convenience store outlets.) Fitter management has asked for an analysis of the Yummy Foods account. They want to determine if there are opportunities to expand the company's relationship with Yummy; however, they want to assess the profitability of the relationship before proceeding. The management team wants to see what products each division sells to Yummy, how much is sold, and on what terms. Assume that in Fitter's current system, all the required data are available only at the sales division level. What steps will be needed to pull this company-wide analysis together? (Review how each division sells its products.) Do you think a sales division manager will be enthusiastic about sharing all data with his or her counterpart in the other division? Do you think there might be some reluctance? Why?

4. Continuing the Yummy Foods example, now assume that Fitter has an SAP ERP system installed. Each sales division records sales in the same way. Sales records exist in real time and are kept in the company's common database. What steps will be needed to pull this company-wide analysis together? Do you expect that the divisions will meet the new system with enthusiasm or reluctance?

5. Assume you are a new summer intern at Fitter Snacker, working directly under the CIO. Your first job is to write a memo describing the poor information flow between three functional areas in the company: Marketing and Sales, Accounting and Finance, and Supply Chain Management. Focus on the lack of information flow to and from Marketing and Sales, in particular.

6. How does an ERP system like SAP simplify looking up customer numbers, setting a delivery date, and charging a unique price to a given customer? Include a discussion of master data.

7. What is document flow? Why is it important for auditors of a company?

8. A CIO of a major pharmaceutical company once stated that the reason the corporation used ERP systems could be summed up in one word: *control*. How does an ERP system give management control?

9. How can a business better serve its customers using the APO tool in SAP ERP?

10. Assume you are the marketing manager for a large pet food company, such as Iams. You need to launch a new marketing campaign. What social media channels would you use for this campaign? How can CRM help your new strategy?

For Further Study and Research

Beal, Barney. "SAP Takes Another Shot at CRM On-Demand." *SearchCRM.com*, March 2, 2011. http://searchcrm.techtarget.com/news/2240032955/SAP-takes-another-shot-at-CRM-on-demand.

Cafasso, Rosemary. "CRM Buyers Say Goodbye to Cloud CRM/On-Premises Debate." *SearchCRM.com*, August 23, 2011. http://searchcrm.techtarget.com/news/2240063219/CRM-buyers-say-goodbye-to-cloud-CRM-on-premise-debate.

Diana, Alison. "Social CRM Rush Projected for Enterprises." *InformationWeek*, March 4, 2011. www.informationweek.com/news/software/productivity_apps/229300370.

Hildreth, Sue. "Measuring the ROI of Social CRM No Easy Task." *SearchCRM.com*, May 3, 2010. http://searchcrm.techtarget.com/news/2240018288/Measuring-the-ROI-of-social-CRM-no-easy-task.

Kontzer, Tony. "Better Late Than Never? SAP Spices Up On-Demand CRM." *Information Week*, February 6, 2006. www.informationweek.com/news/178601884.

Information Age. "Salesforce.com – The Facebook of Business?" September 5, 2011. www.information-age.com/channels/business-applications/company-analysis/1652743/salesforcecom-the-facebook-of-business.thtml.

Levine, Barry. "Salesforce Conference Pushes 'Social Enterprise'." *destinationCRM.com*, August 26, 2011. www.destinationcrm.com/Articles/Web-Exclusives/Viewpoints/Six-Myths-of-Social-Media-77185.aspx.

Lopez, Maribel. "Mobile Strategy: It's Not About the Gadgets." *Information Week*, August 30, 2011. www.informationweek.com/thebrainyard/news/mobile/231500273.

Mittal, Saurabh. "Six Myths of Social Media: Understanding the Evolving Customer Service Landscape." *destinationCRM.com*, August 19, 2011. www.destinationcrm.com/articles/Web-Exclusives/Viewpoints/Six-Myths-of-Social-Media-77185.aspx.

Pombriant, Denis. "When Will CRM Join the Analytics Revolution?" *SearchCRM.com*, February 3, 2011. http://searchcrm.techtarget.com/news/2240031716/When-will-CRM-join-the-analytics-revolution.

Rosenbaum, David. "Now You See (Some of) It." *CFO Magazine*, July 15, 2011. www.cfo.com/article.cfm/14586485.

Wagner, William, and Zubey, Michael. *Customer Relationship Management*, 1st edition. Boston: Cengage Learning, 2007.

Weiss, Todd R. "Social CRM for the Enterprise: How Analytics Can Move You to Greater Success." *CIO*, July 06, 2011. www.cio.com/article/685754.

CHAPTER 4

PRODUCTION AND SUPPLY CHAIN MANAGEMENT INFORMATION SYSTEMS

LEARNING OBJECTIVES

After completing this chapter, you will be able to:

- Describe the steps in the production planning process of a high-volume manufacturer, such as Fitter Snacker
- Describe Fitter Snacker's production and materials management problems
- Explain how a structured supply chain management planning process enhances efficiency and decision making
- Understand how production planning data in an ERP system can be shared with suppliers to increase supply chain efficiency

INTRODUCTION

In Chapter 2, you learned that Enterprise Resource Planning (ERP) has its roots in materials requirements planning (MRP) processes and software. Materials requirements planning, and the extension of that process to partners in the supply chain, are important parts of today's ERP systems. In fact, effective supply chain management is critical to the success of companies such as Fitter Snacker. In this chapter, we will first examine how Fitter manages its production activities, and then we will explore some supply chain management functions in an ERP system. We will also we will look at the broader concept of supply chain management.

In Chapter 3, we looked at Fitter's sales order process, and we assumed that Fitter had enough snack bars in its warehouse to fill a typical order. Like most unintegrated manufacturing operations, however, Fitter often has problems scheduling production. Consequently, sometimes its warehouse is not adequately stocked, and customer orders cannot be filled in a timely fashion—leading to customer dissatisfaction and lost sales. In this chapter, you will explore Fitter's supply chain management problems and learn how ERP can help solve them.

PRODUCTION OVERVIEW

To efficiently meet customer demand, Fitter must develop an estimate of customer demand, and then develop a production schedule to meet that forecasted demand. Developing a production plan is a complicated task, but the end result answers two simple questions:

- How many of each type of snack bar should we produce, and when?
- What quantities of raw materials should we order so we can meet that level of production, and when should they be ordered?

Developing a good production plan is just the first step: Fitter must also be able to execute the plan and make adjustments when customer demand does not meet the forecast. An ERP system is a good tool for developing and executing production plans because it integrates the functions of production planning, purchasing, materials management/warehousing, quality management, sales, and accounting. To support even better supply chain management, companies can connect ERP systems to supplier and customer information systems as well.

In this chapter, we will use spreadsheet examples to illustrate the logic that Fitter should be using to plan and schedule production of its NRG bars. First, we will look at Fitter's current production process, as well as some of the associated problems that are due to Fitter's unintegrated systems. We will use spreadsheets to further explore the planning and scheduling logic required at each stage of the production planning process, and then we will examine the SAP ERP screens that implement this logic in an ERP environment. Throughout the chapter, you will develop a deeper understanding of why using an integrated information system is superior to using unintegrated systems.

The goal of production planning is to schedule production economically so a company can ship goods to its customers by the promised delivery dates in the most cost-efficient manner. There are three general approaches to production:

- *Make-to-stock*—Items are made for inventory (the "stock") in anticipation of sales orders; most consumer products (for example, cameras, canned corn, and books) are made this way.
- *Make-to-order*—Items are produced to fill specific customer orders; companies usually take this approach when producing items that are too expensive to keep in stock or items that are made or configured to customer

specifications. Examples of make-to-order items are airplanes and large industrial equipment.

- *Assemble-to-order*—Items are produced using a combination of make-to-stock and make-to-order processes; the final product is assembled for a specific order from a selection of make-to-stock components. Personal computers are a typical assemble-to-order product.

Fitter's Manufacturing Process

Fitter uses make-to-stock production techniques to produce its snack bars. The manufacturing process is illustrated in Figure 4-1.

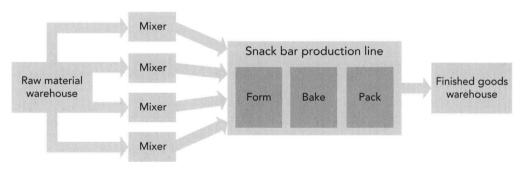

Source Line: Course Technology/Cengage Learning.

FIGURE 4-1   Fitter's manufacturing process

The snack bar production line can produce 200 bars per minute—or 12,000 bars per hour. Each bar weighs 4 ounces, which means the line produces 48,000 ounces (or 3,000 pounds) of bars per hour. The entire production line operates on one shift a day. The next section describes Fitter's production process in more detail.

Fitter's Production Sequence

Raw materials are taken from the warehouse to one of four mixers. Each mixer mixes dough in 500-pound batches. Mixing a batch of dough requires 15 minutes of mixing time, plus another 15 minutes to unload, clean, and load the mixer for the next batch of dough; therefore, each mixer can produce two 500-pound batches of dough per hour. That means the four mixers can produce a total of 4,000 pounds of dough per hour—more than the production line can process. Because only three mixers need to be operating at a time to produce 3,000 pounds of snack bars per hour, a mixer breakdown will not shut down the production line.

After mixing, the dough is dumped into a hopper (bin) at the beginning of the snack bar production line. A forming mechanism molds the dough into bars, which will weigh 4 ounces each. Next, an automated process takes the formed bars on a conveyor belt through an oven that bakes the bars for 30 minutes. When the bars emerge from the oven, they are individually packaged in a foil wrapper, and each group of 24 bars is packaged into a display box. At the end of the snack bar line, display boxes are stacked on pallets (for larger orders the display boxes are first packed into shipping boxes, which are then stacked on the pallets).

Switching the production line from one type of snack bar to the other takes 30 minutes—for cleaning the equipment and changing the wrappers, display boxes, and shipping cases. Each night, a second shift of employees cleans all the equipment thoroughly and sets it up for the next day's production. Thus, changing production from NRG-A on one day to NRG-B the next day can be done at the end of the day without a loss of capacity. (**Capacity** is the maximum amount of bars that can be produced.) On the other hand, producing two products in one day results in a half-hour loss of capacity during the changeover.

Fitter's Production Problems

Fitter has no problems *making* snack bars, but it does have problems deciding *how many* bars to make and *when* to make them. The manufacturing process at Fitter suffers from a number of problems, ranging from communication breakdowns and inventory issues to accounting inconsistencies, mainly stemming from the unintegrated nature of its information systems.

Communication Problems

Communication breakdowns are an inherent problem in most companies, and they are magnified in a company with an unintegrated information system. For example, at Fitter, Marketing and Sales personnel do a poor job of sharing information with Production personnel. Marketing and Sales frequently excludes Production from meetings, neglects to consult Production when planning sales promotions, and often fails to even alert Production of planned promotions. Marketing and Sales also typically forgets to notify Production when it takes an exceptionally large order.

When Production must meet an unexpected increase in demand, several things happen. First, warehouse inventories are depleted. To compensate, Production must schedule overtime labor, which results in higher production costs for products. Second, because some materials (such as ingredients, wrappers, and display boxes) are custom products purchased from a single vendor, a sudden increase in sales demand can cause shortages or even a stockout of these materials. Getting these materials to Fitter's plant might require expedited shipping, further increasing the cost of production. Finally, unexpected spikes in demand result in high levels of frustration for Production staff. Production personnel are evaluated on their performance—how successful they are at controlling costs, keeping manufacturing lines running, maintaining quality control, and operating safely. If they cannot keep production costs down, Production staff receive poor evaluations. Managers are especially frustrated when an instant need for overtime follows a period of low demand. With advance notice of a product promotion by Marketing and Sales, Production could use slack periods to build up inventory in anticipation of the increase in sales.

Inventory Problems

As noted earlier, Fitter's week-to-week and day-to-day production planning is not linked in a systematic way to expected sales levels. When deciding how much to produce, the production manager applies rules developed through experience. Her primary indicator is the difference between the normal amount of finished goods inventory that should be stocked and the actual inventory levels of finished goods in the warehouse. Thus, if NRG-A or NRG-B inventory levels seem low, the production manager schedules more bars for production. However, she does not want too many bars in inventory because they have a limited shelf life. Her judgment is also influenced by the information she hears informally from people in Marketing and Sales about expected sales levels.

The production manager's inventory data are maintained in an Access database. Data records are not updated in real time and do not flag inventory that has been sold but not yet shipped. (Such inventory is not available for sale, of course, but employees cannot determine this by looking at the database; thus, workers do not know the level of inventory that is available to ship at any given moment). This is problematic if the Wholesale Division generates unusually large orders or high volumes of orders. For example, two large Wholesale Division orders arriving at the same time can deplete the entire available inventory of NRG-A bars. If Production is manufacturing NRG-B bars at that time, it must halt production of those bars so it can fill the orders for NRG-A. This means delaying production of NRG-B bars and losing production capacity due to the unplanned production changeover.

The production manager lacks a systematic method not only for meeting anticipated sales demand, but also for adjusting production to reflect actual sales. Marketing and Sales does not share actual sales data with the Production Department, partly because this information is hard to gather on a timely basis and partly because of a lack of trust between the Sales and Production departments (as a result of prior negative experiences). If Production had access to sales forecasts and real-time sales order information, the manager could make timely adjustments to production, if needed. These adjustments would allow inventory levels to come much closer to what is actually needed.

Accounting and Purchasing Problems

Production and Accounting do not have a good way to calculate the day-to-day costs of Fitter's production. Manufacturing costs are based on the number of bars produced each day, a number that is measured at the end of the snack bar production line. For the purpose of figuring manufacturing costs, Fitter uses **standard costs**, which are the normal costs of manufacturing a product; standard costs are calculated from historical data, factoring in any changes in manufacturing that have occurred since the collection of the historical data. For each batch of bars it produces, Fitter can estimate direct costs (materials and labor) and indirect costs (factory overhead). The number of batches produced is multiplied by the standard cost of a batch, and the resulting amount is charged to manufacturing costs.

Most manufacturing companies use standard costs in some way, but the method requires that standards be adjusted periodically to conform with actual costs. (These adjustments will be discussed in Chapter 5.) Fitter's actual raw material and labor costs often deviate from the standard costs, in part, because Fitter is not good at controlling raw materials purchases. The production manager cannot give the purchasing manager a good production forecast, so the purchasing manager works on two tracks: First, she tries to keep raw materials inventories high to avoid stockouts. Second, if she is offered good bulk-quantity discounts on raw materials such as oats, she will buy in bulk, especially for items that have long lead times for delivery. These purchasing practices make it difficult both to forecast the volume of raw materials that will be on hand and to calculate an average cost of the materials purchased for profitability planning. Fitter also has trouble accurately forecasting the average cost of labor for a batch of bars because of the frequent need for overtime labor.

Thus, Production and Accounting must periodically compare standard costs with actual costs and then adjust the accounts for the inevitable differences, which is always a tedious and unpleasant job. The comparison should be done at each monthly closing, but Fitter often puts it off until the closing at the end of each quarter, when its financial backers require legitimate financial statements. The necessary adjustments are often quite large, depending on production volumes and costs during the quarter.

Exercise 4.1

a. A convenience store chain offers to buy a very large amount of its store brand health bars (the NRG-B bars with a customized wrapper). The chain wants a lower-than-normal price because the proposed order is quadruple the size of its regular order. The marketing manager asks managers from Production, Purchasing, and Accounting whether the terms of the proposed deal will be profitable. Will the managers in these areas be able to provide a reliable answer on short notice?

b. The production manager notes that current warehouse inventory levels are fairly high, so the production line does not need to be run for a full eight hours each day during the coming week. For several reasons, however, she plans to run the line for eight hours a day anyway. If the line shuts down workers would still need to be paid during the idle time and overhead costs would continue to be incurred as well. Running the line full time decreases the average cost of bars actually produced (indirect costs can be spread over more bars). In addition, some warehoused raw materials will spoil if they are not used soon. Is the production manager's reasoning logical? Why, or why not?

THE PRODUCTION PLANNING PROCESS

In this section, you will examine a systematic process for developing a production plan that takes advantage of an ERP system. Spreadsheet calculations are presented to explain and illustrate the key steps, and the corresponding screens in the SAP ERP system follow the spreadsheet data.

Production planners are employees who interact with the inventory system and the sales forecast to determine how much to produce. Planners follow three important principles:

- Using a sales forecast, and taking into account current inventory levels, create an aggregate (combined) production plan for all products. Aggregate production plans help to simplify the planning process in two ways: First, plans are made for groups of related products rather than for individual products. Second, the time increment used in aggregate planning is frequently a month or a quarter, while the production plans that will actually be executed operate on a daily or weekly basis. Aggregate plans should consider the available capacity in the facility.
- Break down the aggregate plan into more specific production plans for individual products and then into smaller time intervals.
- Use the production plan to determine raw material requirements.

Production planners aggregate products into product groups to reduce the number of variables they must consider when developing a production plan. Developing production groups can be complicated. For example, cereal manufacturers can group together different package sizes, or they might group together product brands (such as kids' cereals, health cereals, and so on). A consumer products company may group by product type (e.g., shampoo, laundry detergent, and disposable diapers). The aggregate production plan for Fitter will combine the only two products, NRG-A and NRG-B bars, into one group to illustrate the process. The plan will be developed using a monthly time increment. Ultimately, the monthly production plan will be disaggregated to determine weekly raw materials orders and daily production schedules.

The SAP ERP Approach to Production Planning

The SAP ERP approach to the production planning process is shown in Figure 4-2. Refer to this figure throughout this discussion to track the stages in the production planning process.

Source Line: Course Technology/Cengage Learning.

FIGURE 4-2 The SAP ERP production planning process

The information at each stage of the production process flows through the following steps, which are explained in detail in the upcoming sections:

- *Sales forecasting* is the process of predicting future demand for a company's products.
- *Sales and operations planning (SOP)* is the process of determining what the company will produce. In the diagram, the Sales forecasting and Starting

83

inventory levels are inputs to this process. At first glance, it might seem that a company should just make products to match forecasted sales, but developing the production plan is often more complicated than that because capacity must be considered. Many products have seasonal demand, and to meet demand during peak periods, production planners must decide whether to build up inventory levels before the peak demand, increase capacity during the peak period, subcontract production, or use some combination of these approaches.

- In the *Demand management* step, the production plan is broken down into smaller time units, such as weekly or even daily production figures, to meet demand for individual products.
- The *Materials requirements planning (MRP)* process determines the amount and timing of raw material orders. This process answers the questions: "What raw materials should we be ordering so we can meet a particular level of production?" and "When should we order these materials?"
- In the *Purchasing* step, the quantity and timing information from the MRP process is used to create raw materials purchase orders, which are transmitted to qualified suppliers.
- The *Detailed scheduling* process uses the production plans developed during the demand management step as an input for a production schedule. The detailed scheduling method used depends on the manufacturing environment. For Fitter, the detailed production schedule will determine when the production line will switch between the NRG-A and NRG-B bars.
- The *Production* process uses the detailed schedule to manage daily operations, answering the questions: "What should we be producing?" and "What staffing do we need to produce those products?"

Let's take a more detailed look at each of these steps in the production process.

Sales Forecasting

Currently, Fitter Snacker has no formal way of developing a sales forecast and sharing it with Production. SAP's ERP system would allow it to take an integrated approach to sales forecasting. Whenever a sale is recorded in SAP's ERP Sales and Distribution (SD) module, the quantity sold is recorded as a consumption value for that material. These consumption values can be updated on a weekly or monthly basis, as desired. If more detail is needed, the Logistics Information system that is part of SAP ERP can record sales with more detail (for example, by region or sales office), or data can be stored in the separate Business Warehouse (BW) system for more detailed analysis. With an integrated information system, accurate historical sales data are available for forecasting.

A range of forecasting techniques can be used to predict consumer demand. One simple forecasting technique is to use a prior period's sales and then adjust those figures for current conditions. To make a forecast for Fitter, we can use the previous year's sales data in combination with information on this year's marketing initiatives to predict future sales. Look at the forecasts that were created for January through June, shown in Figure 4-3.

Sales forecasting	Jan.	Feb.	March	April	May	June
Previous year (cases)	5734	5823	5884	6134	6587	6735
Promotion sales (cases)					300	300
Previous year base (cases)	5734	5823	5884	6134	6287	6435
Growth: 3.0%	172	175	177	184	189	193
Base projection (cases)	5906	5998	6061	6318	6476	6628
Promotion (cases)						500
Sales forecast (cases)	5906	5998	6061	6318	6476	7128

Source Line: Course Technology/Cengage Learning.

FIGURE 4-3   Fitter's sales forecast for January through June

The sales data in Figure 4-3 are for shipping cases, which contain 12 display boxes with 24 bars each, for a total of 288 bars. Note in Figure 4-3 that the forecast starts with the previous year's sales levels, to reflect Fitter's seasonal sales fluctuations (sales are higher in the summer when more people are active). Also note that there was a special marketing promotion last year. The estimated impact of this promotion was an increase in sales of 300 cases for May and June. To get accurate base figures for last year's sales, this promotional increase must be subtracted from the previous year's sales numbers.

Fitter's Marketing and Sales Department anticipates a 3 percent growth in sales over last year, based on current trends and on research reported in trade publications. In addition, Fitter will be launching a special marketing promotion at the end of May to increase sales at the beginning of the summer season. As shown in Figure 4-3, Fitter marketing experts think the promotion will result in a sales increase of 500 cases for June.

Exercise 4.2

Following the format of the spreadsheet in Figure 4-3, develop a spreadsheet to forecast Fitter's sales for July through December. Calculate the base projection using the previous year's values (shown in Figure 4-4), and factor in the 3 percent estimated growth rate. Assume that the special marketing promotion last year resulted in an increase in sales of 200 cases for July, and that a special marketing promotion this year will result in an increase in sales for July of 400 cases.

Sales volume	July	Aug.	Sept.	Oct.	Nov.	Dec.
Previous year	6702	6327	6215	6007	5954	5813

Source Line: Course Technology/Cengage Learning.

FIGURE 4-4   Fitter's sales for last year, July through December

Sales and Operations Planning

Sales and operations planning (SOP) is the next step in the production planning process. The input to this step is the sales forecast provided by Marketing and Sales. The output is a production plan designed to balance demand with production capacity. The production plan becomes the input to the next step, demand management. The goal is to develop a production plan that meets demand without exceeding capacity and that maintains "reasonable" inventory levels (neither too high nor two low). This process requires judgment and experience.

A sales and operations plan is developed from a sales forecast, and it determines how Manufacturing can efficiently produce enough goods to meet projected sales. In Fitter's case, there is no way to make this determination, because Fitter does not produce a formal estimate of sales. If Fitter had an ERP system, the calculation would be done as described here.

We know that Fitter can produce 200 bars per minute, so we can estimate the production capacity required by the sales forecast. Figure 4-5 shows Fitter's sales and operations plan for the first six months of the year.

Sales and operations planning		Dec.	Jan.	Feb.	March	April	May	June
1) Sales forecast			5906	5998	6061	6318	6476	7128
2) Production plan			5906	5998	6061	6318	6650	6950
3) Inventory		100	100	100	100	100	274	96
4) Working days			21	20	23	21	21	22
5) Capacity (shipping cases)			6999	6666	7666	6999	6999	7333
6) Utilization			84%	90%	79%	90%	95%	95%
7) NRG-A (cases)	70.0%		4134	4199	4243	4423	4655	4865
8) NRG-B (cases)	30.0%		1772	1799	1818	1895	1995	2085

Source Line: Course Technology/Cengage Learning.

FIGURE 4-5 Fitter's sales and operations plan for January through June

The first line in Figure 4-5 is the sales forecast, which is the output of the sales forecasting process shown in Figure 4-3. The next line is the production plan, which the production planner develops—in a trial-and-error fashion—by observing the effect of different production quantities on the lines in the spreadsheet that calculate inventory levels and capacity utilization (the amount of plant capacity that is being consumed).

The third line, inventory, calculates what the inventory should be based on the previous periods inventory, sales forecast, and production plan. The plan in this example assumes an inventory of 100 cases as of the end of December. Adding production of 5,906 cases to this inventory and subtracting the forecast sales of 5,906 cases will leave an inventory of 100 cases at the end of January, if things go according to plan. The production planner has developed a plan that maintains a minimum planned inventory of approximately 100 cases. This inventory, called *safety stock*, is planned so if sales demand exceeds the forecast by no more than 100 cases, sales can be met without altering the production plan. Notice that in May, the production plan is greater than the May sales forecast and the inventory is 274. Why? Because the planner wants to build up inventory to handle the increased demand in June, which results from the normal seasonal increase in snack bar sales and additional demand from the planned promotional activities.

The fourth line shows the number of working days in a given month, an input based on the company calendar. Using the number of working days in a month, the available capacity each month is calculated in terms of the number of shipping cases:

- 200 bars per minute × 60 minutes per hour × 8 hours per day = 96,000 bars per day
- 96,000 bars per day ÷ 24 bars per box ÷ 12 boxes per case = 333.3 cases per day

- Multiplying the number of working days in a month times the production capacity of 333.3 shipping cases per day gives you the monthly capacity in shipping cases, which is shown in line 5.

With the available capacity (assuming no overtime) now expressed in terms of shipping cases, it is possible to determine the capacity utilization for each month by dividing the production plan amount (line 2) by the available capacity (line 5). The result is expressed as the utilization percentage (line 6). This capacity calculation shows whether Fitter has the capacity necessary to meet the production plan. While higher levels of capacity utilization mean that Fitter is producing more with its production resources, this percentage must be kept below 100 percent to allow for production losses due to product changeovers, equipment breakdowns, and other unexpected production problems. The sales and operations plan in Figure 4-5 shows that Fitter's highest level of capacity utilization is 95 percent in May and June.

The last step in sales and operations planning is to disaggregate the plan, that is, to break it down into plans for individual products. Lines 7 and 8 in Figure 4-5 disaggregate the planned production shown in line 2, based on the breakdown of 70 percent NRG-A and 30 percent NRG-B snack bars. This 70/30 breakdown was established using previous sales data for these products. The monthly production quantities in lines 7 and 8 are the output of the sales and operations planning process, and they are the primary input to the demand management process.

Suppose that Fitter is regularly able to achieve production levels at 90 percent of capacity. If the sales forecast requires more than 90 percent capacity, Fitter management can choose from among the following alternatives to develop a production plan:

- Fitter might choose not to meet all the forecasted sales demand, or it might reduce promotional activities to decrease sales.
- To increase capacity, Fitter might plan to use overtime production. Doing that, however, would increase labor cost per unit.
- Inventory levels could be built up in earlier months, when sales levels are lower, to reduce the capacity requirements in later months. Doing that, however, would increase inventory holding costs and increase the risk that NRG bars held in inventory might pass their expiration date before being sold by retailers.
- To find the right balance, management might try a hybrid approach to the capacity problem: reduce sales promotions slightly, increase production in earlier months, and plan for some overtime production.

The monthly production quantities (in lines 7 and 8 of Figure 4-5) create some inventory in May to meet June's sales; in addition, some overtime production is likely in May and June because capacity utilization is over 90 percent.

This example illustrates the value of an integrated system: it provides a tool for incorporating data from Marketing and Sales and Manufacturing and for evaluating different plans. Whereas Marketing and Sales may want to increase sales, the company might not increase its profits if overtime costs or inventory holding costs are too high. This sort of planning is difficult to do without an integrated information system, even for small companies like Fitter. Having an integrated information system helps managers of all functional areas meet corporate profit goals.

Sales and Operations Planning in SAP ERP

In SAP ERP, the sales forecast can incorporate historical sales data from the Sales and Distribution (SD) module, or the forecast can be created using input from plans developed in the Controlling (CO) module. In the CO module, profit goals for the company can be set, which can then be used to estimate the sales levels needed to meet the profit goals. Figure 4-6 shows the sales and operations planning screen from the SAP ERP system. The title of this screen is "Create Rough-Cut Plan." **Rough-cut planning** is a common term in manufacturing for aggregate planning. As described above, rough-cut plans are disaggregated to generate detailed production schedules.

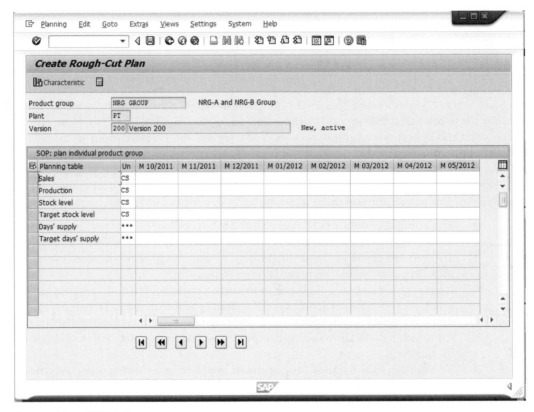

Source Line: SAP AG.

FIGURE 4-6   Sales and operations planning screen in SAP ERP

The sales forecast is entered in the first row (Sales) of the rough-cut plan. Data can be entered manually by the user, a sales forecast can be transferred from a profitability analysis performed in the CO module, or the user can perform a forecast in this screen, calling up historical sales data from the SAP ERP system. The second row, Production, represents the production that is planned to meet the sales forecast. Production figures can also be entered manually, or the SAP system can generate values that meet sales goals. The third row shows inventory as the Stock level. The gray shading of that row indicates it is a calculated result. The fourth row allows for the entry of a Target stock level. If the user enters a value in this row, then SAP ERP will propose production levels to meet the Target stock level. Once the Target stock level is entered, the system will calculate the number of days' worth of supply, so the fifth row (Days' supply) is a calculated result. The sixth row lets the user specify a target stock level in terms of the number of days of demand it would cover, known as Target days' supply. The SAP system uses the factory calendar, which specifies company holidays and planned shutdowns, to determine the number of working days in a month when calculating the Target days' supply.

If the sales plan (the first line in Figure 4-6) is to be developed using forecasting tools, the SAP ERP system can provide the planner with historical sales values based on sales data stored in the system. Without an integrated system such as SAP, the planner would likely have to request sales figures from the Sales Department, and he or she might not be sure how accurate the data were. Figure 4-7 shows how the SAP ERP system displays historical sales figures.

☞ Forecast: Historical Values		Sales provided from SD module			✕	
Historical values					▲ ▼	Field where planner can "correct" the sales value
Period	Val. fld	Corr.value	F	C	⠿	
M 09/2011	6214	6214	☐ ☐			
M 08/2011	6326	6326	☐ ☐			
M 07/2011	6501	6501	☐ ☐			
M 06/2011	6434	6434	☐ ☐			
M 05/2011	6286	6286	☐ ☐			
M 04/2011	6133	6133	☐ ☐			
M 03/2011	5883	5883	☐ ☐			
M 02/2011	5822	5822	☐ ☐		▲ ▼	
	⟳ Forecasting	✎ Correct	🖺 ✕			

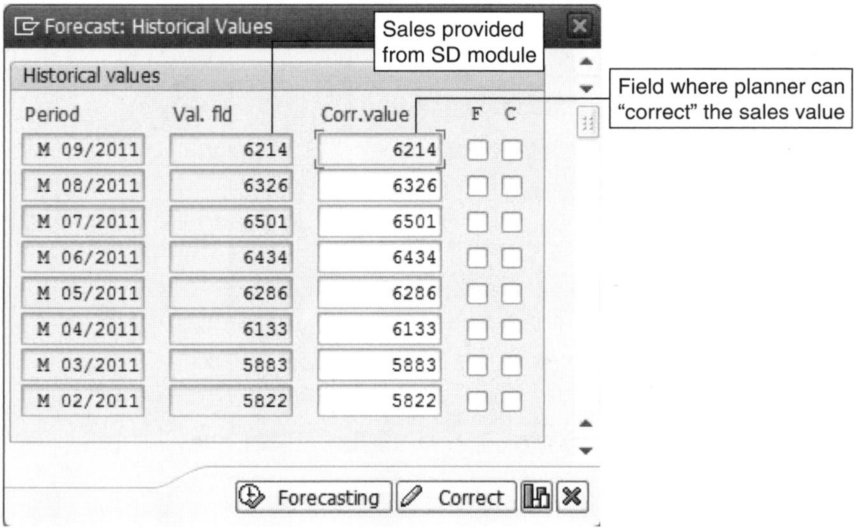

Source Line: SAP AG.

FIGURE 4-7   Historical sales figures in SAP

In addition to providing the historical sales values from the Sales and Distribution module, this screen allows the planner to "correct" the sales values. For example, sales may have been low in the past due to unusual weather conditions, or the planner might know that sales would have been higher if the company was able to meet all the demand. The sales figures used for forecasting should represent the best estimate of what *demand* was in the past, not necessarily what the actual sales were.

The SAP ERP system can automatically graph these data to help the planner determine if there are any unusual patterns in the historical sales values that require investigation. The planner can correct these values as well, to adjust sales values that were unusually high or low, or to back out (or subtract) the effects of previous sales promotions. After the sales forecast is made, it can be adjusted to incorporate increased sales from planned sales promotions. Once the historical data are acceptable, the user can select one of the SAP ERP tools shown in Figure 4-8 to prepare the forecast.

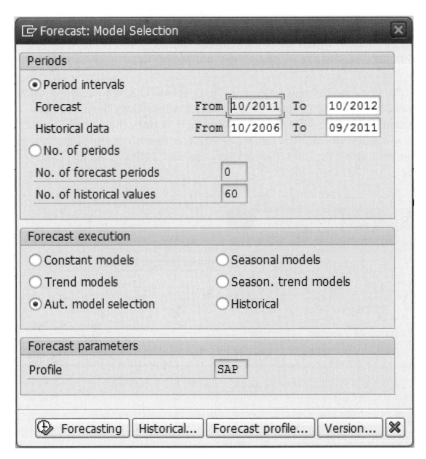

Source Line: SAP AG.

FIGURE 4-8   Forecasting model options in SAP ERP

This screen allows the user to specify a number of forecasting parameters, including whether the model should allow for trends and seasonal variations. Once the SAP ERP system generates a forecast, the planner can view the results graphically, as shown in Figure 4-9. While the SAP ERP system also provides the standard statistical measures of forecast accuracy, human judgment is frequently the best determinant of whether the forecast results make sense.

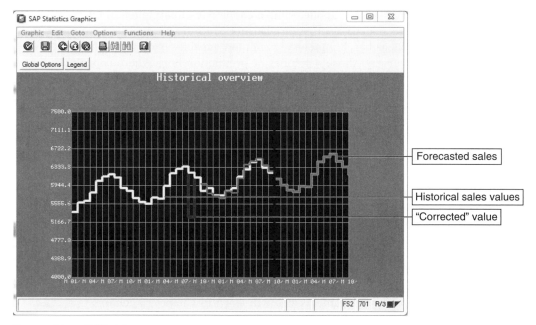

Source Line: SAP AG.

FIGURE 4-9　Forecasting results presented graphically in SAP ERP

Another feature of the SAP ERP sales and operations planning process is the integration of rough-cut capacity planning. A sample screen is shown in Figure 4-10.

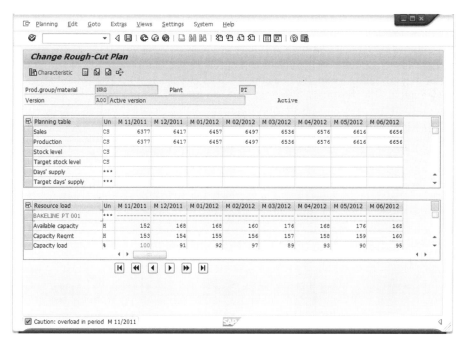

Source Line: SAP AG.

FIGURE 4-10　Sales and operation plan with rough-cut capacity calculation in SAP ERP

Rough-cut capacity planning applies simple capacity-estimating techniques (like those shown in the spreadsheet example in Figure 4-5) to the production plan to see if the production plan is feasible. Frequently, rough-cut capacity planning techniques are applied to critical resources—those machines or production lines where capacity is usually limited. For a company with a simple manufacturing process, these estimates can be very precise. For more complex manufacturing processes, these estimates will not be completely accurate, but they will ensure that the production plans are at least reasonable. Managers can use SAP ERP's more sophisticated planning tools at the detailed scheduling level, when the plans that are developed will actually be converted into manufacturing decisions.

While an integrated ERP system like SAP can provide sophisticated tools to support the sales and operations planning process, the plan will only be successful if the interested parties are committed to the process. If Marketing and Sales and Manufacturing cannot agree on sales forecasts, promotions, and production plans, then the company will find it is overstocking some items, running out of others, and spending a lot of money on overtime production and expedited shipping. Successful sales and operations planning depend on developing a culture of cooperation between Marketing and Sales and Manufacturing; that requires continuous support, encouragement, and enforcement from top management. As you will learn in Chapter 7, changing a company's culture is usually a much more difficult challenge than the technical challenge of installing new hardware and software.

ANOTHER LOOK

Sales and Operations Planning for Blood Banks

Sales and operations planning (SOP) is typically used in for-profit manufacturing organizations; however a recent article in the *Journal of Blood Services Management* suggests there could be significant advantages to applying sales and operations planning concepts to the blood-banking process. The supply chain necessary to supply blood is significant and complex. For example, the nonprofit America's Blood Centers is a network of more than 600 donor centers supplying over 3,500 hospitals and healthcare facilities in North America.

In the article "Benefits to Blood Banks of a Sales and Operations Planning Process," authors Donald A. Keal and Phil Hebert make the argument that sales and operations planning concepts are applicable to blood-banking systems. The key reason, they argue, is that sales and operations planning is a process "that links high-level strategic plans to day-to-day operations." Through the use of sales and operations planning, managers can better manage change by proactively addressing potential problems and opportunities.

One of the unique features of blood banking is that there are customers at both ends of the supply chain. Blood donors are the suppliers but are also customers for the donation centers. While there are still a significant number of blood plasma centers that pay for donations, most blood donation is unpaid. On the distribution end, while hospital patients are the recipients of donated blood, the healthcare provider is the blood bank's customer.

(continued)

The authors provide an example of how sales and operations planning could impact the supply and demand of a particular blood product, single-donor platelets (SDPs). As with any business, a blood center must quickly identify variations in forecasted supply and demand and take action to lessen the potential negative effects of those variations. For instance, if the demand for SDPs at a blood center falls below projections, "the excess SDPs may be exported if they have sufficient shelf life remaining, or donors may be rescheduled to reduce supply. If SDP demand spikes, recruitment and collections may have to work overtime to recruit more donors."

Blood banks may not be for-profit companies, but they cannot operate at a loss either. The authors note that an advantage of a sales and operations planning process is that it requires performance measurement. By using measurements, such as RONA (return on net assets), a blood center can help blood centers avoid situations in which "the cost per unit (CPU) collected is higher than the sales cost of a unit to the health care provider or what an imported unit would cost."

One of the major challenges to applying the sales and operations planning process to blood banks is data accuracy. The authors note that it is not uncommon to have data inconsistencies between the blood management system and the financial system. Without accurate and consistent data, the results of the sales and operations planning process would not be valid.

Question:

1. Write a memo to the director of a blood donation center in your geographic area recommending the implementation of the sales and operations planning process to their blood banking system. Explain the benefits of such a system, and make sure that you identify and address arguments that might be made against your proposal. Specifically address the issue of performance measures in a nonprofit environment.

Disaggregating the Sales and Operations Plan in SAP ERP

As mentioned previously, companies typically develop sales and operations plans for product groups. Product groups are especially important for companies that have hundreds of products, because developing unique plans for hundreds of individual products is extremely time consuming. Furthermore, it would be hard to develop that many different plans in a coordinated fashion while also taking in consideration production capacity. Fitter's product group is very simple; 70 percent of the group consists of NRG-A bars, and 30 percent consists of NRG-B bars.

Figure 4-11 shows how product groups are defined in the SAP ERP system. The system allows any number of products to be assigned to a product group. Product groups can have other product groups as members, as well, so complicated aggregations can be defined.

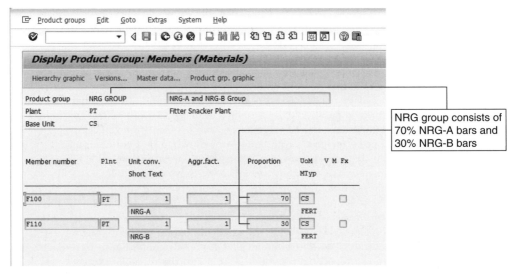

Source Line: SAP AG.

FIGURE 4-11   Product group structure in SAP ERP

When the sales and operations plan is disaggregated, the production plan quantities specified for the group are transferred to the individual products that make up the group, according to the percentages defined in the product group structure.

The results of the disaggregation process can be seen in the Stock/Requirements List screen shown in Figure 4-12.

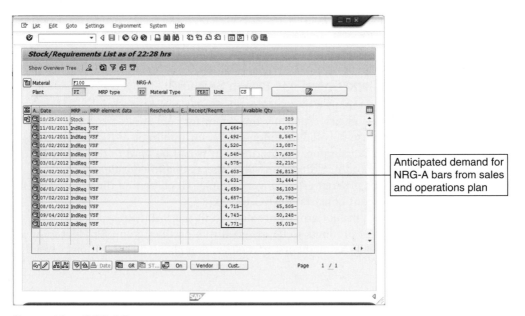

Source Line: SAP AG.

FIGURE 4-12   Stock/Requirements List for NRG-A bars after disaggregation

The Stock/Requirements List screen displays the inventory level for an individual product, including all planned additions and reductions. In Figure 4-10, the production plan for November is 6,377. Seventy percent of 6,377 is 4,464, which is shown in Figure 4-12 as an independent requirement (IndReq). The independent requirements are the output of the disaggregation of the sales and operations plan, and they are used in master production scheduling to determine the schedule for finished product production.

Exercise 4.3

Using the Fitter sales forecast for July through December that you created in Exercise 4.2, develop a spreadsheet for sales and operations planning for those same months. Use the format of the spreadsheet shown in Figure 4-5. The number of working days for each month is shown in Figure 4-13.

	July	Aug.	Sept.	Oct.	Nov.	Dec.
Working days	20	23	21	21	20	21

Source Line: Course Technology/Cengage Learning.

FIGURE 4-13   The number of working days at Fitter, July through December

For your production plan, try to keep the capacity utilization at 95 percent or less. To disaggregate the plan for the group into plans for NRG-A and NRG-B bars, use 70 percent of sales for NRG-A bars and 30 percent for NRG-B bars.

Demand Management

The demand management step of the production planning process links the sales and operations planning process with the detailed scheduling and materials requirements planning processes. The output of the demand management process is the **master production schedule (MPS)**, which is the production plan for all finished goods. For Fitter, the master production schedule is an input in the detailed scheduling process, which determines which bars the company should make and when it should make them. The master production schedule is also an input to the materials requirements planning process, which determines what raw materials to order to support the production schedule.

The demand management process splits Fitter's monthly production planning values into finer time periods. Figure 4-14 shows January's production plan by week and by day.

	Week 1	Week 2	Week 3	Week 4	Week 5	
Demand management	1/3–1/7	1/10–1/14	1/17–1/21	1/24–1/28	1/31	2/1–2/4
Monthly demand NRG-A	4134	4134	4134	4134	4134	4199
NRG-B	1772	1772	1772	1772	1772	1799
Working days in week	5	5	5	5	1	4
Working days in month	21	21	21	21	21	20
MPS NRG-A	984	984	984	984	1037	
Weekly demand NRG-B	422	422	422	422	444	

Demand management	Jan 3	Jan 4	Jan 5	Jan 6	Jan 7
Monthly Demand NRG-A	4134	4134	4134	4134	4134
NRG-B	1772	1772	1772	1772	1772
Working days in month	21	21	21	21	21
MPS NRG-A	197	197	197	197	197
Daily demand NRG-B	84	84	84	84	84

Source Line: Course Technology/Cengage Learning.

FIGURE 4-14   Fitter's production plan for January: The first five weeks of production are followed by a day-by-day disaggregation of Week 1

Fitter will use the weekly plan (which is derived from the sales and operation plan in Figure 4-5) for purchasing materials management. Daily plans will be used for the product(s) that are to be produced on the snack bar line. To get the results shown in Figure 4-14, the following calculations were performed:

- For the weekly plan, the MPS plan for NRG-A bars in Week 1 was calculated as: (4,134 cases in January [the monthly demand from Figure 4-5] ÷ 21 working days in month of January) × 5 working days in Week 1 = 984.3 cases per week.

This figure was rounded to 984 cases in Figure 4-14.

- Because Week 5 consists of the last day in January and the first four days in February, the MPS for NRG-A bars in Week 5 was calculated as:
  - (4,134 cases in January [monthly demand] ÷ 21 working days in month of January) × 1 working day in Week 5 = 196.9 cases
  - (4,198 cases in February [monthly demand] ÷ 20 working days in month of February) × 4 working days in Week 5 = 839.6 cases
  - Week 5 Total = 196.9 + 839.6 = 1,036.5 cases

In Figure 4-14, the master production schedule (MPS) cases for Week 5 were rounded to 1,037 for the NRG-A bars.

In Figure 4-14, the daily production plan values for NRG-A and NRG-B bars were calculated by taking the monthly production plan value and dividing it by the number of working days in the month.

Notice that the demand management process involves no user input. Input is from the sales and operations planning step. The SAP ERP software also uses information from the factory calendar (working days in week and month) to calculate the MPS.

Fitter does not currently do this sort of planning because it has no way to formally share sales forecast data between Marketing and Production. The company cannot relate its possible sales to its capacity and to the time available to make the product. Thus, Fitter cannot produce an accurate master production schedule.

The MPS is an input to the detailed scheduling and materials requirements planning processes. Materials requirements planning (MRP) is discussed next, followed by a discussion of detailed scheduling.

Exercise 4.4

Develop a weekly production plan for August, like the one for January shown in Figure 4-14. For the weekly sales periods, the last week will include two days in September. The factory calendar information is shown in Figure 4-15.

	Week 1	Week 2	Week 3	Week 4	Week 5	
	8/1–8/5	8/8–8/12	8/15–8/19	8/22–8/26	8/29–8/31	9/1–9/2
Demand management						
Working days in week	4	5	5	5	3	2
Working days in month	20	20	20	20	20	23

Source Line: Course Technology/Cengage Learning.

FIGURE 4-15   Fitter's factory calendar for August

Materials Requirements Planning (MRP)

Materials requirements planning (MRP) is the process that determines the quantity and timing of the production or purchase of subassemblies and raw materials required to support the master production schedule. The materials requirements planning process answers the questions, "What quantities of raw materials should we order so we can meet that level of production?" and "When should these materials be ordered?" In this section, you will see how Fitter could accurately plan its raw materials purchases if it had an ERP system.

In Fitter's case, all product components (ingredients, snack bar wrappers, and display boxes) are purchased, so the company could use the materials requirements planning process to determine the timing and quantities for purchase orders. To understand materials requirements planning, you must understand the bill of material, the material's lead time, and the material's lot sizing, which we will discuss in the following sections.

Bill of Material

The **bill of material (BOM)** is a list of the materials (including quantities) needed to make a product. The BOM for a 500-pound batch of the NRG-A or NRG-B bars is shown in Figure 4-16.

Ingredient	Quantity	
	NRG-A	NRG-B
Oats (lb.)	300	250
Wheat germ (lb.)	50	50
Cinnamon (lb.)	5	5
Nutmeg (lb.)	2	2
Cloves (lb.)	1	1
Honey (gal.)	10	10
Canola oil (gal.)	7	7
Vit./min. powder (lb.)	5	5
Carob chips (lb.)	50	
Raisins (lb.)	50	
Protein powder (lb.)		50
Hazelnuts (lb.)		30
Dates (lb.)		70

Source Line: Course Technology/Cengage Learning.

FIGURE 4-16   The bill of material (BOM) for Fitter's NRG bars

The BOM for Fitter's NRG bars is fairly simple because all ingredients are mixed together to form the dough; there are no intermediary steps. Many other products, however, are produced by joining component parts into subassemblies that are then joined to form the finished product. It is obviously more complicated to calculate the raw material requirements for products with more complex BOMs.

Lead Times and Lot Sizing

The BOM can be used to calculate *how much* of each raw material is required to produce a finished product. Determining the *timing* and *quantity* of purchase orders, however, requires information on lead times and lot sizing.

For example, if a manufacturer orders a make-to-stock item, the **lead time** is the cumulative time required for the supplier to receive and process the order, take the material out of stock, package it, load it on a truck, and deliver it to the manufacturer. The manufacturer might also include the time required to receive the material into its warehouse (unloading the truck, inspecting the goods, and moving the goods into a storage location).

Lot sizing refers to the process of determining production quantities (for raw materials produced in-house) and order quantities (for purchased items). In Fitter's case, many raw materials can only be ordered from a supplier in certain bulk quantities. For example, because Fitter uses large quantities of oats, the most cost-effective way to purchase oats is in bulk hopper-truck quantities, which means that the material must be ordered in 44,000-pound quantities. Wheat germ, however, is used in smaller quantities, and to avoid having wheat germ become stale, Fitter orders it in 2,000-pound bulk containers. Protein powder is packaged in 50-pound bags that are loaded 25 to a pallet, so the most cost-effective way to order protein powder is by the pallet load (1,250 pounds).

Let's look at the materials requirements planning process using oats, which have a two-week lead time and must be ordered in hopper-truck quantities (multiples of 44,000 pounds). To determine when and how many pounds of oats should be ordered, we will start with the weekly master production schedule for NRG-A and NRG-B bars, and then we will complete the following steps:

1. Convert the quantities of NRG bars from cases to 500-pound batches.
2. Multiply the number of batches by the pounds-per-batch quantities (which are given in the BOM) to get the gross requirements for each raw material.
3. Subtract the existing raw material inventory and purchase orders that have already been placed from the gross requirements, to determine the net requirements.
4. Plan orders in multiples of the 44,000-pound lot size, allowing for the two-week lead time required for oats, to meet the net requirements in Step 3.

These calculations are summarized in Figure 4-17. This view of the data is frequently called an **MRP record**, which is the standard way of viewing the MRP process on paper.

Oats Lead time = 2 weeks		Week 1	Week 2	Week 3	Week 4	Week 5
MPS	NRG-A	984	984	984	984	1037
(cases)	NRG-B	422	422	422	422	444
MPS	NRG-A	142	142	142	142	149
(500 lb. batches)	NRG-B	61	61	61	61	64
Gross requirements (lb)		57,850	57,850	57,850	57,850	60,700
Scheduled receipts		44,000	44,000			
Planned receipts				88,000	44,000	44,000
On hand	29,650	15,800	1,950	32,100	18,250	1,550
Planned orders		88,000	44,000	44,000		

Source Line: Course Technology/Cengage Learning.

FIGURE 4-17   The MRP record for oats in NRG bars, Weeks 1 through 5

The first two rows of the MRP record are the MPS that was the output from the demand management step (shown in Figure 4-14). These NRG production quantities are shown in terms of shipping cases. The first step is to convert the MPS from shipping cases to 500-pound batches. Each shipping case weighs 72 pounds (not including packaging), so to convert shipping cases to 500-pound batches, multiply the number of shipping cases by 72 pounds per case, and then divide by 500 pounds per batch. Thus, producing 984 shipping cases of NRG-A bars in Week 1 of the year will require 142 batches, as shown in the third row of Figure 4-17.

The next row in Figure 4-17 is Gross requirements. The Gross requirements figures are calculated by multiplying the MPS quantity (in production batches) by the pounds of oats needed for a batch of snack bars. Fitter uses 300 pounds of oats per batch of NRG-A bar and 250 pounds of oats per batch of NRG-B bar. This information is derived from the BOM (Figure 4-16). Therefore, for Week 1, Fitter needs:

- NRG-A: 142 batches × 300 lb. per batch = 42,600 lb. oats
- NRG-B: 61 batches × 250 lb. per batch = 15,250 lb. oats
- Total = 57,850 lb. oats

The next row in Figure 4-17 is Scheduled receipts. This row shows the expected timing of orders of materials that have already been placed, meaning that the supplier has been given the purchase order and is in the process of fulfilling it. There is a two-week lead time for oats, so for oats to be available in Week 1 and Week 2 of the year, oats orders must be placed in the last two weeks of the previous year.

The next row, Planned receipts, shows when planned orders will arrive. The Planned receipts row is directly related to the Planned orders row at the bottom of the record. A planned order is one that has not been placed with the supplier but will need to be placed to prevent Production from running out of materials. Because there is a two-week lead time for oat orders, the quantities in the planned orders row will be available for production in two weeks, which is indicated by an entry in the Planned receipts row.

The arrows in Figure 4-17 show the relationship between planned orders and planned receipts. For example, the materials requirements planning calculation suggests that an order for 88,000 pounds of oats should be placed in Week 1 so it will arrive in Week 3. To say it differently: the planned order for 88,000 pounds of oats in Week 1 will not be available for use until Week 3, which is shown by the planned receipt of 88,000 pounds in Week 3. There is only one order, but it shows up in two places on the MRP record.

The next row in Figure 4-17 is the On hand row. The first number in this row (29,650) is the inventory of oats on hand at the beginning of Week 1. The On hand number in the Week 1 column (15,800) is a projection of the inventory that will be on hand at the end of Week 1 (and therefore at the beginning of Week 2)—accounting for the beginning inventory, gross requirements, and planned and scheduled receipts. In the case of Week 1, the initial inventory of 29,650 pounds, plus the 44,000 pounds of scheduled receipts, minus the 57,850 gross requirement, leaves 15,800 pounds of oats available at the start of Week 2.

The last row is the Planned orders row. This is the quantity that the MRP calculation recommends ordering, and it is the output from the MRP process that purchasing uses to determine what to order to produce the product, and when to order it.

Many times, a planner will need to intervene to tell the system to adjust the planned order. For example, notice that the on-hand quantity of oats in Week 2 is only 1,950 pounds. In the best case scenario, assume the line is producing the NRG-B bar (as that bar uses less oats). At 250 pounds per batch, 1,950 pounds of oats would be enough oats for 7 full batches. The production line can produce 6 batches an hour, so 7 batches of dough would only support the production line for 70 minutes. If the scheduled order does not arrive early enough on the first day of Week 2, the production line could be shut down. When the purchase order scheduled to arrive in Week 1 was ready to be placed (two weeks prior to the beginning of Week 1), the planner should have evaluated that order, considering the low inventory level projected for the beginning of Week 2. The planner might have decided to place an order for two hopper-truck loads of oats, instead of the planned order for one load. Or he could have ensured that the scheduled receipt shown in Week 2 would actually be delivered at the end of Week 1.

Planning factors such as lead times are just estimates, so planners must evaluate the planned orders suggested by the materials requirements planning calculation before allowing the program to automatically turn them into purchase orders.

Notice once again the need for software to help with this kind of calculation. Of course, a human being can do these computations, but with many products and constituent materials, the calculations become very tedious and prone to error. Even for a small company such as Fitter, doing the calculations with reasonable speed and accuracy requires software help. Notice also the information needed to do the MRP calculation: starting with a sales forecast, the software works down to the master production schedule and then to a schedule of required raw materials.

Exercise 4.5

Develop an MRP record, similar to the one in Figure 4-17, for wheat germ for the five weeks of January. Wheat germ must be ordered in bulk-container quantities, so the planned orders must be in multiples of 2,000 pounds. Use a lead time of one week and an initial on-hand inventory of 3,184 pounds; assume that an order of 8,000 pounds is scheduled for receipt during Week 1. Are there any weeks when you, as a planner, would consider placing an order above or below the minimum required? Why? (Assume that there are no problems with storage capacity or shelf life.)

Exercise 4.6

Fitter's purchasing policy has been to carry high levels of inventory to avoid stockouts. Why can inventory levels be lower with an integrated ERP system and MRP-based purchasing? If you had to calculate the financial advantage of this change, how would you do it?

Materials Requirements Planning in SAP ERP

The MRP list in SAP ERP looks very much like a Stock/Requirements List, which you saw in Figure 4-12 (for NRG-A bars). The MRP list shows the results of the MRP calculations, while the Stock/Requirements List shows those results plus any changes that have occurred since the MRP list was generated (planned orders converted to purchase orders or production orders, material receipts, and so on). Because the materials requirements planning calculations are time consuming to process for a company producing hundreds of products using thousands of parts, the materials requirements planning process is usually only repeated every few days—or perhaps weekly. The Stock/Requirements List, however, allows the users of the system to see what is happening (and what will happen) with a material in real time.

Compare the data shown in the MRP record in Figure 4-17 with the MRP list for oats in Figure 4-18 and the Stock/Requirements List in Figure 4-19.

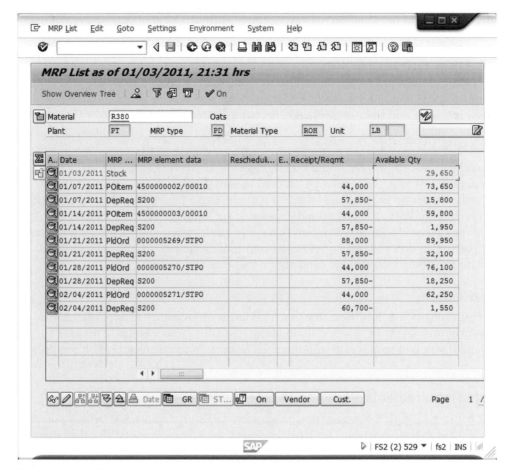

Source Line: SAP AG.

FIGURE 4-18 The MRP List screen in SAP ERP

The MRP list in the third column of Figure 4-18 shows purchase orders (POItem), planned orders (PldOrd), and dependent requirements (DepReq). Dependent requirements represent the demand for oats created by the planned orders for snack bars—the demand for oats *depends* on the production plans for snack bars. The materials requirements planning process creates planned orders to meet these dependent requirements. The planned orders are recommendations by the system to create orders (in this case, purchase orders) for oats.

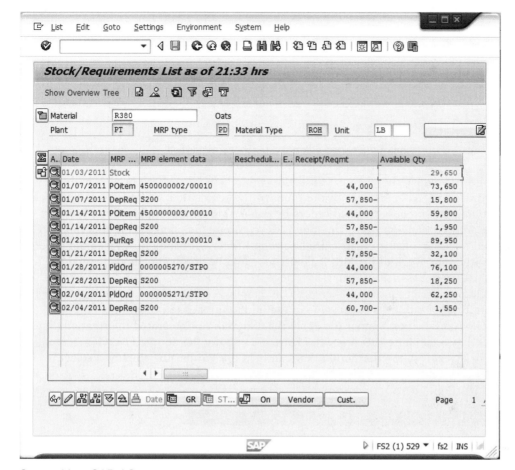

Source Line: SAP AG.

FIGURE 4-19   The Stock/Requirements List screen in SAP ERP

The Stock/Requirements List shown in Figure 4-19 shows purchase orders (POitem), planned orders (PldOrd), and dependent requirements (DepReq), but it also shows purchase requisitions (PurRqs). When a planner decides that it is time for a planned order to become a purchase order, the planned order is converted to a purchase requisition, which is a request to Purchasing to create a purchase order. The planner can convert a planned order to a purchase requisition from the Stock/Requirements List screen by double-clicking the planned order line. This action calls up the Additional Data for MRP Element window, shown in Figure 4-20.

Source Line: SAP AG.

FIGURE 4-20 Conversion of a planned order to a purchase requisition

From this window, the planner can create a purchase requisition or review the planned order and make changes before creating the requisition. SAP ERP also provides the ability to mass-process planned orders by converting groups of planned orders to purchase orders simultaneously. The materials requirements planning process can also be configured to automatically create purchase requisitions; for example, all planned orders created within one week of the MRP calculation could be automatically converted to purchase requisitions.

Once a purchase requisition is created, an employee in the Purchasing department must turn it into a purchase order. One of the important steps in creating a purchase order is choosing the best vendor to supply the material. An integrated information system such as SAP can facilitate this process. Figure 4-21 shows the Source Overview screen, which provides access to information that can help the Purchasing employee select the vendor.

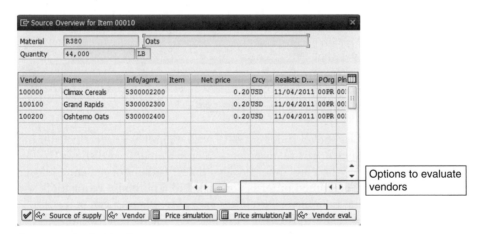

Source Line: SAP AG.

FIGURE 4-21 Source Overview screen for supplier selection

From this screen, the Purchasing employee can view information about each vendor, simulate the price (the SAP system estimates the price from each vendor, which might include quantity discounts and transportation costs), and look at the vendor evaluation—the company's rating of the vendor. The SAP ERP system can be configured to rate vendors based on a number of performance criteria, including quality of goods provided and on-time delivery. The evaluation scores for each vendor are updated automatically as materials are received. The integrated information system allows Purchasing to make the best decision on a vendor based on relevant, up-to-date information.

Once the Purchasing employee decides which vendor to use, the purchase order is transmitted to the vendor. The SAP ERP system can print out a paper order that can be mailed to the vendor. More likely, however, the system will be configured to either fax the order to the vendor, transmit it electronically through EDI (electronic data interchange), or send it via email.

Detailed Scheduling

Finally, let's examine the last portion of the production process, detailed scheduling. The aggregate production plan for product groups developed in sales and operations planning is disaggregated to individual products in finer time increments through the demand management process. In detailed scheduling, a detailed plan of what is to be produced needs to be developed, considering machine capacity and available labor. Detailed scheduling is complex and will not be presented here in spreadsheet form, but we will discuss the important concepts and issues.

A key decision in detailed production scheduling is determining how long the production runs for each product should be. Longer production runs mean that fewer machine setups are required, reducing production costs and increasing the effective capacity of the equipment. On the other hand, shorter production runs can be used to lower the inventory levels for finished products. Thus, the production run length requires a balance between setup costs and holding costs to minimize total costs to the company.

Because the capacity of the Fitter production mixers is much greater than that of the snack bar production line, scheduling mixer production is not an issue. Because the dough must be mixed before the snack bar production line can start, employees who run the mixers at Fitter begin working 30 minutes before the employees who run the production line. During that time, four batches of dough can be mixed so they are ready when the production line starts. With a bit of a head start and a detailed schedule for the production line, it is a simple matter for the personnel operating the mixers to keep ahead of the production line. Thus, the key step for Fitter is to develop a detailed production schedule for the snack bar production line.

The manufacturing process that Fitter uses is known as repetitive manufacturing. **Repetitive manufacturing** environments typically have production lines that are switched from one product to another similar product. Most packaged consumer goods are produced in repetitive manufacturing environments. In repetitive manufacturing, production lines are scheduled for a period of time, rather than for a specific number of items, although it is possible to estimate the number of items that will be produced over a period of time.

For Fitter, the production schedule for a week might be to produce NRG-A bars from Monday morning until the end of day Wednesday, then change over to NRG-B bars for all of Thursday until Friday at noon, when the production line will be switched back to NRG-A bars. Given this schedule, it is possible to estimate the number of bars that will be produced. Figure 4-22 shows the repetitive manufacturing planning screen in the SAP ERP system.

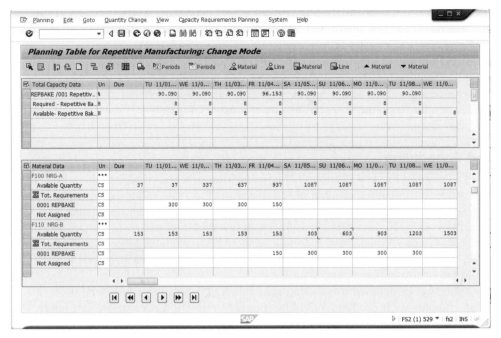

Source Line: SAP AG.

FIGURE 4-22   Repetitive manufacturing planning table in SAP ERP

This screen allows the planner to view capacity, production schedule length, and quantity produced in one screen. Between November 1 and November 8, NRG-A bars are being produced for 3½ days, and NRG-B bars are being produced for 4½ days. The fourth line of the bottom screen shows that a total of 1,050 cases of NRG-A snack bars will be produced from November 1 through November 4 (300 + 300 + 300 + 150 = 1,050), and then production will change over to NRG-B bars from November 4 through November 8 (this screen assumes production shifts continue through the weekend).

The top section of the screen shows the production line capacity requirements for the plan in the bottom section of the screen. The plan shown will require 90.090% of the available capacity of 8 hours per day for all days except November 4, when the capacity requirement will be 96.153%. The second line in the top section of the screen (Required-Repetitive Bakeline) shows the number of hours of capacity used by the plan (rounded to the nearest hour) while the third line (Available-Repetitive Bakeline) shows the planned capacity of the baking line.

In some companies, responsibility for inventory costs belongs to a Materials Management group, and capacity utilization performance is the responsibility of a Production group. Generally, the Materials Management group wants short production runs to keep inventory levels down, while the Production group wants long production runs to keep capacity utilization high. In these circumstances, the decision regarding production run length can become a source of organizational bickering, instead of a decision that minimizes total costs for the benefit of the company.

This conflict points out another advantage of production planning in an ERP system. Because the goal of the company is to maximize profit, the duration of production runs should be decided by evaluating the cost of equipment setup and holding inventory. An integrated information system simplifies this analysis by automatically collecting accounting information that allows managers to better evaluate schedule trade-offs in terms of costs to the company.

Providing Production Data to Accounting

In Chapter 1, you learned that for a company to be successful functional areas must share data. Accounting needs to know what Manufacturing has produced and what resources were used in producing those products, to determine which products, if any, are producing a profit—and then provide information for management to determine how to increase profits. In manufacturing plants, ERP systems do not directly connect with production machines. For example, in Fitter's case, SAP ERP could not directly read the number of bars that came off the packing segment of the snack bar line. The data must be gathered in some way and then entered into SAP ERP for inventory accounting purposes.

Data can be entered into SAP ERP through a PC on the shop floor, scanned using bar-code or RFID technology (discussed in more detail in Chapter 8), or entered using a mobile device. SAP ERP is an open-architecture system, meaning that it can work with automated data-collection tools marketed by third-party hardware and software companies.

In an integrated ERP system, the accounting impact of a material transaction can be recorded automatically. For example, when a shipment of oats arrives at the Fitter plant, someone in the Receiving Department must verify the material and the quantity and quality of the shipment before it is accepted. Once Fitter accepts the shipment, Receiving must notify the SAP ERP system of the arrival and acceptance of the material. This communication is done by completing a goods receipt transaction, which is shown in Figure 4-23.

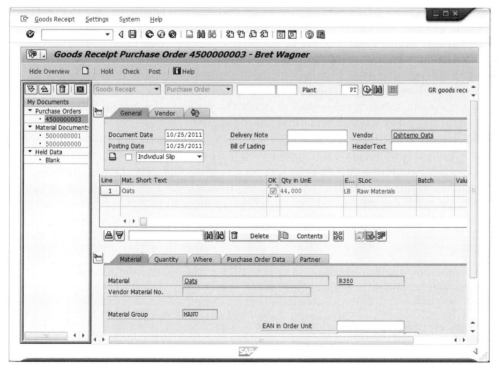

Source Line: SAP AG.

FIGURE 4-23 Goods Receipt screen in SAP ERP

The Receiving department must match the goods receipt with the purchase order that initiated it, to make sure the exact materials ordered have been received, so Accounting can pay the vendor. It is possible for the quantity of material entered in the goods receipt to differ from the quantity specified on the purchase order. Depending on the configuration settings, the SAP ERP system might block entry of the receipt if the discrepancy is too large. If the discrepancy is small, then the receipt may be allowed, with the difference posted to the correct variance account, which allows the transaction to be processed but maintains a record for management to review, to see if there is a consistent problem with a vendor over shipping or "shorting" an order (consistently shipping less than was ordered).

When the receipt is successfully recorded, the SAP ERP system immediately records the increase in inventory levels for the material. On the Accounting side of the system, this causes the value of the inventory shown in the general ledger account to automatically increase as well. This is an important feature of an integrated information system: the goods receipt is recorded once, but the information is immediately available to both Manufacturing and Accounting—and the information is consistent. An integrated information system also has the ability to adjust for changes in material costs. If the cost of the material changes frequently, the system can be configured to reevaluate the value of all the inventory of the material that the company has.

For example, suppose Fitter has 10,000 pounds of cinnamon that it bought at $3 per pound. The company would value its inventory of cinnamon at $30,000. Then suppose the price of cinnamon rises to $4 per pound, and Fitter purchases 1,000 pounds of cinnamon at the higher price. What is the value of the 11,000 pounds of cinnamon that Fitter now owns? The SAP ERP system can be configured to use a moving average formula to reevaluate the inventory based on the current market prices. Depending on the exact nature of the formula, the cinnamon would be valued at somewhere between the $3 per pound previously assumed and the $4 per pound that was just paid. The system can perform this calculation automatically each time material is received.

Using an ERP system to record data does not necessarily make the shop-floor accounting data more accurate. The ERP system allows employees to enter data in real time, but the system requires employees to follow the process. If employees can take material out of inventory without recording the transaction, then the real-time information in the ERP system is worthless. Technologies such as bar-code scanners and RFID tags can help in this process, but accurate data require both a capable information system and properly trained and motivated employees. However, when done accurately, capturing data for manufacturing and inventory purposes on the shop floor means that it is captured at the same time for accounting and inventory management purposes—eliminating any need to reconcile Accounting and Manufacturing records.

Exercise 4.7

Briefly describe how the implementation of SAP ERP might change the relationship between Production and Warehousing at Fitter.

ERP AND SUPPLIERS

Fitter is part of a supply chain that starts with farmers growing oats and wheat and ends with a customer buying an NRG bar from a retail store. Previously, companies used competitive bidding to achieve low prices from suppliers, which frequently led to an adversarial relationship between suppliers and their customers. In recent years, more companies have begun to realize that they are part of a supply chain, and if the supply chain is more efficient, all participants in the chain can benefit. Collaboration can frequently achieve more than competition, and ERP systems can play a key role in collaborative planning.

Working with suppliers in a collaborative fashion requires trust among all parties. A company opens its records to its suppliers, and suppliers can read certain company data because of common data formats. Working with suppliers in this way cuts down on paperwork and response times. Reductions in paperwork, savings in time, and other efficiency improvements translate into cost savings for the company and the suppliers. ERP lets companies and suppliers share information (sales, inventory, production plans, and so on) in real time throughout the supply chain. This allows all parties to eliminate from the supply chain costs that do not add value to the product (such as inventory, overtime, changeovers, and spoilage), while simultaneously improving customer service.

The Traditional Supply Chain

The term **supply chain** describes all the activities that occur between the growing or mining of raw materials and the appearance of finished products on the store shelf. The supply chain for Fitter's NRG bars starts with farmers growing oats and wheat, and it ends with a customer buying a bar from a retail store. In a traditional supply chain, information is passed through the supply chain reactively, as participants change their product orders—as illustrated in Figure 4-24.

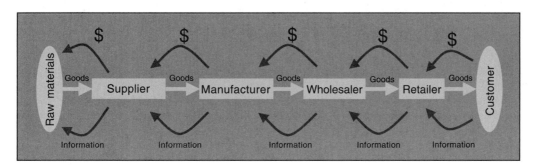

Source Line: Course Technology/Cengage Learning.

FIGURE 4-24 Supply chain—from raw materials to customer

For example, a retailer sees an increase in the sales of Fitter's bars and orders a larger quantity of bars from the wholesaler. If a number of retailers increase their orders, the wholesaler will increase its orders from Fitter. When Fitter gets larger orders from wholesalers, it must increase production to meet the increased demand. To increase production, Fitter will order more raw materials from suppliers.

Because of the time lags inherent in a traditional supply chain, it might take weeks—or even months—for information about Fitter's increased need for raw materials to reach Fitter's suppliers. Raw material suppliers might require time to increase *their* production to meet Fitter's larger orders, resulting in temporary shortages for the supplier. And unusual events such as the "Oprah effect" (where a product is endorsed by a famous name and causes a huge upsurge in demand) can also result in shortages. For example, the Amazon Kindle quickly sold out after the famous talk-show host Oprah Winfrey claimed it was one of her favorite items.

By contrast, if the participants in the supply chain are part of an integrated process, information about the increased customer demand can be passed quickly through the supply chain, so each link in the chain can react quickly to the change.

EDI and ERP

The development of supply chain strategies does not necessarily require an ERP system. Before ERP systems were available, companies could be linked with customers and suppliers through electronic data interchange (EDI) systems. Recall from Chapter 2 that EDI is the computer-to-computer exchange of standard business documents (such as purchase orders) between two companies. A well-developed ERP system, however, can facilitate supply chain management because the needed production planning and purchasing systems are already in place. In addition, the integration of accounting data in the ERP system (described in the next chapter) allows management to evaluate changes in the market and make decisions about how those changes should affect the production plan. With an ERP system, sharing production plans along the supply chain can occur in real time. Using the Internet can make this communication even faster and cheaper than using private EDI networks.

ANOTHER LOOK

Complexities of Supply Chain Management

Over the last few decades, a number of industry trends have focused on making supply chains more efficient and effective. The first of these started in the 1980s when techniques developed at the Toyota Motor Company, now commonly referred to as *lean manufacturing*, started to be accepted and copied by companies around the world. The main idea embodied in lean manufacturing—or the Toyota Production System (TPS)—is that waste must be eliminated. While that seems obvious, the TPS identified inventory resulting from "overproduction" as waste. Much of industrial practice, especially in the United States, was focused on the idea that efficiency should be measured by having each machine produce to its maximum capacity. The TPS approach was that a company should produce exactly what is required when it is required. The TPS emphasized "pull" systems, where customer demand triggers production, rather than "push" systems, where planning methods like MRP are frequently used to push material through the supply chain to the customer in anticipation of demand.

A second important trend has been a decrease in vertical integration of companies. **Vertical integration** means the extent to which a company produces the components and assemblies used in the products it manufactures. In the auto industry, vertical integration reached its peak with Henry Ford and the River Rouge manufacturing complex, where iron ore was deposited at one end of the facility and finished cars rolled out the other. In the 1920s and 1930s, Ford owned iron ore mines and ore freighters, rubber plantations, and a host of businesses and industries that supplied its automobile assembly plants. The goal was to achieve high quality and low costs. Today, efficiency

(continued)

and technology has driven many manufacturers to reduce their level of vertical integration. According to Steve Rodgers, president of AMPA, the Canadian Auto Parts Manufacturers' Association, "65 to 75 percent of the overall component cost of a car comes from outside suppliers." The auto manufacturers now focus on overall design of the vehicle and allow the suppliers to develop the expertise in the braking systems, interiors, and so on, which are then plugged into the designs.

A third trend is supply base rationalization, an effort to determine the "appropriate" number of suppliers a company should have. Many large firms have thousands of suppliers. However, the rationalization concept says that better supplier relationships can be developed when there are fewer suppliers to manage, and costs will be reduced when a smaller number of suppliers have higher production volumes. In 2008, Ford's Senior Vice President of Global Purchasing announced that Ford would be reducing its supply base from over 2,000 suppliers to 700 to 800 over a period of years.

These trends—lean manufacturing, reduced vertical integration, and supply base rationalization—have been implemented by manufacturers in a number of industries over the past 30 years and have resulted in higher efficiencies and reduced cost. But these savings have not come without a cost: increased exposure to disruption. This increased risk was highlighted by the earthquake and tsunami in Japan on March 14, 2011. In addition to the tragic loss of human life and destruction of property, the disaster forced many global companies to severely reduce or shut down production. Japanese-based companies such as Toyota were obviously affected, but the integrated nature of global supply chains meant that the effect of the earthquake rippled throughout the world. For example, the three largest shipbuilders in the world are located in Korea and are dependent on Japanese steel, and the Japanese steel industry was significantly impacted by the Fukushima nuclear power plant disaster, which was triggered by the tsunami that followed the earthquake. (The explosions, fire, and core meltdowns at the power plant made it the worst nuclear disaster since the 1986 Chernobyl explosion.)

Toyota, which has led many of these supply chain trends, is now planning to lead the way in reducing supply chain risk. In September 2011, they announced plans to create a robust supply chain that would recover within two weeks in the event of another massive disruption. This plan consists of three fundamental steps. First, Toyota intends to push for further standardization of parts across Japanese automakers so they can share common components, which could, in turn, be manufactured in several locations. The second element in the plan is the development of technology that would provide more options for parts that require unique materials or components that are only available from one source. Finally, Toyota plans to make each region in the world independent in its parts procurement so that a disaster in Japan would not affect production overseas.

Supply chains have always been complex, but now in addition to speed and efficiency, flexibility and risk reduction must be considered priorities.

Question:

1. What are other potential causes of supply chain disruption? How can ERP systems help minimize the impact when disruptions occur?

The Measures of Success

Performance measurements (sometimes referred to as **metrics**) have been developed to show the effects of better supply chain management. One measure is called the **cash-to-cash cycle time**. This term refers to the time between paying for raw materials and collecting cash from the customer. In one study, the cash-to-cash cycle time for companies with efficient supply chain management processes was a month, whereas the cycle averaged 100 days for those companies without effective supply chain management.

Another metric is total supply chain management costs. These costs include the cost of buying and handling inventory, processing orders, and supporting a company's information systems. In one study, companies with efficient supply chain management processes incurred costs equal to 5 percent of sales. By contrast, companies without supply chain management incurred costs of up to 12 percent of sales.

Other metrics have been developed to measure what is happening between a company and its suppliers. For example, Staples, the office-supply company, measures three facets of the relationship. **Initial fill rate** is the percentage of an order that the supplier provided in the first shipment. Another metric is **initial order lead time**, which is the time needed for the supplier to fill the order. Finally, Staples measures **on-time performance**. This measurement tracks how often the supplier met agreed-upon delivery dates.

Improvements in metrics such as these lead to improvements in overall supply chain cost measurements.

Exercise 4.8

Assume a manufacturer of residential lawn and garden equipment is considering investing in hardware and software that will improve linkages with suppliers. Management expects to save 5 percent of sales by tightening up the supply chain in the first year, 3 percent in the second year, and 1 percent in the third year. The company's annual sales are $1 billion. The company's chief financial officer insists that the investment must pay for itself in cost savings in three years. To meet this requirement, how much should the chief information officer be allowed to spend on improving the supply chain? Explain your answer.

ANOTHER LOOK

Supply Chain Going Green

The retail giant Walmart is trying to compel its suppliers to "go green" as part of its efforts to build a more environmentally sustainable global supply chain. As it did with promoting EDI and RFIDs in the early stages of those technologies, Walmart is leading the curve with its sustainability efforts. In 2008, Walmart's CEO, Lee Scott, told a large gathering in China, "A company that cheats on overtime and on the age of its labor, that dumps its scraps and chemicals into our rivers, that does not pay its taxes or honor its contracts—will ultimately cheat on the quality of its products. And cheating on the quality of products is the same as cheating on customers. We will not tolerate that at Walmart."

As part of this initiative, Walmart will survey its 100,000 global suppliers and ultimately create a "sustainability product index," which will allow the company to evaluate suppliers on their sustainability efforts. Suppliers anxious to keep Walmart as a customer will be motivated to improve their rating on the sustainability index. Some experts think Walmart can change the business climate on sustainability. According to Harvard Professor Rosabeth Moss Kanter, Walmart's determination to use its considerable influence to raise the standards for environmental sustainability "shows that a single company using its unique clout can accelerate public action to reduce greenhouse gases and reverse climate change."

Walmart's new initiative translates into a new burden on suppliers. By some estimates, the company's efforts to improve sustainability could increase the cost of products by 1–3 percent, due, in part, to new requirements that suppliers label products with a green index. However, these costs may be offset if the suppliers, as part of their efforts to reduce their impact on the environment, can also improve their supply chain efficiency.

Question:

1. Do you think consumers will be willing to pay increased prices to ensure their products are sustainably produced and packaged? Would you be willing to pay the extra cost? How much extra?

Chapter Summary

- An ERP system can improve the efficiency of production and purchasing processes. Efficiency begins with Marketing and Sales sharing a sales forecast. A production plan is created based on that forecast and shared with Purchasing so raw materials can be ordered properly.

- Companies can do production planning without an ERP system, but an ERP system that contains materials requirements planning capabilities allow a company to link Production to Purchasing and Accounting. This data sharing increases a company's overall efficiency.

- Companies are building on their ERP systems and integrated systems philosophy to practice supply chain management, a strategy by which a company looks at itself as part of a larger process that includes customers and suppliers. Using information more efficiently along the entire chain can result in significant cost savings. Because of the complexity of the global supply chain, developing a planning system that effectively coordinates information technology and people and that can help a company manage uncertainty is a considerable challenge.

Key Terms

bill of material (BOM)	MRP record
capacity	on-time performance
cash-to-cash cycle time	repetitive manufacturing
initial fill rate	rough-cut planning
initial order lead time	standard costs
lead time	supply chain
lot sizing	vertical integration
master production schedule (MPS)	
metrics	

Exercises

1. In which industries is supply chain management important? In which industries is it not? Why, or why not?

2. Recall from Chapter 1 that a business process cuts across functional lines. When a customer orders a product, such as a custom-built car, the Supply Chain Management function must interact with other functional areas in a company to complete this order. List the functional areas involved in this process. What information must pass between those areas and Supply Chain Management to fill the customer's needs?

3. Create a two-column list, and in the first column, list Fitter's flawed supply chain management process. In the second column, list the ways in which an ERP system could alleviate some of these problems.

4. Metrics are used to measure improvements in supply chain management. What are the benefits of tracking metrics? How often should they be calculated and recorded? Does it depend on the industry? Does it depend on the competitive environment? Why?

5. What are potential sources of risk in Fitter's supply chain? How should Fitter prepare to minimize these risks. Research this topic on the Internet, and use examples to support your reasoning.

6. Compare customer relationship management and supply chain management. How are they similar? How are they different? In which functional areas do they have the most impact? In answering, consider the kinds of technologies used in each.

For Further Study and Research

Beal, Vangie. "SAP to Acquire Right Hemisphere for 3-D Visualization Software." enterpriseappstoday.com. September 8, 2011.

Kim, Chang-Ran. "Toyota Aims for Quake-Proof Supply Chain." *Reuters*, September 6, 2011.

Goetz, Michael. "Suppliers Make Cars, Not Automakers." Sympatico.ca. March 4, 2011. http://autos.sympatico.ca/features/8233/group-project-suppliers-make-cars-not-automakers.

Keal, Donald, and Phil Hebert. "Benefits to Blood Banks of a Sales and Operations Planning Process." *Journal of Blood Services Management* 50, (December 2010): 2785–2787.

Lee, Don, and David Pierson. "Earthquake Damage to a Japanese Silicon Wafer Production Plant Illustrates the Manufacturing Troubles that Can Ensue When Companies Reduce Their Network of Suppliers." *Los Angeles Times*, April 06, 2011.

Overby, Stephanie. "Supply Chain Management to the Rescue." *CIO*, March 16, 2010. www.cio.com/article/580113/Supply_Chain_Management_to_the_Rescue.

Shuldiner, Herb. "Ford Cutting Deep into Supply Base." *Ward's AutoWorld*, December 1, 2008.

Wallgum, Thomas, "Why the Oprah Effect Can Take Down the Best Supply Chains." *CIO*, September 10, 2009. www.cio.com/article/501830/Why_the_Oprah_Effect_Can_Take_Down_the_Best_Supply_Chains.

Wallgum, Thomas. "Wal-Mart Orders Suppliers to Go Green and Some See Red." *CIO*, July 20, 2009. www.cio.com/article/497559/Wal_Mart_Orders_Suppliers_to_Go_Green_and_Some_ee_Red.

Wallgum, Thomas. "Wal-Mart's Green Strategy: Supply Chain Makeover Targets Chinese Manufacturers." *CIO*, Octboer 24, 2008. www.cio.com/article/456625/Wal_Mart_s_Green_Strategy_Supply_Chain_Makeover_Targets_Chinese_Manufacturers?page=1&taxonomyId=3015.

CHAPTER 5

ACCOUNTING IN ERP SYSTEMS

INTRODUCTION

In previous chapters, you learned about functional area activities, both generally and specifically: In Chapter 1, you read an overview of functional area activities; in Chapter 3, you learned about Marketing and Sales activities; and in Chapter 4, you learned about Supply Chain Management. In this chapter, you will learn about the activities in another functional area, Accounting and Finance. You will see how Accounting and Finance is tightly integrated with all the other functional areas and how Accounting activities aid in decision making.

ACCOUNTING ACTIVITIES

Accounting activities can generally be classified as either financial accounting or managerial accounting. An additional area of accounting, tax accounting, is beyond the scope of this text. Because tax accounting is chiefly the external reporting of a business's activities to the Internal Revenue Service, data gathered for financial accounting serves as the basis for tax accounting.

Financial accounting consists of documenting all the transactions of a company that have an impact on the financial state of the organization and then using those documented transactions to create reports for investors and external parties and agencies. These reports, typically called *financial statements*, must follow the prescribed rules and guidelines of various agencies, such as the Financial Accounting Standards Board (FASB), the U.S. Securities and Exchange Commission (SEC), and the Internal Revenue Service (IRS).

Common financial statements include balance sheets and income statements. The balance sheet is a summary of account balances such as cash held; amounts owed to the company by customers; the cost of raw materials and finished-goods inventories; the value of fixed assets such as buildings; amounts owed to vendors, banks, and other creditors; and amounts that the investors have invested in the company. A balance sheet provides an overview of a company's financial health at a point in time, a key consideration for a company's creditors and investors. Figure 5-1 shows a sample balance sheet for Fitter Snacker.

Fitter Snacker Balance Sheet December 31, 2011 (in thousands of dollars)		
Assets		
Cash		$5,003
Accounts receivable		$4,715
Inventories		$9,025
Plant and equipment		$6,231
Land		$1,142
Total assets		$26,116
Liabilities		
Accounts payable	$6,400	
Notes payable	$10,000	
Total liabilities		$16,400
Stockholders' Equity		
Contributed capital	$2,000	
Retained earnings	$7,716	
Total stockholders' equity		$9,716
Total liabilities and stockholders' equity		$26,116

Source Line: Course Technology/Cengage Learning.

FIGURE 5-1 Sample balance sheet for Fitter

The **income statement**, or **profit and loss (P&L) statement**, shows the company's revenue and expenses and the profit or loss for a period of time (typically a quarter or a year). Profitability is important to creditors and investors. It is also important information for managers in charge of day-to-day operations. In general, a manager views profits as indicators of success and losses as indicators of problems to be solved. Figure 5-2 shows a sample income statement for Fitter.

Fitter Snacker Income Statement For the year ended December 31, 2011 (in thousands of dollars)		
Revenue		
Sales revenue	$36,002	
Total revenue		$36,002
Expenses		
Cost of goods sold expense	$25,691	
Selling, general, and administrative expense	$4,251	
Research and development expense	$962	
Interest expense	$521	
Total expenses		$31,425
Pretax income		$4,577
Income tax expense		$1,144
Net income		$3,433

Source Line: Course Technology/Cengage Learning.

FIGURE 5-2 Sample income statement for Fitter

Typically, companies prepare financial statements quarterly, sometimes more frequently. To prepare these statements, a company must "close its books," which means that balances for temporary or nominal accounts (such as revenue, expense, gain, and loss) are transferred to the retained earnings account. The closed nominal accounts will have a zero balance from which to start accumulating revenue and expenses in the next reporting period. Closing entries are made to transfer the balances and establish zero balances for the nominal accounts. To do this, employees must check the accounts to ensure they are accurate and up to date. If a company's information systems routinely generate accurate and timely data, closing the books can go smoothly. If not, "adjusting" entries must be made, in which case, closing the books can be a very time-consuming chore with inaccurate results.

One advantage of an integrated information system is that it simplifies the process of closing the books and preparing financial statements. Accounting staff do not need to assemble data from different systems because all of the required data are contained in a centralized system. Figure 5-3 shows how Fitter's balance sheet and P&L statement would look in the SAP ERP system.

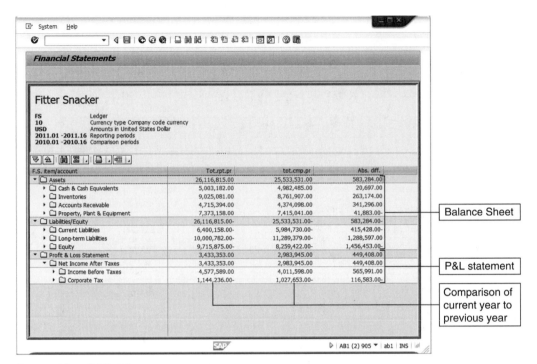

Source Line: SAP AG.

FIGURE 5-3   Balance sheet and income statement for Fitter in SAP ERP system

In an ERP system, the balance sheet and P&L statement are database reports that can be quickly generated at any time, and because the data to prepare the reports are read from the database tables, these reports are always up to date. Another feature of the ERP balance sheet and P&L statement is the ability to quickly display data at different levels of detail, as shown in Figure 5-4. In addition, an ERP system allows the user to create financial statement variants, which are financial statements in other formats, prepared to suit the needs of different users.

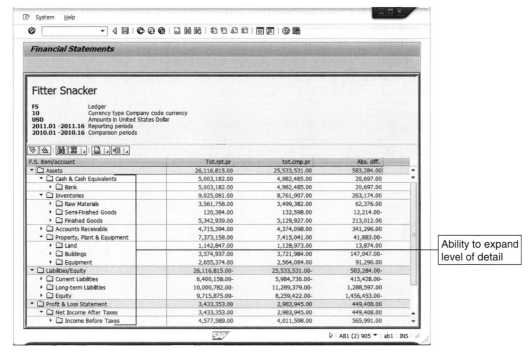

Source Line: SAP AG.

FIGURE 5-4   Balance sheet and income statement in SAP ERP, with several asset categories expanded to show more detail

Managerial accounting deals with determining the costs and profitability of a company's activities. While the high-level information that appears in a company's balance sheet and income statement shows whether a firm is making an overall profit, the goal of managerial accounting is to provide managers with detailed information for making informed decisions, creating budgets, determining the profitability of a particular product, sales region, or marketing campaign, and so on. Managerial accounting produces information that managers use to control a company's day-to-day activities and to develop long-term plans for operations, marketing, personnel needs, repayment of debt, and other management issues. Because managerial accounting provides reports and analyses for internal use, companies can be flexible in how they configure their managerial accounting systems.

Using ERP for Accounting Information

Recall from Chapter 1, that in the past, most companies had separate functional information systems: a marketing information system, a manufacturing information system, and so on—each with its own way of gathering data and its own file system for recording data. Since the 1960s, legions of accountants, analysts, and programmers have tried, often unsuccessfully, to make unintegrated systems work, as prior chapters illustrate. Companies built these unintegrated systems primarily to handle the needs of the individual functional areas, and secondarily to provide data to Accounting so that

Accounting could "keep the books," that is, maintain records of all financial transactions. Data sharing, however, usually did not occur in real time, so Accounting's data were often out of date. Further, because the shared data were often not the only information that Accounting needed to prepare reports for management, accountants and functional area clerks usually had to spend considerable time doing additional research to create those reports.

An ERP system, with its centralized database, avoids these problems. For example, suppose finished goods are transferred from the assembly line to the warehouse. An employee in the warehouse can easily record the transaction, using a terminal or a bar-code scanner. In SAP ERP, the Materials Management module would see the transfer event as an increase in finished goods inventory available for shipment; the Accounting module would see the event as an increase in the monetary value of the finished goods inventory. With ERP, everyone uses the same database to record operating data. This database is then used to generate management reports, produce financial statements, and create budgets.

In accounting, a company's accounts are kept in a record called the **general ledger**. In the SAP ERP system, input to the general ledger occurs simultaneously with the business transaction in the specific module. Many SAP ERP modules cause transaction data to be entered into the general ledger, including:

- *Sales and Distribution (SD)*—The SD module records a sale and then creates an **accounts receivable** entry (a general ledger document that indicates a customer owes money for the goods received by the customer).
- *Materials Management (MM)*—The MM module controls purchasing and records inventory changes. The receipt of goods from a purchase order creates an **accounts payable** entry in the general ledger, which indicates the company has an obligation to pay for goods it has received. Whenever material moves into or out of inventory (purchased materials arrive from the vendor, raw materials are taken out of inventory to support production, or finished goods go from production to inventory), general ledger accounts are affected.
- *Financial Accounting (FI)*—The FI module manages the accounts receivable and accounts payable items created in the SD and MM modules, respectively. The FI module is also where the general ledger accounts are closed at the end of a fiscal period (quarter or year), and it is used to generate financial statements.
- *Controlling (CO)*—The CO module tracks the costs associated with producing products. To make a profit, a company must have an accurate picture of its product costs so it can make correct decisions about product pricing and promotions, as well as capital investments.
- *Human Resources (HR)*—The HR module manages the recruiting, hiring, compensation, termination, and severance of employees; the HR module also manages benefits and generates the payroll.
- *Asset Management (AM)*—The AM module manages fixed-asset purchases (plant and machinery) and the related depreciation.

OPERATIONAL DECISION-MAKING PROBLEM: CREDIT MANAGEMENT

Out-of-date or inaccurate accounting data that result from unintegrated information systems can cause problems when a company is making operational decisions, as illustrated by the discussion of Fitter's credit management challenges in Chapter 3. In this section, we will look at industrial credit granting in general, and then we will examine the problems with Fitter's credit-granting procedures in more detail.

Industrial Credit Management

Companies routinely sell to customers on credit; however, good financial management requires that only so much credit be extended to a customer. At some point, the customer must pay off some of the debt to justify the faith the seller has shown (and so the seller can turn the accounts receivables into cash). Credit management requires a balance between granting sufficient credit to support sales and ensuring the company does not lose too much money by granting credit to customers who end up defaulting on their credit obligations.

In practice, sellers manage this relationship by setting a limit on how much money a customer can owe at any one time, and then monitoring that limit as new orders come in and payments are received. For example, the seller might tell a buyer that her credit limit is $10,000, which means that the most she can owe the seller is $10,000. If the buyer reaches that amount, the seller will accept no further sales orders until she pays off some of her debt. When making a sale on credit, the seller makes an entry on the books to increase the accounts receivable and sales balances. Thus, when the buyer's accounts receivable balance on the seller's books reaches $10,000, the buyer must make some payment.

Continuing the example, assume the buyer calls the seller to order $3,000's worth of goods. If the buyer's accounts receivable balance is already $8,000, the seller should not accept the $3,000 order because it would bring the accounts receivable balance to $11,000, which exceeds the buyer's credit limit. Instead of refusing the order, the seller's sales representative might suggest that the buyer reduce the size of the order, or ask her to send in a payment before processing the order, thus reducing the buyer's debt. Clearly, to make this system work, a sales representative needs to have access to up-to-date accounts receivable balances for all customers.

If Accounting keeps the books up to date and can provide the current accounts receivable balance to Marketing and Sales *when needed*, then credit limits can be properly managed. Marketing and Sales can compare the customer's credit limit to an accurate balance-owed amount (plus the order's value) to make a decision. However, in an unintegrated system, Accounting may not immediately record sales and/or payment receipts as they occur. In that case, accounts receivable balances will not be current. Furthermore, the sales representative may be working from an out-of-date credit-balance printout. If the printout does not reflect recent payments, a customer may be improperly denied credit. The customer would probably challenge the denial, which would trigger a request for updated information in Accounting. The delay entailed in that research could reduce customer satisfaction, and performing the research would consume valuable employee time.

These problems should not arise with an integrated information system. When a sale is made, the system immediately increases the customer's accounts receivable balance. When the company receives and records a payment, the accounts receivable balance is immediately decreased. Because the underlying database is available to Accounting *and* Marketing and Sales, sales representatives have access to up-to-date customer balance information. Thus, sales representatives do not need to make a request to Accounting for the customer's accounts receivable balance.

With that background, we can now consider how Fitter handles credit management, using unintegrated systems.

Fitter's Credit Management Procedures

As described in Chapter 3, when a new order comes in to Fitter, a sales clerk refers to a weekly printout of a customer's current balance and credit limit to see if credit should be granted. Assuming the customer's order would not present credit-limit problems, the sales clerk enters the sale in the sales order entry system, which is a stand-alone computer program. Sales data are transferred to Accounting by transferring files at the end of each day. An accounting clerk uses the data transferred from the sales system to prepare customer invoices.

Accounting must make adjustments for any partial shipments before creating an invoice. The accuracy of the adjustment process depends on whether the warehouse transmits order changes to Accounting in a timely fashion. After creating the invoice, Accounting makes the standard revenue-recognition accounting entries: a debit to accounts receivable and a credit to sales for the amount billed.

Accounting clerks also process customer payments. Clerks receive and manually handle checks. They enter data in the accounting program, increasing the cash balance and decreasing the accounts receivable balance. These data are later used to make updates to individual customer accounts, reducing the amount that customers owe to Fitter. If time permits, accounts are posted (and the bank deposit is made) on the day payment is received; otherwise, the entries are done as soon as possible the next day. Thus, there can be a delay between the time Fitter receives a check from a customer and the actual reduction of the customer's accounts receivable balance, which can lead to mistakes in credit management.

Now let's look at how SAP ERP could improve Fitter's credit management process.

Credit Management in SAP ERP

The SAP ERP system allows a company to set a credit limit for each customer. A company can configure any number of credit-check options in the SAP ERP system, including when to check a customer's credit (for instance, at order creation, at creation of the delivery document, or at the goods issue) and who to notify when an order would cause a customer to exceed its credit limit (for instance, the sales clerk or credit management personnel). Figure 5-5 shows a dynamic credit check with Reaction C selected.

Reaction C means that if the order being saved will cause the customer to exceed its credit limit, the system will issue a warning indicating the amount by which the order exceeds the credit limit. Because the system is issuing a warning, the order can be saved, but it will be blocked from further processing until the credit problem is cleared.

Frequently, companies do not configure the system to provide warnings to sales order clerks because they are not equipped to correct the problem and because the credit problem is an issue between the selling firm's Accounts Receivable Department and the customer's Accounts Payable Department. Rather, a person in the credit management function regularly reviews all blocked sales orders and resolves the credit problem directly with the customer.

Figure 5-5 also shows that the credit check is dynamic and has a two-month horizon. This means that only the next two months of sales orders will be used in calculating the credit check. Customers may place orders for a long-range schedule, but only those that will be shipped in the near term are usually considered in the credit check.

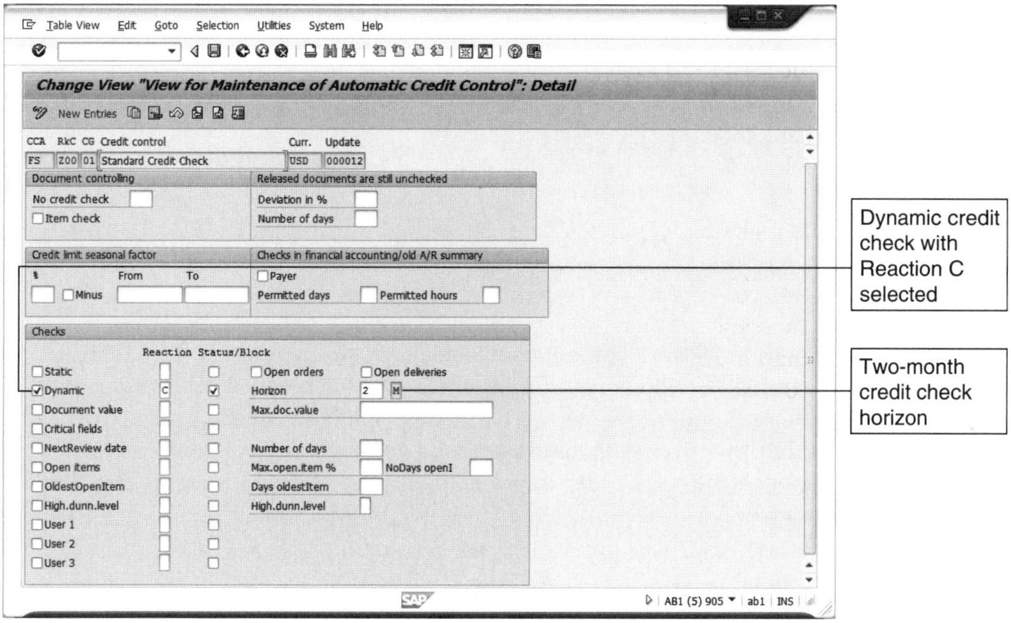

Source Line: SAP AG.

FIGURE 5-5   Credit management configuration

Figure 5-6 shows the credit-checking process in Figure 5-5 applied to a specific customer, Health Express. Health Express has a credit limit of $1,000 and currently has used $590 of this limit. If Health Express places an order for snack bars that totals more than $410, the order will be blocked.

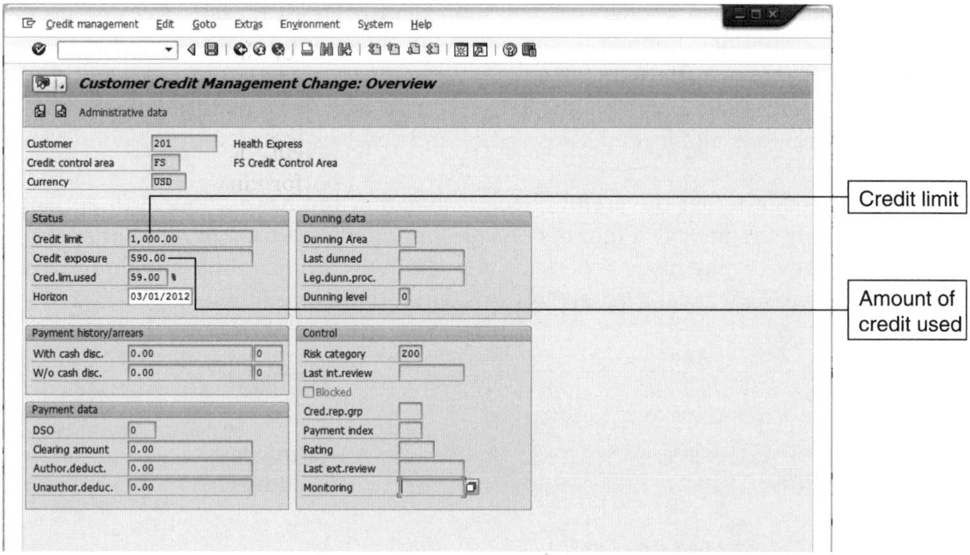

Source Line: SAP AG.

FIGURE 5-6   Credit management for Health Express

Figure 5-7 shows the SAP ERP screen where blocked sales orders are listed. Most companies have an employee who is responsible for reviewing blocked sales orders (perhaps every two hours) and taking corrective action. The advantage of using SAP ERP to manage credit is that the process is automated and the data are available in real time. The user can double-click the sales order to see company information, such as contacts, or to see payment history.

Source Line: SAP AG.

FIGURE 5-7   Blocked sales order

With Fitter's current system, the sales order clerk must manually check credit. If the clerk fails to do this, then a customer who is a bad risk may receive more credit. However, even when the clerk does perform the manual credit check, the credit decision can frequently be made in error, since the data are not current. With the SAP ERP system, the check is automatic, the data are up to date, and it is a simple matter to review blocked sales orders.

Exercise 5.1

1. Create a document that describes Fitter's current credit management procedure. Write this document so it could be used to train a new employee in the credit management process.

2. Create a revised version of your document to reflect the process improvements that would result if Fitter were performing credit checks using an integrated information system.

PRODUCT PROFITABILITY ANALYSIS

Business managers use accounting data to perform profitability analyses of a company and its products. When data are inaccurate or incomplete, the analyses are flawed. There are three main reasons for inaccurate or incomplete data: inconsistent record keeping, inaccurate inventory costing systems, and problems consolidating data from subsidiaries. The following sections will look at each of these causes, using Fitter as an example.

Inconsistent Record Keeping

Each of Fitter's sales divisions maintains its own records and tracks sales data differently. The Direct Sales Division's sales order form includes a code for the appropriate sales region (Northeast, Southeast, and so on). The Wholesale Division's sales order form includes a code for the state. Suppose that a Fitter executive asks for a report that summarizes monthly sales dollars for all Mid-Atlantic states (i.e., some states from Fitter's Northeast sales region and some states from its Southeast region) for each month of the previous year. Neither division's records are set up to easily answer that question. Rather, a Fitter accountant would need to go to the source sales documents for the Direct Sales Division and, by looking at the shipping address, determine whether the sale was to a company in a Mid-Atlantic state. If so, the accountant would need to manually add the relevant information for this sale to an electronic spreadsheet. For the Wholesale Division, the accountant could run sales summary reports for each state in the Mid-Atlantic region by month and add this data manually to the spreadsheet report. Once all the data was gathered, it could be formatted to create the desired reports.

Now, suppose Fitter's management wants to evaluate the efficiency of Production's operations. Production uses paper records, so, again, data must be taken from the paper records and entered into a spreadsheet. As often happens, those paper records might be inaccurate or missing, making the validity of the final report questionable and the creation of the report time consuming.

There are many variations on this theme. Conceivably, a company's divisions could maintain the same data about a function, but if each division's system was created at a different time, each might a different file system. Often, to answer a question about overall company performance, at least one set of data must be rekeyed into a spreadsheet (or some other middleware program) for the merged analysis. While it is possible to get an answer, doing so takes much more time with unintegrated systems.

With an ERP system, this sort of effort is minimized or eliminated because both divisions record and store their data in the same way, in the same database. Ideally, the company's processes would be changed to fit the best practices of the software when it is installed. As part of the system configuration process, the managers of each division would agree on how data would be collected and stored. Then, questions regarding company performance could be answered in a few minutes by any accountant (or manager or salesperson, for that matter) who understands how to execute a query in the database language or how to use built-in management reporting tools.

Inaccurate Inventory Costing Systems

Correctly calculating inventory costs is one of the most important and challenging accounting tasks in any manufacturing company. Managers need to know how much it costs to make individual products, so they can identify which products are profitable and which are not.

In the next section, we will first review the fundamentals of inventory cost accounting. Then, we will explore how an ERP system can improve the accuracy of inventory cost accounting. Finally, we will discuss the rationale behind activity-based costing as a method to further improve the accuracy of inventory cost accounting.

Inventory Cost Accounting Background

A manufactured item's cost has three elements: (1) the cost of raw materials, (2) the cost of labor employed directly in the production of the item, and (3) all other costs, which are typically called **overhead**. Manufacturing overhead costs include factory utilities, general factory labor (such as custodians or security guards), factory managers' salaries, storage, insurance, and other manufacturing-related costs.

Materials and labor are often called **direct costs** because the constituent amounts of each in a finished product can be estimated fairly accurately. On the other hand, the overhead items are **indirect costs**, which are difficult to associate with a specific product or a batch of specific products. In other words, the direct cause-and-effect relationship between an overhead cost (such as the cost of heat and light) and making a particular product (NRG-A bars) is difficult to establish.

Nevertheless, overhead costs are part of making products, so companies must have some way to allocate these indirect costs to the products they make. A common method is to use total machine hours, on the assumption that overhead is incurred to run the machines that make the products. With this approach, overhead costs for a certain time period are added up and then divided by the expected total machine hours for that time period to get an overhead per machine hour rate. This value is then used to allocate overhead costs to products. Suppose Fitter used this approach and calculated its overhead rate at $1,000 per machine hour. If Fitter can make 10,000 bars in an hour, then each bar would be allocated $0.10 of overhead ($1,000 ÷ 10,000). Overhead can also be allocated to a product using direct labor hours or material costs. A company makes the decision on how to allocate overhead costs based on what makes the most sense in its production environment.

Companies such as Fitter that produce goods for inventory typically record the cost of manufacturing during a period using a standard cost. As explained in Chapter 4, standard costs for a product are established by studying historical direct and indirect cost patterns in a company and taking into account the effects of current manufacturing changes. At the end of an accounting period, if actual costs differ from standard costs, adjustments to the accounts must be made to show the actual cost of inventory owned on the balance sheet and the cost of inventory sold on the income statement.

For example, Fitter might determine that each NRG-A bar should cost $0.75 to make—that is, the cost of raw materials, labor, and overhead should equal $0.75 per bar, given the budgeted number of units. That amount would be Fitter's standard cost for a bar. Assume that during a given month, Fitter makes 1 million NRG-A bars. Using the standard cost, it would increase its balance sheet inventory account by $750,000. Also, assume that the company sells 800,000 bars in the month. In the income statement, the cost of the sales would be shown as $600,000 (800,000 × $0.75). The inventory account would be reduced by $600,000, because the company no longer has those units to sell.

If actual costs in the month equaled standard costs, no balance sheet or income statement adjustments would be needed. Actual costs never exactly equal expected costs, however, so adjustments are almost always needed. The differences between actual costs and standard costs are called **cost variances**. Note that cost variances can arise with both direct and indirect costs. These variances are calculated by comparing actual expenses for material, labor, utilities, rent, and so on, with predicted standard costs.

If the company keeps records for the various elements separately, compiling variance adjustments can be difficult. If products are made by assembling parts that are made at different manufacturing sites, and the sites use different information systems, the adjustments may be very imprecise.

ERP and Inventory Cost Accounting

Many companies with unintegrated accounting systems analyze their cost variances infrequently because of the difficulty of doing so. As a result, these companies often do not know how much it actually costs to produce a unit of a product. As the following example illustrates, knowing precisely how much production costs can be very important.

Suppose Fitter has an opportunity to sell 300,000 NRG-A bars to a new customer. This is a huge order for Fitter. The customer wants a price of $0.90 per bar. Fitter's standard cost per bar is currently $0.75—based on information that is two months old. Fitter knows that the costs to manufacture snack bars have been increasing significantly in the past few months. Fitter does not want to sell at a loss per unit, but it also does not want to lose a large order or a potentially good long-term customer. Because of the difficulty of compiling all the data to calculate cost variances, Fitter only analyzes cost variances quarterly, and new data will not be available for another month. Should Fitter accept the large order?

If Fitter had an ERP system, employees throughout the company would have recorded costs in the company-wide database as they occurred. The methods for allocating costs to products and for computing variances would have been built into the system when it was configured. Thus, the system could compute variances automatically when needed. This would simplify the process of adjusting accounts, and Fitter's management would always have accurate, up-to-date information on cost variances. Fitter could make an informed decision on whether it could profitably sell snack bars for $0.90 each. Furthermore, with a properly operating sales and operations planning process, Fitter could determine whether it has the capacity to complete the order on time, as well. If overtime would be required to complete the order, then analysts could use the planning capabilities of the ERP system to evaluate costs using overtime production.

ERP system configurations allow analysts to track costs using many bases—by job, by work area, or by production activity. This means that unit costs can be computed using different overhead allocation bases, allowing an analyst to play "what if" with product profitability decisions. In an unintegrated system, doing such multifaceted tracking would be time consuming and difficult.

Product Costing Example

Suppose Fitter wants to update standard costs for its NRG-A bars. By analyzing the company's recent indirect costs related to the products produced, Fitter's cost accountants have calculated new overhead rates. Because the material costs are much larger than direct labor costs at Fitter, the company has decided to apply production overhead as a percentage of direct material costs. The new rate for production overhead is 100 percent of direct material costs.

Figure 5-8 shows the product cost analysis for the NRG-A bar. The cost analysis is based on seven cases of bars, which is the amount of bars that can be produced by a 500-pound batch of dough. The recipe for a 500-pound batch of NRG-A bars was shown in Figure 4-16 in Chapter 4. This information is repeated in the cost analysis of Figure 5-8, along with the per-unit cost of each of these materials.

| Ingredient | NRG-A Bar Product Cost Analysis (7 cases) | | | |
	Unit of measure	NRG-A	Cost per unit of measure	Direct material cost
Oats	lb	300	$0.20	$60.00
Wheat germ	lb	50	$0.30	$15.00
Cinnamon	lb	5	$3.00	$15.00
Nutmeg	lb	2	$4.50	$9.00
Cloves	lb	1	$5.50	$5.50
Honey	gal	10	$6.40	$64.00
Canola	gal	7	$1.70	$11.90
Vit./min. powder	lb	5	$18.45	$92.25
Carob chips	lb	50	$2.10	$105.00
Raisins	lb	50	$3.20	$160.00
Total direct material cost				$537.65
Production overhead cost (100% of Total direct material)				$537.65
Direct labor				54.50
Cost of goods manufactured (COGM)				1,129.80
Sales and administrative costs (30% of COGM)				338.94
Cost of goods sold (COGS)				1,468.74
COGM per case				$161.40
COGS per case				$209.82

Source Line: Course Technology/Cengage Learning.

FIGURE 5-8 Product cost analysis for NRG-A bar

For example, the per-pound cost of oats is $0.20. Multiplying the quantity of materials by the unit cost gives the direct material cost for that ingredient item; therefore, the total direct material cost of oats is $60.00 (300 × $0.20). Summing the results for all of the ingredients gives a total direct material cost of $537.65 for a 500-pound batch. Applying the production overhead rate of 100 percent to this direct material cost gives a production overhead cost equal to the direct material cost, or $537.65. As shown in the Figure 5-8, the direct labor cost to mix the dough and bake the snack bars is $54.50. It is important to note that the labor cost is only about 10 percent of the direct material cost, which is why Fitter has chosen to apply production overhead costs based on direct material only.

The sum of direct materials, production overhead, and direct labor is the cost of goods manufactured (COGM). Currently, Fitter uses a rate of 30 percent of the cost of goods manufactured to estimate the sales and administrative costs. Adding the sales and administrative costs to the COGM gives the cost of goods sold (COGS). Because the COGM and COGS were estimated based on the BOM (recipe) from Chapter 4 that produces seven cases of snack bars, the figures must be divided by seven to give the COGM and COGS on a per-case basis. Figure 5-8 shows that these are $161.40 and $209.82, respectively.

The product cost analysis allows you to determine whether selling 300,000 NRG-A bars to a new customer for a price of $0.90 per bar would earn a profit for Fitter. Given that there are 24 bars in a box and 12 boxes in a case, the current cost for an NRG-A bar is:

$$\frac{\$209.82/\text{case}}{(24 \text{ bars/box})(12 \text{ boxes/case})} = \$0.73/\text{bar}$$

Based on this calculation, you can see that Fitter can sell the bars at $0.90 and make a profit of $0.17 per bar.

Exercise 5.2

Estimate the COGM and COGS on a per-case basis for the NRG-B bar using the production information in Figure 4-16 and the following product costs:

Protein powder (lb.)	$4.40
Hazelnuts (lb.)	$1.64
Dates (lb.)	$3.55

Use the same direct labor costs and overhead percentages shown in the NRG-A bar product cost analysis in Figure 5-8.

Product Cost Analysis in SAP ERP

A large company may produce thousands of complicated products, and the task of gathering the information required to develop product costs can be a major challenge. An advantage of an integrated information system such as SAP ERP is that timely, accurate information is available in the information system. The key pieces of information for a cost analysis are the direct material costs and the direct labor costs. In SAP ERP, the direct material costs are determined from the bill of material (BOM), which is managed in the Production Planning (PP) module. Direct labor costs are determined from the product routing, which documents the machines and work centers used in the production of a product—along with equipment set-up time, production rates, and labor requirements. The BOM and routing information, combined with other data maintained in the Production Planning module, allows the SAP

ERP system to determine the quantities of direct material and direct labor used in a product. These production data, combined with material cost information stored in the Financial Accounting module, provide the basis for a product cost analysis.

In the SAP ERP system, a product cost is based on a **product cost variant**. In SAP ERP, the term *variant* is used to mean a version of a plan or analysis. A product cost variant is basically the procedure for developing a product cost analysis; many variants can be created for different planning requirements. Once a product cost variant is developed, it only takes seconds for the SAP ERP system to gather the required information to create a product cost estimate. Figure 5-9 shows the result of a product costs analysis in the SAP ERP system. This screen not only provides the cost analysis, but it also allows the user to explore the details about how cost analysis was calculated.

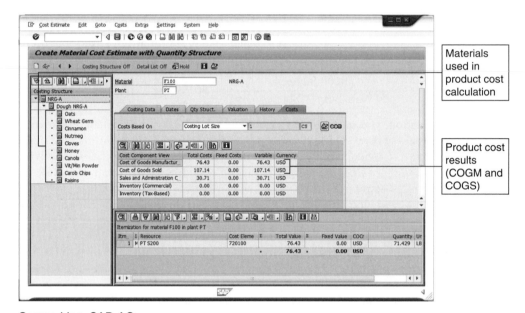

Source Line: SAP AG.

FIGURE 5-9   Product cost analysis result in SAP ERP

The SAP ERP product cost tool greatly reduces the time required to develop cost estimates, and it increases their accuracy because it gets its data directly from system modules, where the data are real time.

Activity-Based Costing and ERP

A trend in inventory cost accounting is toward **activity-based costing**. In activity-based costing, overhead costs are assigned to products based on the manufacturing activities that gave rise to the costs. Accountants identify activities associated with overhead cost generation, and they keep records on the costs *and* on the activities. The activities are viewed as causes (drivers) of the overhead costs. This view treats overhead costs as more direct than traditional cost-accounting methods have treated them. In an attempt to assign costs more precisely to individual products, activity-based costing tries to avoid rough allocation procedures. Although not all overhead costs can be linked to products by their activities, many can be. Activity-based costing is often used when competition is stiff, overhead costs are high, and products are diverse. A company using activity-based costing can determine which products have the highest profit margin, information that is crucial for making strategic decisions on product lines.

Consider this example from Fitter's operations. Suppose that storage of raw materials is considered an activity. Also assume that storage activities differ between NRG-A and NRG-B bars because the ingredients are different, and that some of these storage activities are more labor-intensive than others. In an ERP system, Fitter would track the various storage activities (how often they occur) and the cost of each. When determining the profitability of each kind of bar, Fitter cost accountants calculate storage costs based on the number of storage activities required by each type of bar. This costing is more precise than computing an average storage cost based on total storage costs and machine hours, and then allocating that amount to each kind of bar. Conceivably, if the activities differ enough from one bar to the next, one could be significantly more or less profitable than the other. This fact would be revealed by the activity-based costing approach, but *not* by traditional cost-accounting approaches. An information system that supports activity-based costing allows managers to see that difference.

Activity-based costing requires more bookkeeping than traditional costing methods because a company must do activity-based costing in addition to traditional costing, and because activity-based costing requires a company to keep track of instances of activities, not just the costs. For many companies, the cost and effort required to implement activity-based costing is justified by the value of the information yielded. Companies often use activity-based costing for strategic purposes, while using traditional costing for bookkeeping and taxes. Having an integrated information system allows a company to do both kinds of accounting much more easily. One study of companies with and without ERP revealed that: (1) ERP companies had nearly twice as many cost-allocation bases to use in management decision making, and (2) the ERP companies' managers rated their cost-accounting system much higher. ERP companies also have more faith in the numbers from their accounting systems.

A survey of management accountants revealed some interesting findings in regard to how they perceived their ERP systems. Researchers conducting this survey solicited responses from approximately 500 members of the IMA, the association for accountants and financial professionals in business. ERP systems were looked at by accounting managers as being better than not having ERP systems in the areas of having the attributes of a "single, comprehensive database, providing data on a real-time basis, and making relevant information available to operations management." In addition, ERP systems were found to help in resolving conflicts in goals, standardizing basic processes, and controlling product costs. ERP systems in the accounting field also help shorten the time for making decisions and improve that decision making. On the negative side, the respondents thought the ERP systems were overly complex and took too long to implement.

Problems Consolidating Data from Subsidiaries

Some companies have special operations that make closing their books at the end of an accounting period a challenge. Companies that have subsidiaries or branches face such a challenge, and most large companies have more than one legal entity. Because a company's executive team must understand the big picture in terms of overall operations and profitability, account balances for each entity must be compiled and forwarded to the home office so consolidated financial statements and reports for the company as a whole can be generated.

You might think this would be merely an arithmetic problem: add up cash for all the entities, accounts receivables for all the entities, and so on through the accounts. The job, however, is more difficult than that. Problems can arise due to a variety of issues, including the following: Accounts stated in another country's currency must be converted to U.S. dollars (in the case of a U.S. parent company), and transactions between a company and its subsidiaries must be eliminated from the accounts.

Currency Translation

The following scenario illustrates the problems of **currency translation**, which is the process of converting account balances expressed in one currency into balances expressed in another currency. Assume one euro is worth $1.25 (US), and a company's European subsidiary reports cash of 1 million euros at the end of the year. When the European subsidiary's balances are consolidated with those of the U.S. parent company at the end of the year, $1,250,000 will be recorded. The same sort of translation would be done for all the European subsidiary's accounts. A complicating factor is that exchange rates fluctuate daily; however, an ERP system can be configured to access daily exchange rates and translate daily transactions automatically.

ANOTHER LOOK

International Financial Reporting Standards (IFRS)

The current reporting standard for financial statements in the United States is **U.S. GAAP (Generally Accepted Accounting Principles)**, created by the Financial Accounting Standards Board. Governing bodies, such as the SEC, require companies trading on U.S. stock exchanges to report their finances using the U.S. GAAP reporting standard. However, in an effort to achieve a worldwide standard in accounting, by 2016 publicly traded U.S. companies are likely to be required to report their financial statements under a set of standards called the **International Financial Reporting Standards (IFRS)**, which are a set of international accounting standards issued by the International Accounting Standards Board (IASB). A single set of reporting standards is important to U.S. investors because many large companies in the United States, such as Intel, Coca-Cola, and McDonalds, generate more than one-half of their income from outside the United States. In addition, many investors are now investing in companies worldwide and are interested in comparing financial statements across countries. More foreign companies are also merging with those in other countries, which provides another incentive for countries worldwide to move to a common reporting standard.

Previously, foreign companies trading on U.S. stock exchanges were required by the SEC to report their finances in U.S. GAAP or to provide a translation between IFRS and U.S. GAAP; the SEC now allows those companies to report only using IFRS. Recently, the FASB and the IASB have been working on making the two standards, IFRS and U.S. GAAP, closer. This work is known as *convergence*, because it involves eliminating

(continued)

differences between the two standards, thereby enabling companies to easily transition to IFRS.

An ERP system can help companies adopt IFRS because the financial modules of ERP systems are capable of reporting on multiple standards. Many companies will be reporting their financials under IFRS and at the same time reporting for local tax purposes under a different standard (in this case U.S. GAAP). ERP systems can handle the parallel requirements for filing financial records.

Question:

1. Using the Internet, find an article describing a U.S. company's transition from U.S. GAAP to IFRS. How can an ERP system help ease the transition for organizations?

Intercompany Transactions

Transactions that occur between a parent company and one of its subsidiaries (or between different subsidiaries), known as **intercompany transactions**, must be eliminated from the books of the parent company because the transaction does not represent any transfer of funds into or out of the company.

As an example, suppose that Acme Inc. owns Bennett Manufacturing, and Bennett sells raw materials to Acme for $1 million. Acme then uses the materials to make its product. Bennett's sale to Acme is Acme's cost of sales. From the point of view of an outsider, money has merely passed from one part of the consolidated company to another. A company cannot make a profit by selling to itself.

Companies often do business with their subsidiaries, and for such companies, intercompany transactions occur frequently. Keeping track of those transactions and making the adjustments can be a challenge for accountants.

ANOTHER LOOK

Spreadsheets: A Poor Substitute

Many users of information technology feel comfortable using spreadsheets such as Excel to do large data analysis and reporting projects. And, as Nick Gomersall (a specialist in ERP and accounting systems at The GL Company) notes, it is easy to form a link between a company's ERP system and a personal computer through which an end user can download ERP transaction data into a spreadsheet. These spreadsheets are often used for data analysis and reporting instead of the built-in reporting functionality of the ERP system or its Business Intelligence (BI) tools because these reporting tools are new and sometimes challenging to learn. These "rogue" spreadsheets can create considerable risk for a company in terms of lack of consistency, reliability, and control. For instance, a study by the accounting firm KPMG, found that when spreadsheets contained more

(continued)

than 200 lines, the probability of an error was almost 100 percent. As a result, decisions based on these spreadsheets are likely to be flawed. In addition, financial spreadsheets on laptops taken outside the company create a risk for loss of sensitive data.

Gomersall advocates that companies use "accounting intelligence" applications, which use real-time processing rather than batch processing to pull data from ERP systems and which include built-in reporting templates that can be used to gain insight into the corporate earnings. However, these applications are not always available, or fully utilized, and many companies are not aware of the extent of "rogue" spreadsheet use. According to an analyst with Gartner Research, most companies' IT organizations do not provide technical support for Excel, and are often "unaware of the extent to which sophisticated and complex spreadsheets are being used within the enterprise. Unless explicitly directed by a compliance officer to exert more control over spreadsheet usage, most IT managers avoid intruding too deeply into the area of user-developed applications."

Most CFOs (chief financial officers) are unaware of the extent to which spreadsheets and manual data analysis are involved in closing a company's books. In fact, the area of closing the books and reconciliation are two tangible areas where Accounting can improve its timing and accuracy by taking full advantage of the capabilities of a company's ERP system.

Question:

1. Make a list of the pros and cons of using spreadsheets for financial analysis within a corporation. Alternatively, form two teams in the classroom and debate the pros and cons.

MANAGEMENT REPORTING WITH ERP SYSTEMS

The integrated nature of an ERP system and the use of a common database and built-in management reporting provide numerous benefits. Although the reporting of accounting information is a common Accounting function, it is often very challenging for companies to generate the right reports for the right situation. Without an ERP system, the job of tracking all the data required for a financial report is a monumental undertaking. With an ERP system, a vast amount of information is available for reporting purposes; however, often it is years after an ERP implementation before a company figures out which reports are the most critical for decision making. In this section, we will examine some management-reporting and analysis tools available with ERP systems.

Data Flows in ERP Systems

As you have seen in earlier chapters, with an ERP system, all transactions in all functional areas of a company are posted in a centralized database. It is worth reemphasizing that the database *is* the company's "books." There is no separate set of books for Marketing and Sales or Production or Purchasing.

Thus, even though it is common usage to refer to "data flows" in an ERP system, it is actually a misnomer. Data do not flow from one ERP module to another because they are all in one place—the database. Each area views the same records. It might be better to speak of "data access" than of "data flows" when talking about how these areas use the common database.

Document Flow for Customer Service

As you learned in Chapter 3, each transaction that is posted in SAP ERP gets its own unique document number that allows quick access to the data. If you need to look up a transaction in SAP ERP, you do so by referencing the document number, which acts as an index to the appropriate database table entries.

In SAP ERP, document numbers for related transactions are associated in the database. This provides an electronic audit trail for analysts trying to determine the status of an order. The best example of this concept is the linkage of document numbers for a sales order. Figure 5-10 illustrates the document flow concept for a sales transaction.

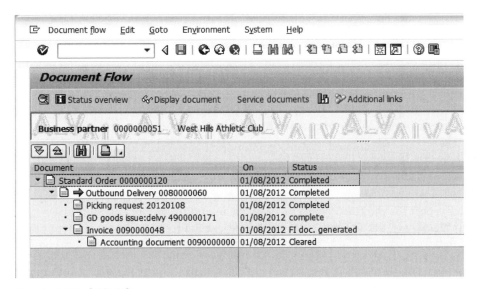

Source Line: SAP AG.

FIGURE 5-10   Document flow of a sales transaction in SAP ERP

The linked events shown in Figure 5-10 progress as follows:

1. When the order was placed, sales order document 120 was created.
2. The system recorded the delivery, which is the transfer of the order's requirements to the Materials Management module; the delivery is denoted by document 80000060.
3. The picking request, which is the document that tells warehouse personnel which items make up the order, was created and given document number 20120108.
4. The goods were removed from inventory on the same day, an event recorded by document number 4900000171.

5. After the goods were issued, an invoice was generated so the customer would be billed; the invoice was given document number 90000048.
6. At the same time, the accounting entries for the sale were generated. The posting document number is 90000000.

The Document Flow screen can be used to drill down to see the details of any one of these events. The term **drill down** refers to the ability to view the details behind a summary of information. For example, the user can double-click the order number (120) and see the details of the order—products ordered, quantity, customer name, and so on. From that display, the user can double-click the product numbers or the customer number for more details on the products or customer. To see the debits and credits in the accounting entry, the user can double-click the accounting document to see the scheduled entries.

Users can access the document flow from any SAP screen that is used in the sales order process. If a customer were to call and ask about the status of an order, the sales representative could access the document flow and see whether the goods had been shipped. If the customer called with questions about an invoice, the representative could use the document flow to access the documents related to that invoice, such as the original sales order or the picking request. This sort of research can be done quickly with SAP ERP. With unintegrated systems, establishing the audit trail and researching source documents can be very difficult and time consuming.

Built-In Management-Reporting and Analysis Tools

Accounting records are maintained in the common database of an ERP system. The advantage of using a database is that accounting employees can query the records to produce standard reports as well as answer ad hoc questions. An ad hoc question is one that is spontaneous. For example, a Fitter manager might walk into an analyst's office and ask for a sales report for the third quarter—by division and by product. Traditional accounting packages are not optimized to set up and execute queries against accounting records, but database packages are. When the records are kept in a database they can be queried because of the built-in database language.

Thus, an analyst at Fitter who wants to identify the 10 largest orders placed by Health Express in the past year could execute a query in SAP ERP to show the answer. In principle, this query could directly access the transaction records to get the answer, which would mean that analysts running queries would be accessing the records at the same time as current transactions are being recorded. This competition for resources can slow down processing in even a large database system, such as those used by ERP packages.

Early on, SAP addressed the need to minimize the demands on the database system from queries on the transaction records by providing special reporting capabilities within the ERP system in the form of database tables that store aggregated data. For example, a table could store sales data summarized by customer on a weekly or monthly basis. Using data from these special tables reduces the demands on the database because less data needs to be pulled from the database; the data comes from special database tables created for reporting, not from the tables used to process sales transactions. For example, SAP ERP provides the Sales Information System (SIS) tool for analyzing sales data and the Logistics Information System (LIS) tool for analyzing production and logistics (shipping) questions. Both the SIS and the LIS come embedded with SAP ERP and use special summary tables to improve reporting efficiency.

As mentioned in Chapter 2, SAP and other manufacturers improved the ability to analyze data without reducing system performance by creating Business Warehouse (BW) products. A BW system is a completely separate information system that extracts data from the ERP system. With BW, users have the ability to create reports and perform analyses in a system that does not compete for system resources with transaction processes. However, current BW systems do require aggregation of data, a process that is complicated and time consuming. In addition, data aggregation creates limits on what data can be analyzed.

A new era of data analysis is dawning with the introduction of in-memory computing. With in-memory computing, aggregation of the data is not required, eliminating the time-consuming process that limits analyses. With in-memory computing, detailed records (rather than aggregated data) are maintained in a separate system so the ERP system performance is not affected, and because the system works on the detailed data records, there is no limit on the types of analyses that can be performed. Chapter 8 provides more detail on in-memory computing.

As the previous sections illustrate, an ERP system is a key component in creating management reports. Managerial accounting reports help the company's managers understand how the company is making money—what products are profitable, where costs may need to be reduced, and so on. Financial accounting reports are used to inform external parties—shareholders and government agencies—how well the company is doing financially. The importance of accurate accounting reports cannot be overstated, as you will see in the next section.

THE ENRON COLLAPSE

On October 16, 2001, Enron Corporation, then one of the world's largest electricity and natural gas traders, reported a $618 million third-quarter loss and disclosed a $1.2 billion reduction in shareholder equity, related in part to transactions between the company and several partnerships run by its chief financial officer (CFO), Andrew Fastow. Until that time, Enron had been a rapidly growing firm that was revolutionizing the energy trading business and making millionaires out of its investors. CEO Jeffrey Skilling, who resigned on August 14, 2001, for personal reasons, had helped transform the company from a natural gas pipeline company to a global marketer and trader of energy. Along the way, the company had encouraged its employees to invest large portions of their 401K retirement savings accounts in Enron stock by matching employee contributions.

On October 17, the day after Enron reported its tremendous third-quarter loss, the SEC—which is dedicated to protecting investors and maintaining the integrity of the securities markets—sent a letter to Enron asking for information about the loss. Enron's high-flying business practices immediately began unraveling. On October 22, 2001, Enron announced that the SEC was conducting an inquiry into a possible conflict of interest related to the company's dealings with the partnerships run by CFO Fastow. Shares of Enron sank more than 20 percent on the news. Two days later, Enron ousted CFO Fastow in an attempt to restore investor confidence. On November 8, Arthur Andersen, Enron's financial auditing firm, received a federal subpoena for documents related to Enron, and on December 2, Enron made the largest Chapter 11 bankruptcy protection filing in U.S. history. Clearly, the accounting records made public by Enron, which were released quarterly and were not audited, did not reflect the financial health of the company.

Enron began as an oil pipeline company in Houston in 1985. With the deregulation of electrical power markets, starting in the mid-1990s, Enron began working as an energy broker—trading electricity and other commodities. As a broker, Enron entered into separate contracts with sellers and buyers of energy, making money on the difference between the selling price and the buying price. Because Enron kept its books private, it was the only party that knew both prices. Enron's business evolved over time, extending to practices that allowed customers to insure themselves against a range of risk factors, including changes in interest rates, weather, and a customer's inability to pay. The volume of these financial contracts eventually became far greater than the volume of contracts to actually deliver commodities.

To manage the risk in these contracts, Enron employed a team of people with Ph.D.s in mathematics, physics, and economics. Risk management balances the opportunities offered by a business against the risks inherent in taking that business. As Enron's business became more complex and its stock soared, the company created partnerships between Enron and companies involved in Internet broadband technologies, computer technology, and energy, to name a few. While some of the partnerships were set up legitimately, others were created for the sole purpose of masking billions of dollars in debt, allowing Enron managers to shift debt off the books.

The partnerships that Fastow engineered were the subject of discussion long before Enron's bankruptcy. In a June 1, 1999, article in *CFO* magazine, Ronald Fink noted that the Financial Accounting Standards Board was looking at rule changes that would affect companies using creative financing techniques, such as those used by Enron. Enron owned a number of subsidiaries, but it made sure that it owned no more than 50 percent of the voting stock, which allowed it to keep the debt and assets of these subsidiaries off Enron's own books. If Enron had not used these creative accounting practices, the company would have had to report a much higher percentage of debt, which would have increased the costs that Enron paid to borrow money.

For years, Enron's financial statements had been audited by Arthur Andersen, a highly regarded accounting firm. As Enron's auditor, Andersen issued annual reports attesting to the validity of Enron's financial statements; it was supposed to function as an unbiased, incorruptible observer and reporter. Enron's October 16, 2001, press release characterized numerous charges against income for the third quarter as "nonrecurring," even though Andersen had determined that Enron did not have a basis for concluding that the charges would in fact be nonrecurring. Andersen advised Enron against using that term and documented its objections internally in the event of litigation, but the firm did not report its objections or take any other steps to correct the public statement. On March 7, 2002, Arthur Andersen was charged with obstruction of justice.

Perhaps the most damning part of Andersen's obstruction of justice indictment related to the destruction of documents. On October 23, 2001, the day after Enron publicly acknowledged the SEC inquiry, Andersen personnel in Houston were called to mandatory meetings where they were instructed by Andersen partners and others to immediately destroy documentation relating to Enron; Andersen employees were told they should work overtime if necessary to accomplish the destruction. Over the next few weeks, employees in several Andersen offices worldwide undertook a concerted initiative to shred tons of paper documentation and to delete hundreds of computer files relating to Enron.

Outcome of the Enron Scandal

The effects of the Enron scandal were felt both within and well beyond the company. Many of Enron's shareholders were Enron employees who invested their 401K accounts in

Enron stock. Shareholders lost an estimated $40 billion dollars—in many cases, individuals lost their entire life savings. A class-action lawsuit against financial institutions that had dealings with Enron (including Canadian Imperial Bank of Commerce, JPMorgan, and Citigroup) produced more than $7 billion in settlements, although legal fees consumed a significant portion of this.

Thousands of Enron workers lost their jobs, and 31 individuals were either charged or pled guilty to criminal charges. J. Clifford Baxter resigned as Enron's vice chairman on May 2, 2001. He was found shot to death in his car on January 15, 2002, in an apparent suicide. In 2006, Andrew Fastow, Enron's former chief financial officer, was sentenced to six years in prison. His sentence had been limited to a maximum of 10 years as part of a plea agreement in which he agreed to testify against former CEO Jeffrey Skilling and CEO Ken Lay. Fastow's wife, Lea, also received a one-year prison sentence for filing a false income tax return. In October 2006, Jeffrey Skilling was convicted on 19 counts of conspiracy, fraud, insider trading, and making false statements to auditors. He was ordered to pay nearly $45 million into a restitution fund for Enron's victims, and was sentenced to 24 years in jail. Although he is appealing his conviction, he began serving his sentence in late 2006. Ken Lay was convicted on fraud and conspiracy charges in May 2006, but two months later, prior to being sentenced, he died of a heart attack.

On June 15, 2002, jurors convicted the accounting firm Arthur Andersen of obstructing justice by destroying Enron documents while on notice of a federal investigation. Andersen executives had claimed that the documents were destroyed as part of general housekeeping duties, and not as a ruse to keep Enron documents away from the regulators. That October, U.S. District Judge Melinda Harmon sentenced Andersen to the maximum: a $500,000 fine and five years' probation. Those events were anticlimactic, however, as the former auditing giant had been all but dismantled by then. Once a world-class firm with over 85,000 employees globally, Andersen has since been whittled down to almost nothing. As of early 2012, Andersen has not declared bankruptcy or been dissolved, but it is no longer an active company.

As a result of the failure of Enron, as well as the high-profile bankruptcies of WorldCom and Global Crossing, the United States Congress passed the Sarbanes-Oxley Act of 2002. This act was intended to prevent the kind of fraud and abuse that led to the Enron downfall.

Key Features of the Sarbanes-Oxley Act of 2002

The Sarbanes-Oxley Act is designed to encourage top management accountability in firms that are publicly traded in the United States. Frequently, top executives involved in corporate scandals claim that they were unaware of abuses occurring at their company. Title IX of the Sarbanes-Oxley Act requires that financial statements filed with the SEC include a statement signed by the chief executive officer and chief financial officer, certifying that the financial statement complies with the SEC rules. Specifically, the statements must certify that "the information contained in the periodic report fairly presents, in all material respects, the financial condition and results of operations of the issuer." Anyone who willfully certifies a statement "knowing that the periodic report accompanying the statement does not comport with all the requirements set forth in this section shall be fined not more than $5,000,000, or imprisoned not more than 20 years, or both."

Title II of the act addresses auditor independence. Among other things, this section of the act limits the nonaudit services that an auditor can provide to an audit client; the prohibited nonaudit services include the following:

- Bookkeeping or other services related to the accounting records or financial statements
- Financial information systems design and implementation services
- Legal services
- Expert services unrelated to the audit
- Management functions
- Human resources functions
- Any other service that the Public Company Accounting Oversight Board (PCAOB) determines to be impermissible. (The PCAOB was created in Title I of the act with broad powers to regulate audits and auditors of public companies.)

Title IV of the act covers enhanced financial disclosures, and it specifies more stringent requirements for financial reporting. Section 404 of Title IV requires that a public company's annual report contain management's internal control report. The control report must outline management's responsibility for establishing and maintaining adequate internal control over financial reporting, and it must also assess the effectiveness of the company's internal control structure and procedures. Section 409 of Title IV addresses the timeliness of reports, and may require companies to file an SEC report within two days of a significant trigger event—for example, completion of an acquisition or a default by a major customer.

IMPLICATIONS OF THE SARBANES-OXLEY ACT FOR ERP SYSTEMS

The Sarbanes-Oxley Act has had significant ramifications for the design of information systems of publicly traded companies. To meet the internal control report requirement, a company must first document the controls that are in place and then verify that they are not subject to error or manipulation.

An integrated information system provides the tools to implement internal controls, as long as the system is configured and managed correctly. However, even the passage of the Sarbanes-Oxley Act and the availability of state-of-the-art ERP technology cannot prevent the type of insidious and systematic fraud that was involved in the Enron scandal. An ERP system relies on a central database with accurate information. ERP systems make it difficult to hide fraudulent dealings, and perhaps Enron's problems would have been more obvious to stakeholders of the company had the company implemented an ERP system. But it is unlikely that an ERP system or the Sarbanes-Oxley Act can prevent all fraud.

ANOTHER LOOK

Sarbanes-Oxley Ten Years Out

Ten years has passed since the passage of the Sarbanes-Oxley Act of 2002, and to date, the SEC—the organization in charge of prosecuting violations of the law—has filed cases against only 20 companies accused of violating the act. The backbone of the act was increased responsibility placed on company executives. The act allows the SEC to seize pay from the CEOs and CFOs of companies found to have filed fraudulent financial statements, even if the executives were not directly involved in the fraud. However, some experts, such as Jack T. Ciesielski, president of R. G. Associates and the editor of *The Analyst's Accounting Observer*, believe the act is a "dormant enforcement tool" and is not a deterrent because it is not really being used. A primary challenge to enforcing the Sarbanes-Oxley Act is that much of the language in the bill was poorly drafted and ambiguous. In addition to the small number of cases filed under Sarbanes-Oxley, half of the companies that have been charged have been small companies, and many cases have yet to be resolved.

Recently, however, some larger companies have been charged with violations of the act. For instance, Navistar was charged by the SEC with overstating its income from 2001 to 2005, and, as a result, the chief executive of the company, along with the former chief financial executive, were forced to give back stock they had earned during that time frame. Similarly, the former CEO at Diebold (a maker of automated teller machines) was forced to repay cash and stock after the SEC charged the company with overstating its results over the course of five years. And in a recent case against Beazer Homes and two of its former executives, the SEC collected $8 million and 119,000 shares of Beazer stock. While these cases do involve larger companies, with executives being forced to return at least some portion of their compensation, many feel that enforcement is still lacking. According to Harvey Goldschmid, a professor at Columbia Law School and a former SEC commissioner, "The trick is to create deterrents and accountability in the system. You don't do it if you're soft on individuals."

Question:

1. Use the Internet to research the latest news surrounding the Sarbanes-Oxley Act. Make a list of companies that have been charged with fraudulent activities in the last three years. Can you see any patterns of an increase or decrease in fraud over the past few years?

The next section explores ways in which SAP ERP and other ERP systems can prevent corporate fraud and abuse.

Archiving

One of the first things a new SAP ERP user typically notices is that the software offers very few ways to delete items. For example, the menus in the SAP ERP system related to material master data (master records that describe material characteristics) are shown in Figure 5-11.

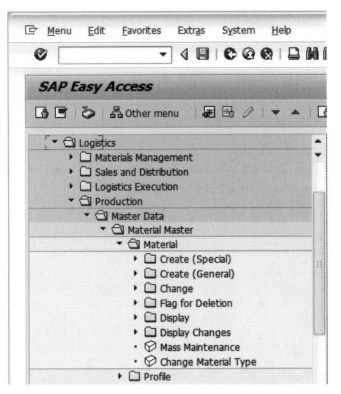

Source Line: SAP AG.

FIGURE 5-11   Transaction options for material master data

This screen offers options for creating, changing, and displaying, but not simply deleting—the closest alternative is an option to flag data for deletion. Before material data can be deleted from the SAP ERP system, a user must create an auditable record of its existence. Data are removed from the SAP ERP system only after they have been recorded to media (tape backup, DVD-R) for permanent storage. This permanently stored data, or **archive**, allows auditors to reconstruct the company's financial position at any point in the past.

Suppose data could be freely deleted from an ERP system. An unscrupulous employee could create a fictitious vendor, post an invoice from the vendor, have payment made for the bogus invoice to a Swiss bank account, and then delete all records of this transaction. It would be very hard to detect the fraud and probably impossible to find out who committed it, because the records would no longer exist.

Not only does the SAP ERP system require archiving before data can be deleted, but it also keeps track of when data are created or changed. Figure 5-12 shows the change record for the material master. Each time a user changes the material master, the change record tracks the change in the data, who changed them, and when the change occurred. For example, in Figure 5-12, you can see that Cindy made changes to the material's basic data (such as the description, measurement units, or weight) on April 28, 2010.

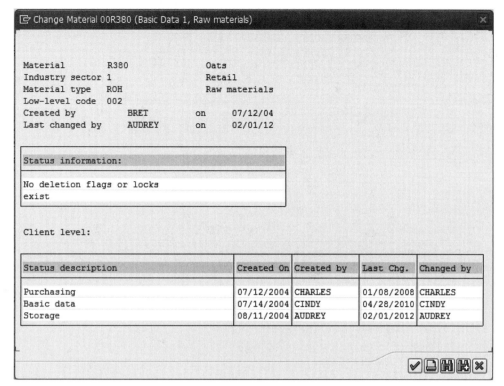

Source Line: SAP AG.

FIGURE 5-12   Change record for material master

User Authorizations

Another way that an ERP system can prevent employee theft is through user authorizations and separation of duties. SAP ERP has sophisticated user administration tools that allow different levels of authorization management, to ensure that employees can perform only the transactions required for their jobs. The system controls user authorizations through its Profile Generator, which provides a simple method for selecting the functions a user should be allowed to perform.

Figure 5-13 shows a predefined role in the SAP ERP system for a user whose job involves managing material master data and bills of material. This employee can perform any transactions shown on the role menu in Figure 5-13.

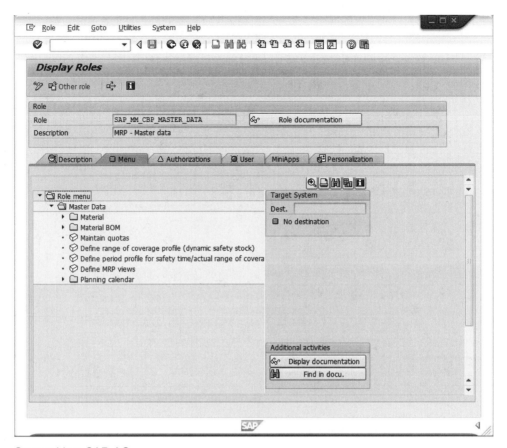

Source Line: SAP AG.

FIGURE 5-13 Display Roles screen in SAP

Managing authorized usage can be one of the most complex tasks in an ERP system. The joke in the world of authorizations is "If you're doing your job, we're not doing ours." It may be a challenge to provide users with the proper authorizations in a timely manner, but most companies take the position that it is better to err on the side of caution, by taking a little longer to grant the right level of authorization, than to give users too much authority quickly.

Tolerance Groups

As another way to make sure employees do not exceed their authority in financial transactions, companies using an ERP system can set limits on the size of transaction an employee can process. In the SAP ERP system, this is done using tolerance groups. As you learned in Chapter 2, tolerance groups are preset limits that define transaction limits. Tolerance groups are used to set limits on the dollar value for a single item in a document as well as on the total value of the document. Just as importantly, they are used to set a limit on payment differences. For instance, suppose a customer has been invoiced for $1,005 but accidentally sends in a check for $1,000 to pay the invoice. The cost of requesting and processing a second payment for the $5.00 would cost both parties more than $5.00. In this case it is better to accept the $1,000 check as payment in full and account for the difference as a variance. Figure 5-14 shows the SAP ERP Change View screen for tolerance groups. The Permitted payment differences section in this figure shows that the system would allow the user to process a payment that was in error by no more than 1 percent or $10.00. In Figure 5-14, the group field is blank, which indicates that this group is the default tolerance group. If an employee is not assigned to any other tolerance group, then by default the limits in the default group apply. As with authorizations, it is a safe policy to define a default tolerance group with low limits and to err on the side of less authority rather than more authority.

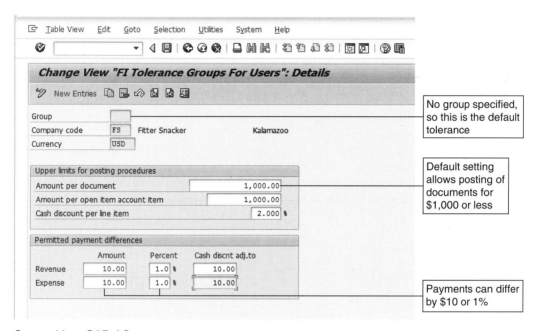

Source Line: SAP AG.

FIGURE 5-14 Default tolerance group

Financial Transparency

A key feature of any ERP system is the ability to drill down within a report to get to the source documents (transactions) that were used to create the report. For example, if sales figures for a region look unusually high, the user can verify the results by double-clicking the figure in the report to drill down to review the specific sales orders that constitute the overall sales figures. The ability to drill down from within reports to get to transaction information makes it easier for auditors to confirm the integrity of the reports. Figure 5-15 shows a general ledger account balance for raw material consumption. This general ledger accounts for all raw material usage at the company.

148

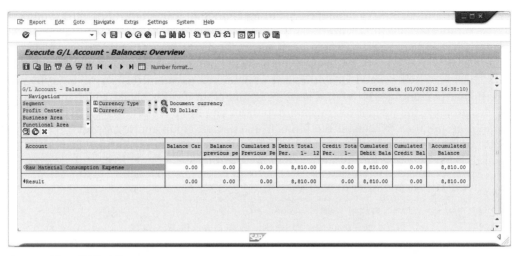

Source Line: SAP AG.

FIGURE 5-15   G/L (general ledger) account balance for raw material consumption

To see the source of the figures in this report, a user can double-click on the 8,810.00 figure for the Accumulated Balance of the Raw Material Consumption Expense row to bring up the Account Line Item Display screen, shown in Figure 5-16. Figure 5-16 shows that two items make up the $8,810.00 raw material consumption total.

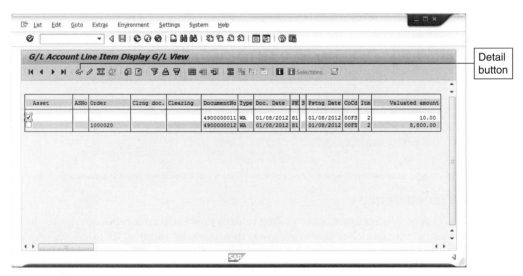

Source Line: SAP AG.

FIGURE 5-16   Documents that make up G/L account balance for raw material consumption

A manager might be intrigued by the $10 expense and want more information on what caused it. Clicking the Detail button on the Account Line Item Display screen brings up more detailed information on the $10 expense, as shown in Figure 5-17. Fifty pounds of material were charged to cost center R010, which is a research and development cost center.

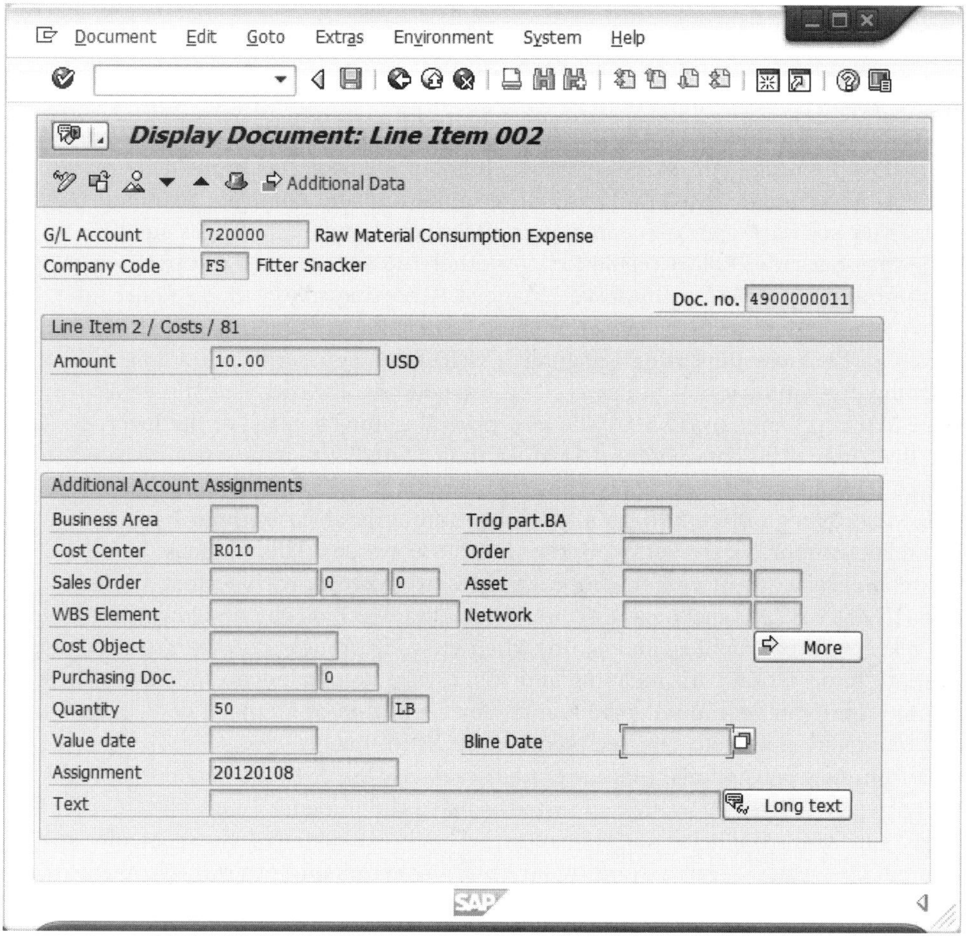

Source Line: SAP AG.

FIGURE 5-17   Details on $10 line item in G/L account for raw material consumption

From this screen even more details can be displayed. With a few mouse clicks, an auditor could move from a summary statement of the general ledger account to screens showing the details related to an employee in the Research and Development Department taking 50 pounds of oats from inventory for product development. With a properly configured and managed ERP system, direct links between the company's financial statements and the individual transactions that make up the statements help an auditor more easily detect fraud and abuse.

Exercise 5.3

Assume that you are the manager of the Accounting Department at Fitter, which still does not have an ERP system. What changes must you make in your accounting practices to get the company in compliance with the Sarbanes-Oxley Act? Write a proposal to your manager outlining your plan to be ready for the additional amount of reporting necessary. For this exercise, assume that Fitter does not have an ERP system in place.

TRENDS IN FINANCIAL REPORTING—XBRL

The finance departments of most corporations are under pressure from a variety of sources. The financial crisis of 2008 along with the global recession has affected almost all companies. Profit margins are being squeezed, market volatility has brought increased risk, and new government regulations are more numerous and complex. As noted previously, ERP software can help companies effectively handle challenges such as complying with Sarbanes Oxley regulations. Another regulation, put forth by the SEC in 2009, is the Interactive Data to Improve Financial Reporting rule, which requires the gradual implementation of XBRL tags in financial reporting documents.

Extensible Business Reporting Language (XBRL) is a standards-based language for the electronic communication of business and financial data. XBRL is a subset of **Extensible Markup Language (XML)**, the new programming language of the Internet. XML uses tags that define the data contained within them. Similar to data types assigned to records in a database, XML tags apply specific meaning to the data within a Web page. XML-coded data can go directly from a Web page into a database without having to pass through middleware or, worse yet, be rekeyed into the system. This reduces the chance of errors. In comparison, most current Internet pages are written in Hypertext Markup Language (HTML). HTML specifies only how your data will look (by assigning text styles, coloring, placement of graphics, and so on) when viewed through a browser. XML changes that data into information with meaning and usefulness. For financial reporting, XBRL provides an identifying, computer-readable tag for each item of financial data. For instance, "company net profit" has its own unique XBRL tag.

Apart from new regulations, there are other reasons why XBRL is becoming prevalent. Reports written in XBRL are processed faster because the imbedded tags directly relate to a database, and XBRL financial reports can more easily be validated electronically and then compared to other reports. More importantly, investors and other interested parties are concerned with transparency in reporting. To assess the risk of a given investment, the investor must understand the financial aspects of the investment. If a report is obscure or hiding information, then the risk is not easily assessed. XBRL results in more transparency of reporting.

XBRL is controlled by a nonprofit group of 600 international companies and other organizations, including governmental agencies. The group is responsible for creating and standardizing these financial tags. In addition to the SEC, entities such as the U.S. Federal Deposit Insurance Corporation (FDIC), which provides deposit insurance guaranteeing the safety of deposits in member banks, and Her Majesty's Revenue & Customs (the United Kingdom's customs and tax-collection departments), are beginning to require the use of XBRL tags.

ERP systems can accept data in XML and XBRL format. For example, SAP's Business Objects XBRL Publishing tool allows users to avoid complex tags and simply use a drag-and-drop system for categorizing financial data.

Chapter Summary

- Companies need accounting systems to record transactions and generate financial statements. Accounting activities can generally be classified as either financial accounting or managerial accounting.

- Financial accounting consists of documenting all the transactions of a company that have an impact on the financial state of the organization, and then using those documented transactions to create reports for investors and external parties and agencies. Managerial accounting deals with determining the costs and profitability of a company's activities. The goal of managerial accounting is to provide managers with detailed information so they can make informed decisions, create budgets, determine the profitability of a particular product, sales region, or marketing campaign, and so on.

- An accounting system should let a user summarize data in meaningful ways so the data can then be used to assist managers in their day-to-day work and in long-range planning.

- Unintegrated information systems are more likely to result in accounting data that is inaccurate or not current, which can affect decision making and therefore profitability.

- Closing the books means that balances for temporary or nominal accounts (such as revenue, expense, gain, and loss) are transferred to the retained earnings account. An integrated information system simplifies the process of closing the books and preparing financial statements. Using an integrated information system and a common database to record accounting data has important inventory cost-accounting benefits. More precise record keeping is possible, which can lead to more accurate product cost calculations. These, in turn, can help managers determine which products are profitable and which are not.

- The use of an integrated system and a common database to record accounting data has important management-reporting benefits. With an ERP system, a user can use the built-in query tools to build reports as well as drill down within reports to the source documents (transactions) that were used to create the report.

- The Sarbanes-Oxley Act of 2002, passed in the wake of the Enron collapse and other high-profile bankruptcies, promoted management accountability by requiring extra financial approval and reporting. Because ERP systems can help companies meet the requirements of this legislation, the act has increased the demand for integrated data reporting.

- Extensible Business Reporting Language (XBRL), a subset of XML (Extensible Markup Language), is a standards-based language for the electronic communication of business and financial data. For financial reporting, XBRL provides an identifying, computer-readable tag for each item of financial data. For instance, "company net profit" has its own unique XBRL tag.

Key Terms

accounts payable

accounts receivable

activity-based costing

archive

balance sheet

cost variance

currency translation

direct costs

drill down

Extensible Business Reporting Language (XBRL)

Extensible Markup Language (XML)

financial accounting

general ledger

income statement

indirect costs

intercompany transactions

International Financial Reporting Standards (IFRS)

managerial accounting

overhead

product cost variant

profit and loss (P&L) statement

U.S. GAAP (Generally Accepted Accounting Principles)

Exercises

1. Outline the way an ERP system's handling of transactions affects a company's general ledger. List three specific SAP modules and how they cause changes to the general ledger.

2. This exercise tests your understanding of the information needed to trace a sale through a multistep ERP sales cycle: sales order, inventory sourcing, delivery, billing, and payment. Assume that an order has been placed with your company and entered into your ERP system. The following events then take place:

   a. The system automatically checks the customer's credit and finds it to be acceptable. The order is recorded for the delivery date requested.

   b. The system schedules the production of the goods. (There is not enough inventory to ship from stock.)

   c. The system schedules raw material orders from the vendors to produce the goods ordered.

   d. The raw materials are received and stored.

   e. The goods are produced and reserved for shipment to the customer.

   f. The system schedules the delivery, and an invoice is printed and included with the shipment. The goods are then put on the delivery truck

   g. Shipping notifies Accounting of the shipment's details.

   h. A month later, the customer sends in payment, which is recorded in accounting.

   For each of these events, list the information that must be recorded in the common database. You do not need to know how to use a database to do this, nor do you need to understand bookkeeping. For example, for the credit-check step, think about what information is needed to perform a credit check on a given customer.

   At each step, did the wealth of the company increase or decrease? At each step, how did the company's obligations to outside entities change? At each step, how did the obligations of outside entities to the company change?

3. Assume that you are the manager of Accounting at Fitter, which is privately owned by a family and headed by a board of directors. The board members are set to visit the company tomorrow morning and would like to see sales data for today, as an example of a typical day. Your boss calls you up and asks you to work with the employees on your team to complete the table shown in Figure 5-18, in anticipation of the board members' visit tomorrow.

Sales data September 29	Distributor Division	Direct Sales Division	Total
# Bars sold			
NRG-A			
NRG-B			
Total			
$ Value of bars sold			
NRG-A			
NRG-B			
Total			
# Customers sold to			
NRG-A			
NRG-B			
Total			

Source Line: Course Technology/Cengage Learning.

FIGURE 5-18   Table for sales report

Given Fitter's current sales order data-processing practices, why will this be a difficult task to complete? Explain the business practices that would cause difficulty in quickly and accurately gathering this data. Why would this task be easy to complete if Fitter had an ERP system? To answer this question, review Chapters 3 and 4 to see how sales orders are processed.

4. The following exercise will test your understanding of Fitter's current credit-check system. In each situation, you are given background data and information about documents in the system.

SITUATION 1

Background data	
Today's date	6/29/13
Current list price, NRG-A	$1.50/bar
Current list price, NRG-B	$1.60/bar
Accounts receivable balance at start of business day, ABC Corporation	$9,000
Credit limit, ABC Corporation	$12,000
Current order	
Product	NRG-A
Amount	4 cases (1,152 bars)
Price	List
Ship to	ABC headquarters
Date desired	7/5/13
Next invoice number	A1001
Documents in system	
No documents relating to ABC are in the system.	

Source Line: Course Technology/Cengage Learning.

    a. Given the information currently in the system, will credit be granted or denied for ABC Corporation's current order?

    b. If the system processed data in a more timely way, would it change the answer as to whether or not credit be granted?

SITUATION 2

Background data	
Today's date	7/3/13
Current list price, NRG-A	$1.50/bar
Current list price, NRG-B	$1.60/bar
Accounts receivable balance at start of business day, KLM Corporation	$6,000
Credit limit, KLM Corporation	$8,000
Current order	
Product	NRG-B
Amount	5 cases (1,440 bars)
Price	List
Ship to	KLM headquarters
Date desired	7/8/13
Next invoice number	A1200
Documents in system	
Purchase order KLM 82332 for three cases (864 bars) of NRG-A. This order is in the sales order entry program, but it has not been transferred to the accounting program (thus, Accounting does not yet know about this sale).	

Source Line: Course Technology/Cengage Learning.

c. Given the information currently in the system, will credit be granted or denied for KLM Corporation's current order?

d. If the system processed data in a more timely way, would credit be granted or denied?

SITUATION 3

Background data	
Today's date	7/13/13
Current list price, NRG-A	$1.50/bar
Current list price, NRG-B	$1.60/bar
Accounts receivable balance at start of business day, ACORN Corporation	$6,000
Credit limit, ACORN Corporation	$6,000
Current order	
Product	NRG-A
Amount	150 boxes (3,600 bars)
Price	List
Ship to	ACORN headquarters
Date desired	7/15/13
Next invoice number	A1300
Documents in system	
A check from ACORN was received in yesterday's mail and entered into the accounting system. The check is for $2,000, applied to invoices from June's sales. The sales clerks are working from credit-limit printouts prepared at the beginning of the week (two days ago).	

Source Line: Course Technology/Cengage Learning.

    e. Given the information currently in the system, will credit be granted or denied for ACORN Corporation's current order?

    f. If the system processed data in a more timely way, would credit be granted or denied?

5. ERP systems save time for accountants in many ways. Some researchers expected that job opportunities for accountants would diminish with the implementation of an ERP system. In reality, accountants are needed more than ever in industry. Use an online job search Web site and look at the jobs available for accountants. How many positions require experience with ERP systems? Do any positions require data analysis capabilities that involve Business Warehouse technology?

6. Companies usually prepare annual division- and company-wide budgets that show projected monthly results, such as: sales, cost of sales, inventory levels, cash on hand, and other key data. Such budgets are effective for planning and controlling operations if they are designed as "flexible" budgets. A flexible budget is restated as conditions change from month to month, so goals remain reasonable and useful for evaluating performance. If not kept up to date, budgets are not useful for planning and controlling operations.

If information systems are unintegrated, getting data from the company's departments to create the initial budget is a chore, and keeping the data current is often so difficult that it is not done. Thus, while the flexible budget concept is a good idea, it is difficult to achieve with unintegrated systems. Because ERP makes flexible budgeting more achievable, ERP helps management discharge its planning and controlling roles better. Why do you think flexible budgeting would be more achievable with an ERP system? List your reasons, and explain.

7. Using the Internet, research the status of the government regulations in the United States concerning the requirements of companies publicly traded to adopt IFRS. The SEC Web site (*www.sec.gov*) is a good source of information on this topic. Report any updates to the requirements.

8. Review Fitter's unintegrated production and purchasing procedures, described in Chapter 4. How would its current job-scheduling, production, and purchasing procedures result in variances from standard costs? Why would Fitter have trouble researching these costs at month's end to adjust the "standard costs per unit" to accurate "actual costs per unit"?

9. Investigate the adoption of XBRL by companies, and report on the status of XBRL implementation at this point in time.

For Further Study and Research

Barnhart, Todd M. "The Financial Supply Chain." *Darwin Magazine*, April 2004.

Bloomberg News. "Lawyer Who Negotiated Enron Settlements Retiring." August 28, 2007.

The Economist. "Sarbanes-Oxley: Five Years Under the Thumb." July 26, 2007. www.economist.com/business/displaystory.cfm?story_id=9545905&CFID=19771870&CFTOKEN=7941782.

Fink, Ronald. "Balancing Act: Will a New Accounting Rule Aimed at Off-Balance-Sheet Financing Trip up Enron?" *CFO*, July 1, 1999.

Flood, Mary. "Andersen Conviction Affirmed." *Houston Chronicle*, July 1, 2004.

Gaskin, James E. "XML Comes of Age." *InternetWeek.com*, April 3, 2000.

Goff, John. "They Might Be Giants." *CFO*. January 12, 2004. www.cfo.com/article.cfm/3011295?f=related.

Hays, Kristin. "Ex-Enron CFO Fastow Sentenced to 6 years in Prison." *Houston Chronicle*, September 26, 2006.

Herm, Marcus. "XML - An Opportunity for Small and Medium-Sized Enterprises." Software AG. http://webmethods.com/xml/library/herm.htm.

Johnson, Carrie. "Enron's Lay Dies of Heart Attack." *Washington Post*, July 6, 2006. www.washingtonpost.com/wp-dyn/content/article/2006/07/05/AR2006070500523.html.

Information Age. "Spreadsheet Creep." 27 May 2008. www.information-age.com/research/information-integrity/331821/spreadsheet-creep.thtml.

Kimmel, Paul D., Jerry J. Weygandt, Donald E. Kieso. *Financial Accounting Tools for Business Decision Making*, 5th edition. New Jersey: Wiley; 2009.

KPMG LLP. "Sarbanes-Oxley Section 404: Management Assessment of Internal Control and the Proposed Auditing Standards." White Paper, March 2003. www.kpmg.ca/en/services/audit/documents/SO404.pdf.

KPMG LLP. "Sarbanes-Oxley: A Closer Look." White Paper, January 2003.

Krumweide, Kip R., and Win G. Jordan. "Reaping the Promise of Enterprise Resource Systems." *Strategic Finance*, October 2000, 49–52.

List, Allison. "The Lax Enforcement of Section 304 of Sarbanes-Oxley: Why Is the SEC Ignoring Its Greatest Asset in the Fight Against Corporate Misconduct?" *Ohio State Law Journal* 70, no 1 (2009).

Lubin, Joann S., and Kara Scannell, "Critics See Some Good from Sarbanes-Oxley." *Wall Street Journal*, July 30, 2007.

McClenahen, John S. "The Book on the One-Day Close." *IndustryWeek.com*. April 1, 2002. www.industryweek.com/ReadArticle.aspx?ArticleID=1058.

Morgenson, Gretchen. "Clawbacks Without Claws." *New York Times*. September 10, 2011. www.nytimes.com/2011/09/11/business/clawbacks-without-claws-in-a-sarbanes-oxley-tool.html?pagewanted=all.

Preacher, Debbie. "Sarbanes-Oxley: A Business Blessing in Disguise." *ebizq.net*. July 17, 2005. www.ebizq.net/topics/com_sec/features/6116.html.

SAP.com. "SAP ERP Financials: IFRS Compliance." 2011. www.sap.com/solutions/business-suite/erp/financials/ifrs.epx.

SAP.com. "SAP Customer Success Story: NB Power: Deferred Restructuring Elicits Impressive Flexibility from SAP Consulting." 2004. www.sap.com/platform/netweaver/pdf/CS_NB_Power.pdf.

SAP.com "SAP Delivers New XBRL Publishing Software to Enable Easier Communication of Financial and Business Data." February 18, 2009. www.sap.com/news-reader/index.epx?pressid=10944.

Sarbanes-Oxley Act, H.R. 3763, Title III, Section 302, §1350 (a)(3).

Sarbanes-Oxley Act, H.R. 3763, Title IX, Section 906, §1350 (c).

U.S. Securities and Exchange Commission. "The Investor's Advocate: How the SEC Protects Investors, Maintains Market Integrity, and Facilitates Capital Formation." www.sec.gov/about/whatwedo.shtml.

VanVuren, Ken, W. Mark Wilder, and Rick Elam. "An Empirical Investigation of the Effectiveness of ERP Systems as Assessed by Management Accountants." *Journal of Business and Public Affairs*, (Fall 2006): 57–76.

Washington Post. "Timeline of Enron's Collapse." July 9, 2004. www.washingtonpost.com/wp-dyn/articles/A25624-2002Jan10.html.

White, Clinton Jr. *The Guide & Workbook for Understanding XBRL*, 5th edition Newark: SkipWhite.com; 2011.

XBRL International. "XBRL Basics." www.xbrl.org.

CHAPTER 6

HUMAN RESOURCES PROCESSES WITH ERP

INTRODUCTION

A company's employees are its most valuable resource, which means that the human resources (HR) department plays a critical role within an organization. The human resources department is responsible for many of the activities that a company performs to attract, hire, reward, train, and, occasionally, terminate employees. The decisions made in the human resources department can affect every department in the company. Companies are increasingly aware of the importance of an experienced, well-trained workforce, and many organizations have begun using the term **human capital management (HCM)** to describe the tasks associated with managing a company's workforce.

As a company grows, the need for an organized and effective human resources department becomes increasingly important. The responsibilities of a human resources department usually include the following:

- Attracting, selecting, and hiring new employees using information from résumés, references, and personal interviews

- Communicating information regarding new positions and hires throughout the organization and beyond

- Ensuring that employees have the proper education, training, and certification to successfully complete their duties

- Handling issues related to employee conduct

- Making sure employees understand the responsibilities of their jobs

- Reviewing employee performance and determining salary increases and bonuses

- Managing the salary and benefits provided to each employee and confirming that the proper benefits are disbursed to new and current employees

- Communicating changes in salaries, benefits, or policies to employees

- Supporting management plans for changes in the organization (expansion, retirements, reorganizations, and so on) so competent employees are available to support business processes

Ensuring that these tasks are accomplished and that valid human resources-related information is communicated throughout the organization requires a system that effectively controls the flow of information. In this chapter, we will explore the role of an integrated information system in human resources.

PROBLEMS WITH FITTER'S HUMAN RESOURCES PROCESSES

Fitter Snacker's has just three employees in its Human Resources Department, and some problems arise simply because of the large number and variety of department responsibilities (from hiring and firing to managing health benefits) as well as the number of people with whom Human Resources interacts. A lack of integration among all departments often results in inaccurate, out-of-date, and inconsistent information.

As with Fitter's other departments, Human Resources' information systems are not well integrated with the company's other information systems. The department relies heavily on paper records and a manual filing system, which creates problems because information is not readily accessible or easy to analyze. The Human Resources Department's recruiting, hiring, and postplacement processes would operate more efficiently with an integrated information system.

Recruiting Process

When a department within Fitter has an opening for a new employee, the department supervisor communicates this need to the Human Resources Department by filling out a paper job vacancy form that describes the position, lists the qualifications a candidate must have, specifies the type of position (temporary, part-time, full-time, or internship), and states when the position will become available. Using this information, Human Resources gets final approval from the president of Fitter to begin the recruiting process. Because there is no central information system, the details on the job vacancy form are frequently inconsistent among, and sometimes within, departments. For example, the requirements for a clerical position in one department includes experience with Microsoft Word, while in another department, the specification is for experience with Microsoft Office.

Usually a job is initially posted internally so current employees have the first opportunity to apply for the position. If no current employees are acceptable for the position, then Fitter posts the position externally.

Problems can occur throughout Fitter's recruiting process. First, the description of the required job qualifications may be incomplete or inaccurate—sometimes because the supervisor is in a hurry, sometimes because the supervisor is not aware of all of the functions required for the position, and sometimes because the supervisor assumes that all candidates will have certain basic skills. Second, if the job vacancy form is lost or not routed properly, the Human Resources Department will not know that the position is available, while the supervisor assumes that the paperwork is in process. When this happens, the department can end up shorthanded, creating productivity issues as well as the possibility of tension or animosity between the departments. Obviously, this problem is more likely to occur when job openings are circulated by paper. With an integrated information system, job information is available immediately and is easier to monitor. Another serious recruiting problem related to a paper-based hiring process is the potential loss of a good candidate due to drawn-out hiring practices or lost data.

Although Fitter does not use recruiting agencies or Internet job sites such as Monster.com to find candidates, it does use several other methods. The company publishes its job vacancies on the company's Web site, in local newspapers, and, in the case of management positions, in national publications. In addition, a representative from the Human Resources Department attends career fairs and recruits on college campuses for prospective candidates. Occasionally, referrals are made by other Fitter employees, and sometimes individuals searching for open positions at Fitter send unsolicited résumés.

Filing and keeping track of résumés and applications is an ongoing challenge. Fitter has dozens of jobs with different titles and descriptions, and the company receives dozens of résumés and applications each day. The Human Resources Department must classify and file all applications and résumés according to the appropriate description. For example, if the résumé of a mechanical engineer is accidentally filed with résumés of candidates applying for jobs in the accounting department, the mistake may not be discovered in time to include the engineer in the search process. In this case, Fitter may not hire the best person for the engineering position, and the mistake might damage Fitter's competitiveness as well as its reputation.

Keeping the applicant's data on a paper form means that retrieving the applicant data and using it to evaluate candidates is also challenging. To generate a list of potential candidates, Human Resources evaluates the résumés and applications it receives in response to a job posting; it also reviews applications that have been on file for less than a year. These résumés and applications must be photocopied and then circulated through the department making the job request. Frequently, more than one person in the requesting department reviews the applications, and because the applicant data are on paper, managers review the applicant files sequentially, slowing the review process.

The Interviewing and Hiring Process

At Fitter, the requesting department develops a **short list** of candidates for the position by selecting up to three applicants, based on the data provided by the Human Resources Department. Human Resources contacts the candidates on the short list, schedules interviews, and creates a file for each candidate. A candidate's file includes a form that shows when the application was received, the position(s) applied for by the candidate, and the date and time of any interviews. If this is not the first time the candidate has applied for a job with the company, the form indicates the more recent status of the candidate: whether the candidate was interviewed and rejected, whether the candidate rejected a job offer, and so on.

If a candidate accepts the interview offer, the Human Resources Department makes the arrangements for the job candidate, including travel arrangements and a schedule of interview activities. A representative from the Human Resources Department conducts an interview that includes a discussion of the applicant's experience and questions relevant to the position for which the candidate has applied. The supervisor of the department in which the position exists also interviews the candidate, and other employees in the department are usually given time to talk to the candidate as well. For most professional positions at Fitter, the candidate is interviewed by the plant manager and, frequently, the company president.

After the initial interview process, a Human Resources' staff member updates the candidate's file to indicate whether he or she is still a possibility for hire. In some cases, a second interview is scheduled. Once someone in Human Resources has interviewed all the candidates on the short list, a representative of the Human Resources Department and the supervisor of the requesting department rank the candidates on the short list. If there is an acceptable candidate, the Human Resources employee makes that person a verbal job offer over the phone. If the candidate accepts the verbal offer, a written offer letter is sent, which the candidate must sign and return. Once the candidate formally accepts the written offer, his or her file is again updated, showing that the candidate has accepted the offer. The Human Resources person then schedules a background check and drug test for the candidate, determines the employee's start date and makes plans for the new employee's orientation session.

If no acceptable candidates were found, or if none of them accepts the job offer, then the process must be repeated, which at a minimum will require the development of a new short list but may involve starting over with a new job posting.

Many of Fitter's problems in the interviewing and hiring process have to do with information flow and communication. Fitter does not have group appointment calendar software, which would allow Human Resources staff to easily find a time when all key personnel would be available to interview a candidate. A group appointment calendar (available in email systems and ERP systems such as SAP) allows users to check others' calendars to schedule meetings. Without such a calendar tool, scheduling interviews is frequently a cumbersome process, requiring the Human Resources employee to coordinate the interview schedule between the candidate and the appropriate personnel at Fitter. Because this is done by email and phone, it can take days and sometimes weeks to schedule an interview. A similar problem occurs after the interviews have been completed. Gathering feedback from all involved parties and ranking the candidates takes time and may require multiple meetings. Managing the travel arrangements and reimbursing candidates for their travel expenses are also cumbersome tasks. More than once, Fitter has lost a promising candidate to another company because of delays in the Fitter interviewing and hiring process.

Fitter hires a human resources consulting firm to perform drug tests and conduct background checks to verify that candidates have not falsified any information and do not have serious criminal records. Fitter outsources this work because of the special skills required. If the background check and drug test are satisfactory, this information is added to the candidate's file, and the job offer stands. If the consultant finds evidence of falsified information or legal troubles or the candidate fails the drug test, the file is likewise updated, and the job offer is rescinded with a written explanation.

On a new employee's first day of work, he or she attends an orientation meeting, which includes completing additional paperwork covering employment terms and conditions, tax withholding, and benefits. All Fitter employees must sign a form that states that the employee has been given a copy of—and agrees to abide by—the company's policies and procedures. The new employee must complete an IRS W-4 form, which tells the employer the correct amount of tax to withhold from the employee's paycheck. Next, a Human Resources representative reviews Fitter's benefits plan. Fitter offers a comprehensive benefits plan that gives employees a range of choices for healthcare plans, life insurance, retirement plans, and medical savings accounts. The employee's dependents may also be covered under Fitter's health insurance plan. If the employee elects dependent coverage, then the Human Resources Department must obtain basic information about each dependent to include in the employee's file.

Because employees must provide a significant amount of detailed data to properly manage compensation and benefits, it is not surprising that Fitter frequently has problems enrolling new employees in the correct benefits plans and establishing the proper payroll deductions. It can often take months to manage the new employee's compensation and benefits correctly. The enrollment issues can generate many time-consuming phone calls to Human Resources management—calls that would not be needed with an integrated system.

ANOTHER LOOK

Human Resources Data in the Cloud

Cloud computing, discussed in more detail in Chapter 8, is the use of computing services provided by another company. Programs and data are stored on servers operated by the cloud computing company and are accessed via the Internet. This arrangement can be

(continued)

cost effective and flexible, but companies must consider several important factors (the first of which is data security) when deciding whether to use cloud computing for sensitive data such as human resources records.

Numerous laws impact a company's relationship with its employees, and much of the data maintained for human resources' purposes is sensitive and governed by privacy laws that vary by country. Companies must develop procedures to control access to this information. If a company's human resources data is stored on the cloud, it is much more difficult to ensure that the data is managed in a manner that meets privacy laws.

A company cannot simply assume that the cloud-computing supplier provides this security. For example, in 2011, German data protection authorities adopted an "orientation guide" to cloud computing that emphasizes that German cloud computing customers are responsible for compliance with all data protection requirements under German law. This compliance includes all subprocessors involved in providing cloud computing services. Thus, it is not sufficient for a company to just accept the cloud computing provider's assurance that its systems are secure. Cloud computing customers should "access logs, tour the data center, go through data center questionnaires and see who has the administrator's password," according to Grady Summers, principal, information security, at Ernst & Young. "Make sure that the service provider can meet regulatory requirements as well."

Questions:

1. What modifications would be required to a company's standard human resources security procedures to address using a cloud-based human resources information system? What documentation would you require from the service provider?

2. Will laws and regulations affecting cloud-based human resources systems become more standardized and simpler in the future, or will there be a growth in complexity with an increase in associated costs? Provide the reasoning behind your answer.

Human Resources Duties After Hiring

A human resources department has responsibilities that continue beyond the hiring and job start of an employee. The human resources department must maintain an ongoing line of communication with the employee and his or her supervisor to make sure the employee is performing well.

Fitter, like most companies, issues performance evaluations to new and current employees. As part of the process, the supervisor performs an evaluation and reviews it with the employee. After the review, the supervisor may modify the evaluation, which both the supervisor and the employee then sign. The employee may also submit a written response to the review, listing any disagreements or explanations. The employee's department manager is expected to review the performance evaluation and employee response, and may add a separate written comment. The completed package is then forwarded to the Human Resources Department, where all documents become part of the employee's file. These files are critically important if an employee fails to perform adequately over a period of time. If an employee must be terminated, the company needs sufficient documentation to demonstrate that the termination is warranted; otherwise, if the employee sues the company for wrongful termination, the company may have problems substantiating the termination decision.

Because Fitter does not have an effective information system, it is difficult to manage performance evaluation data. This makes it more challenging for the Human Resources Department to identify problems with an employee and take corrective action (such as job performance counseling or a transfer) before the problems lead to termination. With Fitter's paper-based system, an employee's file can be viewed by only one person at a time, and it is possible to lose track of an employee's file—temporarily or permanently. Also, it is difficult to maintain proper control of sensitive personal information when it is maintained in paper files.

Employee turnover can be a significant problem for a company. The cost of hiring an employee has been estimated from thousands of dollars to over $50,000. When evaluating the cost of hiring an employee, a company should consider both the direct costs of hiring an employee and the less tangible costs that occur during a new employee's first year or so. For example, while new employees are learning their jobs, other employees have to take time from their normal jobs to train them, which can negatively impact their productivity.

Another cost that is difficult to quantify is an employee's experience and job knowledge, which is lost when he or she leaves a company. For example, if a purchasing manager leaves a company, then all of the manager's knowledge about supplier relations may be lost. The company would have records of the contracts signed with various suppliers, but details of the negotiations that led to each contract may not be documented. Such details can be crucial in successfully negotiating the next contract. The manager may have developed good relations with a certain supplier and know whom to contact when problems arise. These relationships are not specified as part of the purchasing manager position but accrue over time with the individual holding the position. When companies experience high rates of turnover, they lose knowledge and skills that may be crucial to keeping them competitive.

Employee turnover is strongly tied to job satisfaction and compensation. If employees have satisfying jobs and are well compensated, they are less likely to leave the company. Human resources can help maintain a satisfying work environment through a number of means, such as by holding training programs for supervisors and managers, conducting periodic employee satisfaction surveys, and gathering data from employee exit surveys. Human resources also has a critical role to play in compensation, which should be related to the skills and tasks required by the job and the performance of the employee. One important function of a human resources department is to make sure compensation levels are competitive and are applied fairly to all employees. Failure to do so can result in high rates of turnover as well as discrimination lawsuits.

ANOTHER LOOK

At Novartis, Reputation Did Not Match Reality

After 10 years of being on *Working Mother* magazine's "100 Best Companies for Working Mothers" list, Novartis pharmaceutical settled a gender discrimination class action lawsuit in 2010 for $175 million dollars. The settlement covered more than 6,000 female

(continued)

current and former sales representatives who alleged systemic discrimination in pay, promotions, and other working conditions at Novartis.

How did this happen? Novartis had numerous programs designed to help working mothers. As noted in a 2009 article in *Working Mother* magazine, Novartis offered "lunch and learn" sessions on pediatric issues ranging from sleep to nutrition. The company also offered a variety of childcare benefits, including discounts on full-time care at national daycare chains and in-home sick care, and the company made a $1,000 childcare contribution to anyone who saved $4,000 in a pretax childcare account.

Unfortunately, these innovative programs apparently did not reflect the culture of the sales organization at Novartis. The class action lawsuit included numerous charges of sexual harassment and unfair denial of pay raises and promotions. As noted in a *Wall Street Journal* article, the court found that new mothers or pregnant women were singled out. For example, one mother was passed over for promotion because the company felt that she would not be able to leave home for the travel involved in the job because she had four children. In another instance, one woman who was highly-rated in her company evaluations was overlooked for further management education. And some pregnant women were given an extra workload because a manager thought the maternity leave policy at Novartis was too generous.

In addition to the financial payment to the plaintiffs, the settlement requires Novartis to implement a number of changes to its human resource processes, including:

- Revising its policies and processes for investigating discrimination claims
- Implementing specified changes to its performance evaluation system and conducting mandatory training for all managers regarding that system
- Creating an appeals process for employees who disagree with their performance ratings
- Implementing changes to its management development program training
- Implementing changes to its tracking and monitoring of promotional opportunities

Probably the most important factor in avoiding workplace discrimination is making sure the culture of the company does not tolerate it, but good Human Resource information processes can provide the data and tools to analyze and monitor a company's Human Resource practices to avoid discrimination.

Questions:

1. In addition to the damages assessed against it in the discrimination case, what other costs were incurred by Novartis in association with this lawsuit? How do these compare to the financial cost of the settlement?
2. How could an integrated human resources information system be used to detect potential pay discrimination before it becomes systematic?
3. How would you design a compensation system so that pay discrimination is not likely to occur?

HUMAN RESOURCES WITH ERP SOFTWARE

Now that you are familiar with the numerous business processes required to manage a company's human capital, you can begin thinking about how ERP software can improve those processes—leading to overall improvements in a company's performance. With an integrated system, a company can store employee information electronically, eliminating the piles of papers and files that make the retrieval of information difficult. A good information system allows human resources staff members to retrieve relevant employee information in a matter of seconds and to maintain proper controls so sensitive information is not compromised and privacy rules are not violated. An integrated information system is a key component in this process.

ANOTHER LOOK

Data Analytics for Enhancing Performance and Recruiting in Professional Sports

An organization's human resources department is typically responsible for a large amount of data, and sports teams are no exception. Many teams collect and analyze huge volumes of data in hopes of improving player performance and recruiting high-quality players. Recently, Gartner Research named data analytics one of the most important "strategic technologies" in 2011, and the London Irish rugby club can attest to that. During games, the team collects video data (including GPS data) to analyze factors such as distances run and the g-force of various tackles. Injury analysis can be correlated with this rich data set to teach players to use techniques that will minimize the potential for injury. This rich data set not only aids in future game direction but also helps in training. However, the business director of the team, Chris Miles, adds a caveat, "You can't use analytics to replace judgment—it supports it." The Manchester City football (soccer) club also uses data analytics to assess performance during game play. The club measures about 180 actions during a game, but it does not rely solely on data analysis. As with the rugby team, coach intuition supersedes any data result.

In England, players are often traded from football club to another, in hopes of improving a team's performance. Trading is common because of the heavy pressure on clubs to win. Hence football clubs spend a large amount of money obtaining top experienced players. In hopes of nurturing new, younger players, and alleviating some of the enormous expense of trading experienced players, a new rule—called the Home Grown Player rule— has been enacted by the England's top football league. This requires teams to have at least eight players that have been with the team for three seasons starting before that player turned 21. With fewer opportunities to improve teams through trades, teams must make better recruiting decisions to be successful. Prozone, a software tool accessed through the cloud, allows teams to analyze performance data on players and perform what-if analyses on potential trades. It takes football performance data—such as video, shots, percentage passes, tackles won, along with age and nationality, and uses statistics to determine performance ratings. Prozone markets the product as "recruiter software."

(continued)

Questions:

1. Assume you are the human resources manager at Fitter. What metrics or measurements would you develop to assess the potential of an applicant for a production supervisor position? A sales manager position? A chief accountant?

2. Choose a type of sports you enjoy watching. What elements of player performance would you track to analyze? Make a list of at least 20 attributes. Would these attributes also work well for recruiting new players? Explain your answer.

Successfully using a human resources ERP system requires managing a significant amount of detailed information. The SAP ERP Human Resources (HR) module provides tools for managing an organization's roles and responsibilities, definitions, personal employee information, and tasks related to time management, payroll, travel management, and employee training. Figure 6-1 shows the SAP Personal Data screen, which is where basic data for an employee is managed in the SAP system.

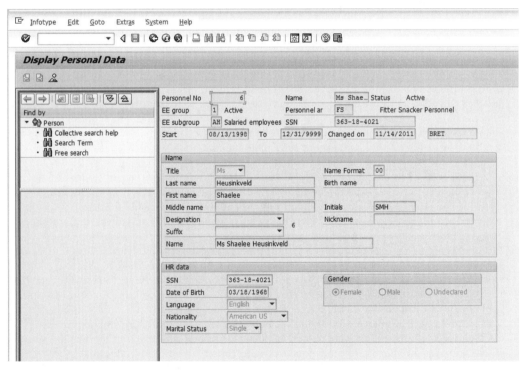

Source Line: SAP AG.

FIGURE 6-1　Personal data stored in SAP Human Resources software

Most companies have an organizational chart or plan that helps define management responsibilities. Without an ERP system, the organizational chart typically defines only the managerial relationships among employees. With an ERP system, it is possible to create an organizational chart with more detail that supports human resources tasks, such as recruiting employees and planning organizational changes.

SAP ERP provides an Organization and Staffing Plan tool that is used to define a company's management structure and the positions within the organizational structure as a whole. The Organization and Staffing Plan tool also names the person who holds each position. Figure 6-2 shows how the Fitter organizational structure could be defined in SAP ERP. The figure shows that Fitter consists of three main organizational units: Manufacturing, Marketing, and Administrative. The Accounting and Human Capital Management organizational units are part of the Administrative organization. Within the Human Capital Management organizational unit are three positions: the manager and two analysts.

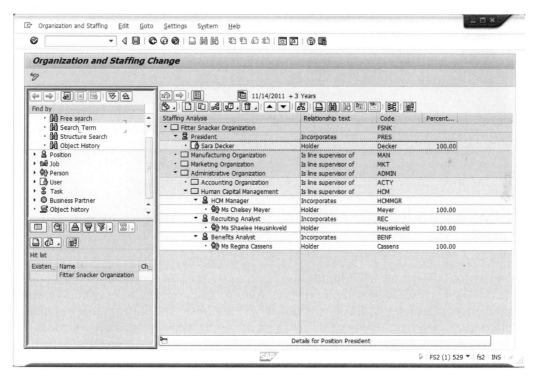

Source Line: SAP AG.

FIGURE 6-2   Organization and staffing plan in SAP ERP

SAP ERP distinguishes between a person, task, job, and position. In SAP, a **person** is a unique individual who holds a position and who performs **tasks**, which are the assigned responsibilities related to a specific job or position. Tasks can be assigned to a position directly, or they can be grouped together in a job. A **job** is a general classification of tasks that are routinely performed together. For example, the job of department head could be defined by assigning it tasks such as review employee performance and prepare monthly budget reports.

A **position** is an individual employee assignment within the organization. Tasks can be assigned directly to a position, or they can be assigned to the position by assigning a job to that position. For example, the position of purchasing manager could be defined with the department head job assigned to it. The purchasing manager would then be responsible for the review employee performance and prepare monthly budget reports tasks. The purchasing manager position could also have tasks such as review monthly spending assigned to it directly. Figure 6-3 shows the relationships among persons, tasks, jobs, and positions in a marketing organization.

Source Line: Course Technology/Cengage Learning.

FIGURE 6-3 Relationships among persons, positions, jobs, and tasks

In Figure 6-3, the job of administrative assistant is assigned a number of tasks, such as reviewing employee time charges, reviewing employee expense reports, and preparing monthly budget reports for the department. These are tasks the company requires of any administrative assistant, whether that job is in marketing, engineering, or production. In SAP, the job of administrative assistant can be defined once—by assigning it specific tasks—and that definition can be used to create administrative assistant positions in different organizational units. The administrative assistant job in marketing is one position, while the administrative assistant job in accounting is a different position. Additional tasks can be added to an administrative assistant position to tailor it to the specific requirements of the organizational unit. For example, in Figure 6-3, the position of marketing administrative assistant has the marketing-specific task of preparing sales reports; an administrative assistant in procurement would not be required to perform that task.

Figure 6-4 shows the SAP ERP screen where tasks are assigned to jobs; in this case, the task "Prepare budget reports" is assigned to the job "Administrative assistant."

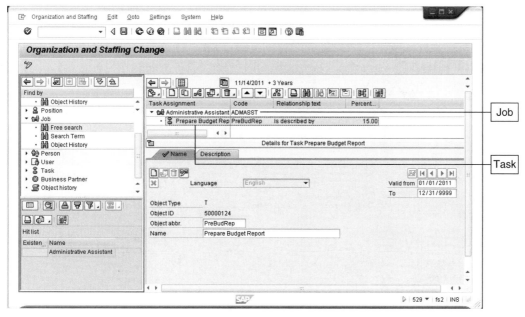

Source Line: SAP AG.

FIGURE 6-4   Assignment of a task to a job in SAP ERP

If the tasks associated with jobs and positions are well defined and current, recruiters in human resources can more easily determine whether candidates have the necessary qualifications for a job. Determining appropriate compensation for a position is also simplified if the tasks required for each position in a company are clearly and consistently defined.

Complete and accurate human resources data simplify a manager's duties. The Manager's Desktop tool within the SAP Human Resources module provides access to all the human resources data and transactions in one location. Figure 6-5 shows the Personal Data portion of the Manager's Desktop, which provides all of the data maintained in the Human Resources module for all employees who report to the manager—which in this case is Fitter's president, Sara Decker. In Figure 6-5, the

Human Capital Management organizational unit is expanded to show the individual employees in that unit.

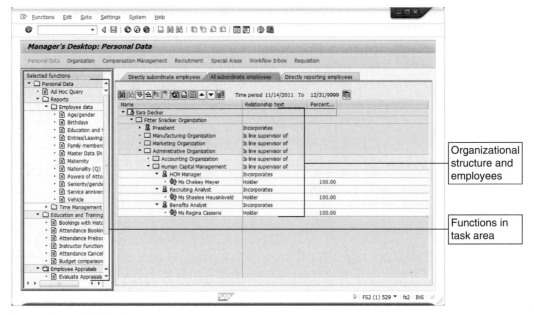

Source Line: SAP AG.

FIGURE 6-5   SAP's Manager's Desktop provides a single point of access to human resources functions

Human resources data includes employees' personal information, so controlling access to that data is critical. An advantage of an integrated information system over a paper-based system is that controlling access to data is automated; managers can use the system to determine which users should have access to various data.

ADVANCED SAP ERP HUMAN RESOURCES FEATURES

Discussing in detail the many SAP Human Resources processes is beyond the scope of this text; however, some of the advanced features of the Human Resources module, including time management, payroll processing, travel management, and training and development coordination are presented in the following sections.

Time Management

Hourly employees, who are paid for each hour worked, must record the hours they work so they can be paid. Salaried employees are not paid based on the number of hours worked, but typically their time must still be tracked. For cost-accounting purposes, it is often important to be able to attribute an employee's time to a cost object—such as a cost center (which may be a department or division), project, or production order—and any time not worked must be attributed to vacation or leave. The SAP Human Resources module uses Cross Application Time Sheets (CATS) to record employee working times and provide data to other modules, including the following:

- *SAP Controlling module*—Monitors and manages costs
- *SAP Payroll module*—Calculates employee pay; payroll data is then transferred to the Financial Accounting module for payroll processing (issuing paychecks as well as making payments for taxes, health insurance payments, retirement contributions, etc.)
- *SAP Production Planning module*—Determines whether enough labor is available to support production plans

Payroll Processing

Payroll processing is probably the most important function of a human resources department. Employees are, not surprisingly, very particular about being paid the correct amount at the correct time. Without proper management of the payroll process, employees might not be paid for all of the hours they worked, they might not be paid at the appropriate rate, or they might have too much or too little money withheld from their pay for taxes and benefits. Mistakes in payroll can cause significant job dissatisfaction.

The two key processes in determining the pay an employee receives are calculation of the remuneration elements and determination of statutory and voluntary deductions. The **remuneration elements** of an employee's pay include the base pay, bonuses, gratuities, overtime pay, sick pay, and vacation allowances the employee has earned during the pay period. The **statutory and voluntary deductions** are paycheck withholdings, including taxes (federal, state, local, Social Security, and Medicare), company loans, and benefit contributions. Properly determining the pay for an employee requires accurate input data and correct evaluation of remuneration elements and deductions.

The process of determining each employee's pay is called a **payroll run**. In the payroll run, the SAP ERP system evaluates the input data and notes any discrepancies in an **error log**. Payroll employees review the error log, make any necessary corrections, and repeat the payroll run until no errors are recorded. Then the payroll run is used to generate employee pay statements, process electronic funds transfers to individual employees' bank accounts, submit tax payments to the appropriate government entities, and perform other calculations as required by human resources and accounting.

Travel Management

Many companies spend a substantial amount of money on employee travel, and managing travel and its associated expenses can be a significant task. A travel request, which may originate with the employee or the employee's manager, is the first step in the travel management process. Travel requests usually require management approval, and the organizational level at which travel must be approved may depend on the duration, location, and cost of the travel. Once management has approved the travel, employees must make their travel reservations. Because airfare, hotel, and rental car costs can vary widely, companies frequently require employees to make reservations through either a company travel office or a travel agency that is under contract to the company. The employee must keep receipts for expenses incurred during the trip in order to complete an expense report and receive reimbursement. The SAP ERP Travel Management system facilitates this process by maintaining travel data for each employee—including flight, hotel, and car preferences—and integrating this data with the Payroll module (to administer reimbursements) and with the Financial Accounting and Controlling modules (to properly record travel expenses). Companies using the SAP ERP Travel Management system can also make use of a Web-based application that allows employees to submit expense reports through a Web browser.

Travel management is also getting easier—and mobile—with SAP's Travel OnDemand product, which is hosted by SAP and accessed via the Internet. (As noted in Chapter 2, this software delivery model, called software as a service, or SaaS, is a subset of cloud computing and is discussed in more detail in Chapter 8.) With Travel OnDemand, employees can use their smartphones to automatically categorize their travel expenses by simply taking a picture of each receipt. The system then reads the receipt and puts it in the correct expense category. For instance, a receipt from a restaurant would be categorized under meals, while a train ticket receipt would be placed under transportation. When the employee returns to the office after a trip, the expense report is already almost complete. This is a huge help to employees who spend a large portion of their time on the road; the hassle of gathering receipts and filling out paperwork is often a source of significant source of job dissatisfaction for employees who travel frequently. In addition, employees using Travel OnDemand are able to query the system about travel and expense policies, such as the company policy on taking clients out to dinner.

ANOTHER LOOK

What's New in Human Capital Management (HCM)

The goals and aspirations of a company's employees should be aligned with the strategic goals of organizations. Surprisingly, research shows that 95 percent of employees are unaware or do not understand their company's strategic goals. In addition, newly recruited employees often do not perform as well as hoped because the employee's personal goals are not aligned with those of the organization. Tools now exist that allow hiring organizations to assess potential candidates not only on their intelligence but also on other, harder to define characteristics, such as motivation and behavior.

Once an employee is hired, new performance evaluation tools allow companies to assess employees in a consistent manner across the organization. Traditionally, individual managers within a company perform evaluations, which might be based on criteria that is inconsistent between different managers. This variation can cause problems when employees are evaluated across departments, perhaps for an internal promotion or a new job. Tools that improve the consistency of evaluations help to alleviate this problem. Many companies are also working to improve their performance assessment process through the use of the "360-degree evaluation," in which employees perform their own evaluations, and are also evaluated not only by their managers, but also by their coworkers, and perhaps even their customers.

Although many organizations are still using spreadsheets to analyze their workforce, those that use the SAP ERP software have the advantage of fast prediction. Using SAP's new in-memory computing (HANA) feature, the Human Capital Management module can now handle large volumes of employee data—such as data related to hiring, promotion, and termination—to predict the three- and five-year makeup of the workforce. SAP is

(continued)

planning an expansion of social networking into the Human Capital Management module in the near future as well.

Question:

1. In what ways could social networking improve human capital management software?

Training and Development Coordination

The Personnel Development component of the SAP ERP Human Resources module allows companies to plan and implement employee development and training activities that maximize an employee's ability to contribute to the organization. Because advances in technology can quickly render an employee's knowledge obsolete, employees will not remain productive without continuing development and training efforts. In addition, many positions require certifications that must be updated, and continuing education is frequently required for recertification. Without an effective human resources information system, managing the training, development, and certification needs for a company's employees can be both time consuming and prone to error.

In the SAP ERP system, employee development is driven by qualifications and requirements. **Requirements** are skills or abilities associated with a position, while **qualifications** are skills or abilities associated with a specific employee. Requirements and qualifications refer to the same concept from a different perspective. By using the SAP Personnel Development tool, a manager can compare an employee's qualifications with the requirements for a position to which the employee aspires. This comparison enables the manager to identify gaps and to plan development and training efforts to close those gaps. It can also serve as a basis for employee evaluation, and it can help motivate the employee by providing a goal and the means to achieve it.

One of the most important reasons companies must manage the development and training of employees is the need for **succession planning**. A succession plan outlines the strategy for replacing key employees when they leave the company or move to another position within the company. The success of a company depends in large part on the skills, abilities, and experience of its management team. This is especially true for small companies like Fitter. Savvy customers have been known to avoid establishing long-term relationships with companies that do not have well-developed succession plans. The Career and Succession Planning components of the SAP ERP Human Resources module allow human resources professionals to create, implement, and evaluate succession planning scenarios. Human resources departments use career planning tools when working with individual employees, identifying potential career goals and drawing up career plans. Companies use succession planning tools to find people to fill unoccupied positions. Succession planning allows human resources employees to meet staffing requirements by proactively identifying candidate employees within the company and ensuring that their training and development plans will prepare them for the new position when it becomes available. Using the career and succession planning tools in an ERP system ensures that human resources will have accurate and timely employee and position data when developing those plans. The system also lets human resources staff more easily track and integrate personnel changes (such as new employees starting and current employees leaving or getting promoted to a new position), and it gives all approved users easy access to data.

ANOTHER LOOK

Executive Succession Planning for the CIO Position

As with any executive search, finding the right CIO (chief information officer) can be very challenging since often the requirements for an individual company's CIO are somewhat subjective. The average CIO lasts three to five years at a company, and about two-thirds of the time a replacement is found outside the organization. At E. & J. Gallo Winery, the current CIO, Kent Kushar, has made it a point to work with the Human Resources Department to find himself a successor. He found one possible candidate in the Sales and Marketing Department, a vice president named Kevin Barnes. Barnes understood Gallo's strategy of linking technology with a customer-oriented approach. Barnes was sent on a CIO training course, so to speak. The course, run by Harvard Professor Jim Cash, is a six-month training course with workshops, teleconferences, and personal advisers. The cost of the course is $35,000, but those who complete it generally find themselves ready to step into a CIO job.

Experienced CIOs have put together a list of key ideas for creating a good succession plan, as explained in the magazine, *CIO*:

- *Perform needs assessments*—Focus on the skills and the type of information technology leadership that the company will require in the future. HCM software can help a company standardize the assessment of potential candidates for leadership positions. Also, find out who is going to retire over the next several years.
- *Determine how far down the ladder the plan will go*—Ideally, successions plans should also be developed for middle management, so if someone leaves the company, the transition to promotion is smooth. Again, HCM software can be used to track the skill set of each employee to identify those who are ready to move up.
- *Evaluate skills, performance, and goals for growth*—Performance evaluations of employees can accomplish this task. At Marriott International, an employee's performance evaluation is compared to a set of company "key dimensions." This helps Marriott to not only do succession planning, but also to ensure their employees are utilized to their full potential.
- *Identify potential*—This task is usually performed by senior management, such as the CIO. While potential can be difficult to assess, international shipping company, UPS, has a standardized way of assessing employees in four areas of leadership—business, people, results, and self. This balanced evaluation is shared with all groups across the organization and is used when evaluating people for senior-level management positions.
- *Put potential leaders to the test*—Give employees opportunities to show their potential and develop new strengths. UPS rotates upper-level IT

(continued)

managers through different IT functions and business areas to gain experience. CIOs can groom future leaders by putting them in charge of projects or meetings.

- *Keep succession criteria consistent and up to date*—Succession plans should become part of an organization's culture. According to George Hall, senior vice president at Marriott, "Succession planning is not a means to an end; it's the end itself. It's really what falls out of doing other things correctly."

Questions:

1. Assume that Fitter needs to replace their current CIO who is retiring. Make a list of the pros and cons of hiring a new CIO from outside the company as opposed to promoting someone from within the company. Which do you think is the correct approach? Explain your answer.
2. What are the risks to the company if they fail to create a succession plan?

ADDITIONAL HUMAN RESOURCES FEATURES OF SAP ERP

Human resources staff must keep pace with rapidly changing social, technological, and legislative developments that affect the corporate world. Because of that, the SAP Human Resources module has been expanded to include features that assist managers with human resources tasks that have only recently become important to corporations.

Mobile Time Management

Many employees, especially sales personnel who spend a significant amount of time on the road, may not have regular access to a PC. SAP's Mobile Time Management tool allows employees to use smartphones or other mobile devices to record their working times, record absences, or enter a leave request.

Management of Family and Medical Leave

The Human Resources module alleviates some of the administrative burden imposed by the federal Family and Medical Leave Act (FMLA) of 1993. Companies can program the Human Resources module to determine whether an employee is eligible to take FMLA leave and to automatically deduct those absences from the employee's allowable leave.

Management of Domestic Partner Benefits

Many companies provide benefits for domestic (unmarried) partners. The Human Resources module now supports the management of benefits for domestic partners and their children. The system provides companies more flexibility in customizing dependent coverage options for health plans, eligibility for enrollment of dependents, and designation of beneficiaries.

Administration of Long-Term Incentives

An outgrowth of the Sarbanes-Oxley Act (discussed in Chapter 5) is that companies must account for the expected costs that will occur as a result of long-term employee incentives, such as stock options. The Human Resources module provides more options for processing long-term incentives. For instance, the SAP Payroll module enables companies to calculate taxes accurately when employees exercise stock options and sell their shares in the company. The Human Resources module can be programmed to share that incentive data with Accounting so that Accounting can complete the necessary financial reporting.

Personnel Cost Planning

Changes in an organization (including expansions, acquisitions, and downsizing) can affect employee-related expenses, which are usually a significant portion of a company's costs. The Personnel Cost Planning tool allows human resources staff to define and evaluate planning scenarios to generate cost estimates. Performing cost planning allows human resources to forecast cost estimates by integrating data with other SAP ERP modules.

Management and Payroll for Global Employees

Companies who manage a team of employees around the globe face many complicated issues, including managing relocation plans, visas and work permits, housing, taxes, and bonus pay in a variety of countries. SAP ERP has enhanced features to support the management of these issues, with customized functionality for over 50 countries—helping companies ensure their payroll processes meet current legal regulations and collective bargaining agreements in the local business environments.

Management by Objectives

The concept of management by objectives (MBO) was first outlined by Peter Drucker in his 1954 book *The Practice of Management*. In MBO, managers are encouraged to focus on results, not activities, and to "negotiate a contract of goals" with their subordinates without dictating the exact methods for achieving them. SAP ERP supports the MBO approach through a process that incorporates performance appraisal. The appraisal results can affect an employee's compensation, generating annual pay raises that can be significant, depending on the employee's performance. The MBO process in SAP ERP also allows managers to include the results of achieved objectives in the employee's qualifications profile.

ANOTHER LOOK

FMLA Management

Under the Family and Medical Leave Act (FMLA) of 1993, eligible employees can take up to 12 weeks of unpaid time off per year to recover from a serious medical condition or to care for a sick member of their immediate family or a new child. At Banner Health, a company with hospitals and healthcare facilities in seven states, about 5 percent of employees make use of FMLA leave. The company has calculated the cost of that leave at close to $1 million per year, not including the cost of regular sick days, vacations, bereavement leave, and so on. In fact, the Human Resources staff at Banner thinks that cost estimate probably does not reflect leave taken by another 1 percent of employees whose time is not accurately tracked. Some absences are not tracked because they are not documented properly. For example, if an employee takes time off for migraine

(continued)

headaches during the year, but those headaches do not occur in a continuous set of 12 weeks, the absences might not be documented as part of FMLA. By tracking absences with human capital management software, employees might be encouraged to see specialist doctors sooner to get treatment that could reduce future absences.

Part of the challenge of documenting FMLA absences is the complexity of the task. First, in addition to the FMLA, there are many state laws governing medical leave rights, such as the California Family Rights Act (CFRA). Second, the FMLA rules are complex. For example, the following is a small section of the FMLA that defines intermittent or reduced leave:

> Leave under subparagraph (A) or (B) of subsection (a)(1) shall not be taken by an employee intermittently or on a reduced leave schedule unless the employee and the employer of the employee agree otherwise. Subject to paragraph (2), subsection (e)(2), and subsection (b)(5) or (f) (as appropriate) of section 103, leave under subparagraph (C) or (D) of subsection (a)(1) or under subsection (a)(3) may be taken intermittently or on a reduced leave schedule when medically necessary. Subject to subsection (e)(3) and section 103(f), leave under subsection (a)(1)(E) may be taken intermittently or on a reduced leave schedule. The taking of leave intermittently or on a reduced leave schedule pursuant to this paragraph shall not result in a reduction in the total amount of leave to which the employee is entitled under subsection (a) beyond the amount of leave actually taken.

Obviously, understanding and properly accounting for FMLA leave is complex. Software to manage FMLA leaves, such as SAP's FMLA Workbench, can help companies do the following:

- Determine FMLA eligibility based on an employees hours worked and hire date.
- Track concurrent and intermittent FMLA leave simultaneously with other leave types such as vacation or personal leave.
- Generate the necessary forms and documents for managing FMLA events.
- Store doctor's certifications and send alerts when new certifications are required.
- Reduce the likelihood of Department of Labor investigations and employee lawsuits.

The last point is especially important for human resources professionals. In the recent legal case *Narodetsky v. Cardone Industries*, the court held that human resources managers may be individually liable for FMLA violations at an organization.

Question:

1. Using the Internet, investigate the cost of absenteeism for companies in the United States. How can human capital management software help companies reduce their costs for this?
2. Using the Internet, find at least two changes to the FMLA act since its creation in 1993.

Chapter Summary

- Employees are among a company's most valuable assets. Without qualified and motivated employees, a company cannot succeed.

- The human resources department has responsibility for ensuring the company can attract, assess, and, hire the right employees—those that will allow it to achieve its goals. Human resources is also responsible for employee compensation, evaluations, training and development, succession planning, and termination.

- Managing, sharing, controlling, and evaluating the data required to manage a company's human capital are simplified by an integrated information system.

- Some of the advanced features of the SAP Human Resources module include tools to facilitate time management, payroll processing, travel management, and training and development coordination (including succession planning).

- Additional features of the SAP Human Resources system address the rapidly changing social, technological, and legislative developments that affect the corporate world.

Key Terms

error log	remuneration element
human capital management (HCM)	requirement
job	short list
payroll run	statutory and voluntary deduction
person	succession planning
position	task
qualification	

Exercises

1. Go to your school's career and jobs Web site and find a position you would like to have. What type of information must be collected by the hiring company to determine if a candidate is appropriate for this job? List the skills that you think would be required for this position. Do you have those skills? If not, how can you acquire them?

2. Suppose you are designing a system to summarize information from résumés submitted to a company's human resources department. Create a list of the information that you think would be useful to collect from the résumés.

3. Using the Internet to do your research, describe a position in a company that you would like to have after five years of work experience. List the requirements that you think would be necessary to hold this position.

4. Suppose you are a manager of Fitter's Accounting and Finance department. What human resources information do you think you would need to effectively manage your Accounting and Finance employees?

5. List the steps in a typical recruiting process. Highlight the steps that involve interaction with the potential job candidate. Identify problems in the process that might lead a candidate to develop a negative opinion of the company. How might an effective information system

reduce the potential for these problems? Incorporate into your answer experiences you may have had in looking for a job.

For Further Study and Research

Ferguson, Tim. "Goal! How Data Analytics Drives Sport Teams to Victory." Silicon.com. December 6, 2010. www.silicon.com/technology/software/2010/12/06/goal-how-data-analytics-drives-sport-teams-to-victory-39746685/.

Fisk, Margaret Cronin, and Karen Gullo. "Wal-Mart Accused of Bias Against Women." *Bloomberg,* October 28, 2011. www.bloomberg.com/news/2011-10-28/wal-mart-discriminated-against-women-workers-over-pay-suit-in-texas-says.html.

Frank, Diane. "Plan for Succession." *CIO,* April 24, 2008. www.cio.com/article/341072/Plan_for_Succession.

McGee, Marianne Kolbasuk. "Out Sick: New Tools Help Companies Better Manage Employee Absences." *InformationWeek*, May 5, 2005. www.informationweek.com/news/162600186?queryText=out+sick%3A+new+tools+help+companies+better+manage+employee+absences.

Prozone. "Asset Management – The Application of Analytics to Player Recruitment." 2009. www.prozonesports.com/news-article-asset-management—the-application-of-analytics-to-player-recruitment.html.

Reuters. "Novartis Fined $250 Million in Sex Discrimination Suit." *New York Times*, May 19, 2010. www.nytimes.com/2010/05/20/business/20drug.html.

Schuppert, Stefan. "German DPAs Issue Rules for Cloud Computing Use." *Hogan Lovells Chronicle of Data Protection,* October 13, 2011. www.hldataprotection.com/2011/10/articles/international-eu-privacy/german-dpas-issue-rules-for-cloud-computing-use.

Smith, Mark. "SAP Brews New Human Capital Management for the Cloud." *Perspectives by Mark Smith,* May 24, 2011. http://marksmith.ventanaresearch.com/2011/05/24/sap-brews-new-human-capital-management-for-the-cloud.

Soat, John. "Tomorrow's CIO Next in Line." *InformationWeek*, August 18/25, 2008.

Swabey, Pete. "Personnel Development." *Information Age,* September 16, 2008. www.information-age.com/channels/business-applications/features/643106/personnel-development.thtml.

Shellenbarger, Sue, "Novartis Ruling Offers Lesson on 'Family-Friendly' Workplaces." *WSJ.Com*, May 21, 2010. http://blogs.wsj.com/juggle/2010/05/21/novartis-ruling-offers-lesson-on-family-friendly-workplaces.

Wooldridge, Adrian. "A Survey of Talent." *The Economist*, October 7, 2006.

Working Mother. "Novartis Pharmaceuticals." 2009. www.workingmother.com/work-life-balance/2009/08/novartis-pharmaceuticals.

Wright, Aliah D., "Cloud Computing and Security: How Safe is HR Data in the Cloud?" August 15, 2011. www.shrm.org/hrdisciplines/technology/Articles/Pages/CloudSecurity.aspx.

CHAPTER 7

PROCESS MODELING, PROCESS IMPROVEMENT, AND ERP IMPLEMENTATION

LEARNING OBJECTIVES

After completing this chapter, you will be able to:

- Use basic flowcharting techniques to map a business process
- Develop an event process chain (EPC) diagram of a basic business process
- Evaluate the value added by each step in a business process
- Develop process-improvement suggestions
- Discuss the key issues in managing an ERP implementation project
- Describe some of the key tools used to manage an ERP implementation project

INTRODUCTION

The theme of business processes management underlies much of the discussion in this text. In this chapter, we will explore tools, such as flowcharts and process chains, that can be used to describe business processes. You will learn how these tools, which are not specific to ERP, can help managers identify process elements that need to be improved. We will finish by studying the role these process-modeling tools play in ERP implementation projects.

PROCESS MODELING

By now, it should be clear that business processes can be quite complex. Adding to that complexity is the fact that individuals with various skills and abilities are responsible for executing business processes. For business processes to be effective (achieve the desired results) and efficient (achieve the desired results with the minimum use of resources), the processes must be clearly defined, and individuals must be adequately trained to perform their roles and to understand how their roles fit within the overall business process.

We will use the term **process model** to describe any abstract representation of a process. A process model can be as simple as a diagram with boxes and arrows or as complex as computer software that allows for process simulation. Graphical representations are usually easier to understand than written descriptions, and process-modeling tools provide a way to describe a business process so anyone viewing the model can easily understand the process. Frequently, process models are developed by a team of employees involved in the process. The interaction required to develop a process model often reveals misunderstandings and ensures that all team members are "on the same page." A well-developed process model provides a good starting point for analyzing a process so participants can design and implement improvements. Process models can also be used to train employees who will support the business process.

Flowcharting Process Models

Flowcharts are the simplest of the process-modeling tools. A **flowchart** is any graphical representation of the movement or flow of concrete or abstract items—materials, documents, logic, and so on. Flowcharts originated with mathematicians and computer programmers, who used them to trace the logical path of an algorithm. In the early days of computer programming, computer resources were limited, and executing a program used considerable resources. As a result, most programmers spent a significant amount of time clearly defining the logic of their programs using flowcharts before actually writing the code and testing the program.

A flowchart is a clear, graphical representation of a process from beginning to end, regardless of whether that process is an algorithm or a manufacturing procedure. Flowcharting has been used in business applications since the 1960s to help businesspeople visualize workflows and functional responsibility within organizations. Today the term **process mapping** is often used interchangeably with flowcharting, the distinction being that process mapping refers specifically to the activities occurring within an *existing* business process. Process mapping develops an "as is" representation of a process, with a goal of exposing weaknesses that need to be addressed. Once a company develops a process map, it can perform a **gap analysis**, which is an assessment of disparities between how the process currently works and how the organization wants it to work.

Flowcharting uses a standardized set of symbols to represent various business activities. You can use a wide range of symbols for process mapping, but the basic set shown in Figure 7-1 is sufficient to describe even a complicated business process. Using a few simple symbols places the focus on the process rather than on the tool used to represent it.

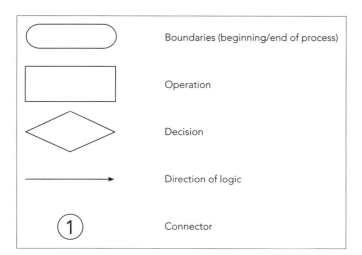

	Boundaries (beginning/end of process)
	Operation
	Decision
	Direction of logic
	Connector

Source Line: Course Technology/Cengage Learning.

FIGURE 7-1 Basic flowcharting symbols

The next section describes Fitter Snacker's process for reimbursing sales personnel for their business expenses; we will use this example to illustrate process mapping.

Fitter Expense-Reporting Process

Maria is a Fitter salesperson who travels frequently for her job. After Maria incurs travel expenses on her personal credit card, she completes a paper expense report, makes a copy for her records, attaches receipts for any expenses over $25, and mails the report to her zone manager at the branch office. The manager, Kevin, reviews the report and either approves it or mails it back to Maria with a note asking for an explanation, verification, or modification. Once Kevin approves the expense report, he mails it to the corporate office. After the administrative assistant sorts the mail at the corporate office, she forwards the expense report to the accounts payable (A/P) clerk, who performs a preliminary check of the report. The clerk contacts Kevin for any necessary clarification, then forwards the expense report to the expense report auditor, who reviews it. If there is a problem with the report, the auditor mails it back to Maria, who revises it and returns it. Then the auditor enters the report into Fitter's PC-based accounting system and files a hard copy with the receipts in a filing cabinet, organized by employee name.

At the end of each week, an A/P clerk uses the PC-based accounting system to print payroll checks, payments to suppliers, and expense reimbursement checks. When Maria receives her reimbursement check, she deposits it into her checking account and mails a payment to the credit card company, which credits her card account. Figure 7-2 shows the process map for the first part of the current Fitter Snacker expense-reporting process.

186

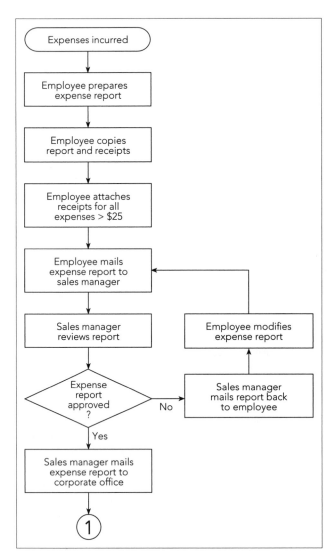

Source Line: Course Technology/Cengage Learning.

FIGURE 7-2   Partial process map for Fitter's expense-reporting process

Establishing process boundaries is one of the most important steps in process mapping. The **process boundaries** define which activities are to be included in the process, and which are considered part of the environment—external to the process. It is important to clearly define the activities that are part of the process and those that are external to the process. Without clearly defined boundaries, a project can expand to the point where it can become unmanageable. Many activities related to sales employee expenses are considered outside of the boundary of Fitter's expense-reporting process map. For example, Fitter might provide cash advances or issue corporate credit cards for travel expenses. Employees might need to make reservations for air travel or hotels through a corporate travel office. The company might require employees to use a preferred hotel, or it might have specific policies regarding car rentals, including preferred rental companies, approved car classes, insurance, and prepaid gas. While all of these considerations are important and should be documented somewhere, the process mapped in Figure 7-2 is the *expense-reporting process*; the process boundaries do not include these additional travel-related activities. Including these external considerations in the process map would greatly increase the size of the process-mapping project and put the process-improvement project at risk. The complete process map for the expense-reporting process begins after travel expenses have been incurred and ends with the receipt by the salesperson of a refund check. These starting and end points are the process boundaries for the expense-reporting process.

All processes should have only one beginning point and one ending point. In Figure 7-2, the beginning process boundary is represented by the oval figure containing the text "Expenses incurred." Next, the process map shows four operation blocks that define the tasks performed by the employee in completing the expense report. The number of operation blocks used and the level of detail in the descriptions are a matter of preference and depend on the purpose for which a process map is created. If the process map will be used to improve a business process, and the members of the process-improvement team are familiar with the process, then less detail is needed. In fact, too much detail could obscure the key features of the process. On the other hand, if the process map will be used to document the process for training new sales employees, more detail is required to ensure that new employees can use the process map to follow the process properly.

Figure 7-2 also contains one decision diamond. A decision diamond asks a question that can be answered with *Yes* or *No*. In this case, the decision diamond asks whether the sales manager approves the expense report. There are only two possible options—*Yes* and *No*. It may tempting for the novice to create process maps with decision diamonds that have more than two outcomes; however, doing so can lead to confused logic. All business processes can be defined using one or more decision diamonds, each with only two outcomes.

Finally, because Figure 7-2 only shows part of the expense-reporting process, the flowchart ends with a connector. Most business processes are too complicated to fit on a single sheet of paper. Connectors provide a way to continue process maps from one sheet to the next.

Exercise 7.1

Complete the process map for the Fitter Snacker expense-reporting process started in Figure 7-2, using the description of the process provided at the beginning of this section and the process-mapping symbols shown in Figure 7-1.

Extensions of Process Mapping

The development of computer technology—specifically, high-quality graphical interfaces—has allowed process-mapping tools to evolve beyond the simple symbols of flowcharting. One helpful tool is **hierarchical modeling**, which is a type of process mapping in which a business process can be described in greater or less detail, depending on the task at hand. Figure 7-3 illustrates a hierarchical model of Fitter's expense-reporting process.

188

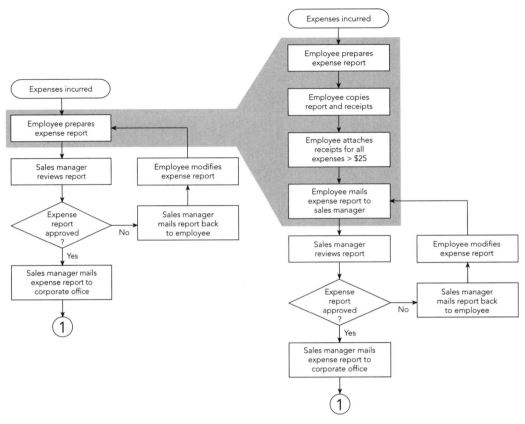

FIGURE 7-3   Hierarchical modeling of Fitter's expense-reporting process

For training purposes, it is important to document the detailed steps a salesperson must follow to complete an expense report; however, the details can make the process map cumbersome for process-improvement activities. In hierarchical modeling, the four steps that the salesperson follows to complete an expense report can be condensed into one step: "Employee completes expense report." Hierarchical modeling software provides the user with the flexibility to move easily from higher-level, less detailed views to lower-level views with more details. Hierarchical modeling can aid in process mapping by allowing a user to create a broad, high-level view of a process and then add more detail as the process is analyzed.

Another widely used and widely recognized type of process-mapping technique is **deployment flowcharting** (also known as **swimlane flowcharting**). This type of flowchart depicts team members across the top, with each step aligned vertically under the appropriate employee or team. Figure 7-4 shows the Fitter expense-reporting process as a deployment flowchart. This process-mapping technique has the advantage of clearly identifying each person's tasks in the process.

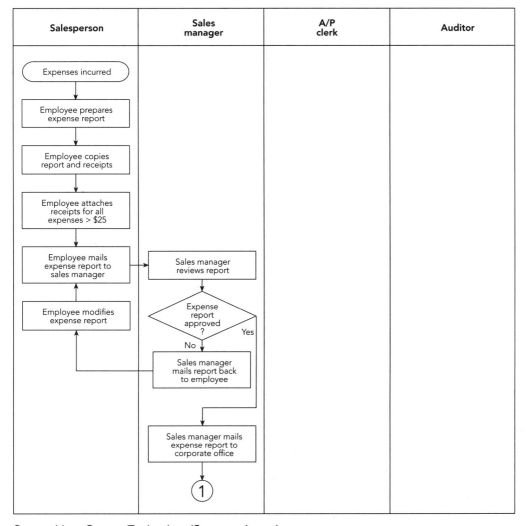

Source Line: Course Technology/Cengage Learning.

FIGURE 7-4 Deployment, or swimlane, flowcharting of Fitter's expense-reporting process

Event Process Chain (EPC) Diagrams

SAP's ERP software supports hundreds of business processes, and SAP has developed graphical models for many of these business processes using the **event process chain (EPC)** format. The EPC format uses only two symbols to represent a business process. The advantage of the EPC format is that it matches the logic and structure of SAP's ERP software design. The EPC modeling technique is available as a software tool through Software AG's ARIS (Architecture of Integrated Information System) platform.

In EPC modeling, the two structures used to represent business processes are *events* and *functions*. Figure 7-5 shows the graphical representations of events and functions in

189

EPC modeling. Events reflect a state or status in the process and are represented by an elongated hexagon, and functions reflect the part of the process where change occurs and are represented by rectangles with rounded corners.

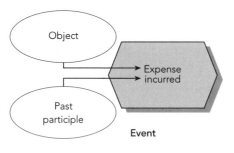

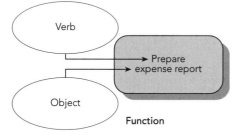

Source Line: Course Technology/Cengage Learning.

FIGURE 7-5 Event process chain (EPC) components

A standardized naming convention for functions and events is also used in EPC modeling. For example, the convention for naming events is object—past participle, as shown in the following examples:

Object	Past Participle
Expense	incurred
Expense report	approved
Hard copy	filed

For functions, the naming convention is verb—object, as shown in the following examples:

Verb	Object
Prepare	expense report
Review	expense report
Mail	refund check

Figure 7-6 shows a simple EPC diagram for part of the Fitter expense-reporting process. EPC diagrams begin and end with events. Furthermore, events must be followed by functions, and functions must be followed by events.

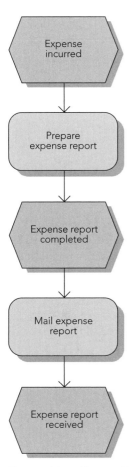

Source Line: Course Technology/Cengage Learning.

FIGURE 7-6   Basic EPC layout

In addition to direct connection of events to functions, EPC diagrams employ three types of branching connectors. Branching occurs when logic either comes from more than one source or proceeds to more than one potential outcome. The three connector types are AND, OR, and Exclusive OR (XOR). Figure 7-7 shows how the AND connector functions. The figure indicates that the expense report must be recorded and a hard copy must be filed.

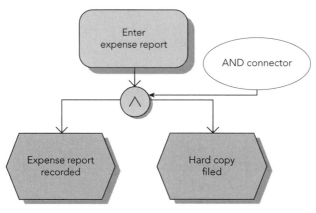

Source Line: Course Technology/Cengage Learning.

FIGURE 7-7   AND connector in an EPC diagram

The OR connector indicates that one or more potential outcomes could occur; it is not exclusive. Figure 7-8 shows an application of the OR connector, which indicates that after a payment is processed, the salesperson is notified, or the sales manager is notified, or both the salesperson and sales manager are notified.

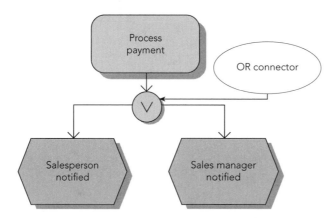

Source Line: Course Technology/Cengage Learning.

FIGURE 7-8   OR connector in an EPC diagram

Figure 7-9 shows how the XOR connector can be used to represent the manager's decision on whether to approve the expense report. Unlike the OR connector, the XOR connector is exclusive; only one event can occur after an XOR connector. Figure 7-9 indicates that only one event can occur after reviewing the expense report: it is approved or it is not approved.

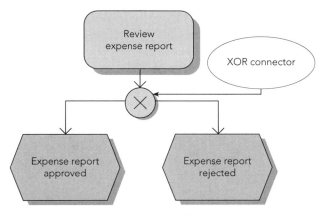

Source Line: Course Technology/Cengage Learning.

FIGURE 7-9   XOR connector in an EPC diagram

Figures 7-7 through 7-9 show one function connecting to two events using a branch connector; however, it is not always the case that functions lead into the connector, nor do multiple events always follow the connector. For example, Fitter could require that salespeople complete expense reports at the end of a short sales trip, but at the end of each week if a trip lasts more than one week. This condition is illustrated in Figure 7-10, where the preparation of the expense report can be triggered by either of two events: the end of the trip *or* the end of the week. It is also possible that more than two events could trigger the function.

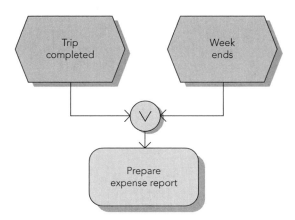

Source Line: Course Technology/Cengage Learning.

FIGURE 7-10   OR connector with two triggering events

Figure 7-11 shows all possible connection combinations. Note that it is not possible to have a single event connect to multiple functions with OR or XOR connectors, because events represent a status or state. When OR and XOR connectors lead to multiple outcomes (functions or events), then a decision is required to decide what path(s) should be followed and an event cannot produce a decision.

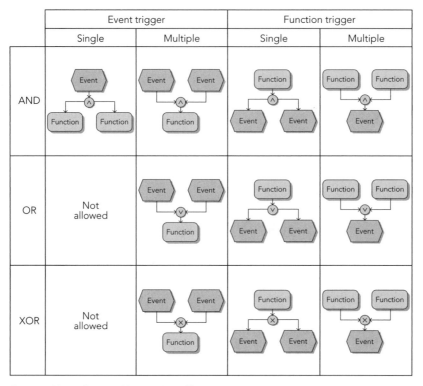

Source Line: Course Technology/Cengage Learning.

FIGURE 7-11 Possible connector and triggering combinations

Finally, Figure 7-12 shows the splitting and consolidating of a path through the process. In this case, the Fitter salesperson can submit her expense report online if she has Internet access; otherwise, she must send in a paper report. Note the same type of connector that is used to split the path must be used to consolidate it.

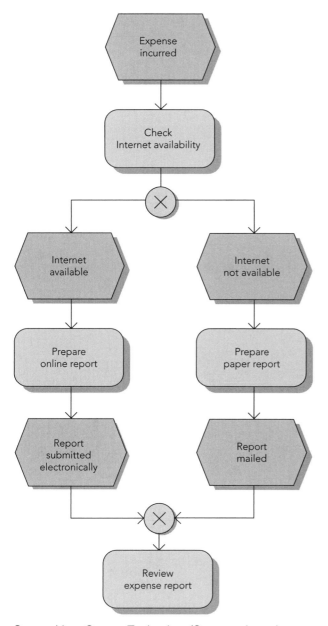

Source Line: Course Technology/Cengage Learning.

FIGURE 7-12   Splitting and consolidating paths

The basic EPC diagram can be augmented with additional information. In EPC terminology, this additional information is called a data element. For example, Figure 7-13 shows the first part of an EPC diagram for the Fitter expense-reporting process; the diagram also shows data elements ("Unapproved multicopy expense report") and organizational elements ("Salesperson," "Sales manager"). The additional elements allow for a more complete description of the process, documenting the "who" and "what" aspects of the process.

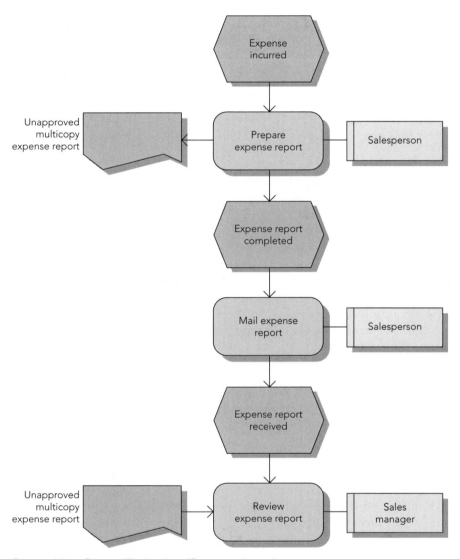

Source Line: Course Technology/Cengage Learning.

FIGURE 7-13   EPC diagram with organizational and data elements

Exercise 7.2

Using the description of the process provided earlier in the chapter, complete the EPC diagram of the Fitter expense-reporting process shown in Figure 7-13. Add both the logic elements (events, functions, and connectors) and the organizational elements.

PROCESS IMPROVEMENT

Process-mapping tools provide the ability to describe business processes in a universally understood format. Generally, the task of mapping a process requires a team consisting of key personnel who are involved in the process. Frequently, the act of accurately describing the process, and understanding how the functional areas interact, make it obvious to the team what steps are necessary to improve the process. This is especially true for organizations that have previously focused on functional responsibilities rather than business processes.

Using the simple technique of value analysis can also generate process-improvement ideas. In **value analysis**, each activity in the process is analyzed for the value it adds to the product or service. The **value added** is an increase in a product's or service's value, from the perspective of the customer. Activities can add:

- *Real value*—Value for which the customer is willing to pay
- *Business value*—Value that helps the company run its business
- *No value*—An activity that should be eliminated

The Fitter expense-reporting process does not provide real value, because Fitter's customers do not care whether sales employees receive prompt and accurate reimbursement of their business expenses. However, the expense-reporting process does add business value, and it should provide this value at a minimum cost. Determining the value of a good or service is easy—it is what someone is willing to pay for it. Evaluating the value of part of a business activity, however, is not an exact science because parts of a process cannot be sold on the open market. Although it is a challenging task, evaluating each activity on the basis of value provided can highlight opportunities for improvement. Activities that cost more than their value added should be improved.

The value analysis concept can be expanded to an evaluation of both the time and cost of each process step. For each step in the current process, you estimate the actual time and cost. Then you estimate the value-added time and cost—determining how much of the actual time is adding value and how much of the cost is worth paying for.

We will use the "Mail expense report" function of Fitter's expense-reporting process to illustrate value analysis. This function could cost upwards of $50, including not just the cost of the envelope and postage, but also the time spent by the salesperson to mail the expense report. The value analysis includes the elapsed time for mailing the expense report, including the time it takes the salesperson to find a mailbox, the time the postal service takes to deliver the expense report to the company headquarters, and the time it takes the company's internal mail system to deliver the expense report to the sales manager.

Suppose that for Fitter the elapsed time is typically three days. To perform value analysis, you would determine how much of this time and cost is value added. To determine this value, you must view the activity "Mail expense report" in terms of what is actually being accomplished. In this case, it is not the physical transmission of paper that matters. Mailing the expense report is a means to transmit expense data and documentation. Email could minimize the time and cost required to transmit that data; therefore, mailing an expense report at a cost of $50, to arrive in three days, is only providing value worth pennies (which is the cost to send an email) in a function that could be executed within seconds. Looking at the current time and cost of each process step, then asking, "What is actually being accomplished, and what is the value?" can help identify areas for process improvement.

Each step in a business process should be challenged to determine if it is providing value. H. James Harrington, in his book *Business Process Improvement*, suggests that companies ask the following questions about their business processes to identify areas for improvement:

- Are there unnecessary checks and balances?
- Does the activity inspect or approve someone else's work?
- Does it require more than one signature?
- Are multiple copies required?
- Are copies stored for no apparent reason?
- Are copies sent to people who do not need the information?
- Is there unnecessary written correspondence?
- Are there people or agencies involved that impede the effectiveness and efficiency of the process?
- Do existing organizational procedures regularly impede the efficient, effective, and timely performance of duties?
- Is someone approving something they already approved (for example, approving capital expenditures that were approved as part of a budget)?
- Is the same information being collected at more than one time or location?
- Are duplicate databases being maintained?

Harrington also suggests using the following approaches to improving processes:

- Perform activities in parallel (for example, approvals).
- Change the sequence of activities.
- Reduce interruptions.
- Avoid duplication or fragmentation of tasks.
- Avoid complex flows and bottlenecks.
- Combine similar activities.
- Reduce the amount of handling.
- Eliminate unused data.
- Eliminate copies.

Evaluating Process Improvement Prior to Implementation

While identifying process improvements can be difficult, implementing them is even more challenging. Disrupting the current process to make changes can be costly and time consuming, and managers are frequently reluctant to risk trying process-improvement ideas—especially if the ideas require a significant change in the way an activity is completed. One way to mitigate this risk is to use dynamic process modeling to evaluate process changes before they are implemented. **Dynamic process modeling** takes a basic process flowchart and puts it into motion, using computer simulation techniques to facilitate the evaluation of proposed process changes. Computer simulation repeatedly generates random variables (such as customer orders) that interact with a logical model of the business process to predict the performance of the actual system. A dynamic process model can estimate the performance of a system, using measures such as cycle time (how long the process takes), productivity, total cost, idle time, and bottlenecks.

198

ANOTHER LOOK

Business Process Management—A Business Responsibility

Although many people may think of automating a process as an IT responsibility, it is not. It is a business responsibility. Business users within an organization must agree on what the old business processes are before the organization can begin to think about adopting—and automating—new business processes. That is exactly what happened with the Royal Pharmaceutical Society of Great Britain (RPSGB).

The RPSGB is the professional body for pharmacist professionals in Great Britain. The RPSGB's responsibilities include investigating complaints against pharmacists and pharmacy technicians, and recommending criminal prosecutions, when appropriate.

The RPSGB's business process management project began in response to challenges the organization was experiencing with the Access database system that handled complaints. By 2006, the database could no longer effectively handle the volume of complaints the RPSGB was receiving, so the organization established a team to introduce new software to help manage its complaint process. Initially, the team could not decide which processes the new software should automate. Team members also disagreed on what level of automation was required and on what type of documentation needed to be maintained. Therefore, the team decided they needed to define the organization's current business processes before determining how to make the complaint management process more efficient. The team created various process maps to develop a graphic representation of the existing processes.

The complaint process begins when a complaint is filed against a pharmacist. For example, complaints might be triggered by a rude pharmacist or, more seriously, by a drunk pharmacist dispensing the wrong medication. Some types of complaints require specific actions, which were documented with the process map.

Only after the team had mapped all the current processes and identified ways to make them more efficient was software applied to automate those processes. The team also worked with the British government to ensure the new processes had the flexibility to be changed quickly if new rules governing the pharmaceutical industry were passed in Parliament.

The entire project took almost two years to complete. During that time, the RPSGB focused considerable energy on change management to convince those involved that changing the processes was worthwhile. In this case, many employees were more easily convinced of the merits of the project because legislation that would require certain process changes was due to be passed shortly. The new automated system greatly reduced the RPSGB's dependence on paper, and it helped the organization achieve its goal of having 80 percent of all cases requiring further action being filed with the organization's Investigation Committee within three months of the completion of the initial investigation.

Questions:

1. Why is it important to understand your current business processes before trying to improve them?

2. Why might it be difficult for a group of workers to come to an agreement about what their current business processes are?

ERP WORKFLOW TOOLS

Most business processes are performed regularly, enabling employees responsible for the process to become efficient in the tasks involved in the process. For example, the sales order process is fundamental to a manufacturing business; the salespeople, sales order clerks, warehouse managers, accounts receivable clerks, and others spend most of their day supporting the process. If the process is efficiently designed and managed, and the employees are properly trained, workers will experience enough repetition to become efficient in their daily tasks.

Some business processes, however, are performed only sporadically. Often, such processes are inefficient, especially when the processes involve more than one functional area. Work may "fall through the cracks," not necessarily through negligence, but due to a lack of repetition. For example, the process of establishing credit limits may occur only occasionally and may require coordination between the Sales Department, which identifies new customers and gathers basic data (contact names, addresses, contract terms and conditions) and the Accounts Receivable Department, which evaluates a customer's credit history to establish a credit limit. Unless employees manage the process of establishing a credit limit properly, a new customer's order may be blocked for an unacceptable length of time. For sporadic processes such as this, a workflow software tool can help employees avoid "dropping the ball" by providing tools for tracking and monitoring the tasks in the project and providing reminders to the employees involved.

Workflow tools are software programs that automate the execution of business processes and address all aspects of a process, including the process flow (the logical steps in the business process), the people involved (the organization), and the effects (the process information that documents the process steps). ERP software provides a workflow management system that supports and speeds up business processes. It enables employees to carry out complex business processes and track the current status of a process at any time.

The SAP ERP workflow tool, called SAP Business Workflow, links employees to the business transactions that need to be performed. In a normal business process, an employee uses his or her knowledge to determine what transactions to process at what times. Sometimes this work is triggered by an external source, such as a customer call that causes the sales order clerk to perform the sales order creation transaction. In other cases, an employee uses a reporting tool to determine what transactions need to be processed. For example, as discussed in Chapter 5, industrial credit management is implemented by blocking sales orders when there is a credit issue. The blocked sales order report (shown in Figure 5-7) is the report that an employee can use to decide what transactions must be processed to resolve the credit issue.

In the case of sporadic processes, the SAP Business Workflow tool proactively connects employees with business transactions using SAP's internal email system and **workflow tasks**, which are email messages that can include basic information, notes, and documents, as well as direct links to business transactions. The SAP system can monitor workflow tasks, and if the tasks are not completed on time, the workflow system can automatically take various actions, including changing the workflow task priority and sending email reminders to the employees responsible for the work.

Consider vacation requests. Employees performing critical operational tasks within an organization may be required to request time off from work in advance. The process of requesting time off is likely a relatively infrequent process that can create operational and employee morale problems if not handled properly. As such, it is a prime candidate for a workflow tool. In SAP, the Workflow Builder is used to define the process behind a workflow. In addition to defining the steps in a business process, the software identifies individuals involved in the process and sets other process parameters. Figure 7-14 shows a Workflow Builder screen for the workflow that manages an employee's request for time off.

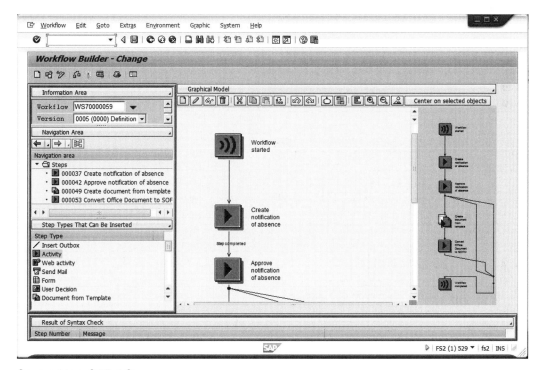

Source Line: SAP AG.

FIGURE 7-14   SAP ERP Workflow Builder screen

In the first step in this process, an employee completes the Create Notification of Absence screen (shown in Figure 7-15) to request time off from work.

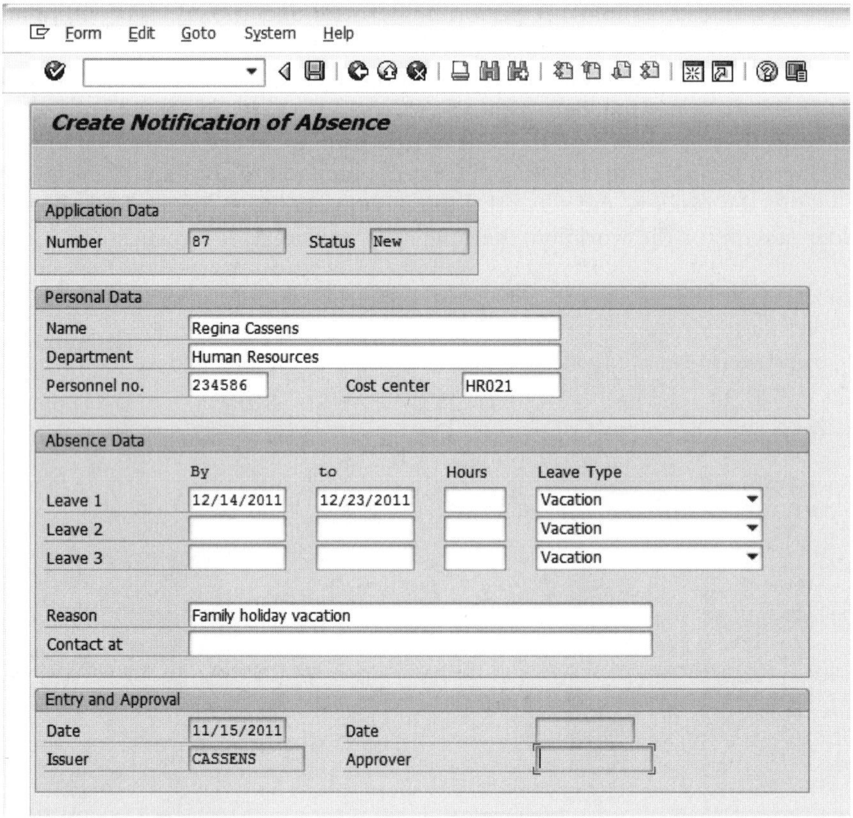

Source Line: SAP AG.

FIGURE 7-15   Create Notification of Absence screen

Once the employee completes this screen, the time-off request becomes a workflow item in the Business Workplace for the employee's supervisor. The Business Workplace is an interface for accessing a variety of SAP functions, including email, a calendar, and workflow—similar to other comprehensive communication and collaboration software packages such as Microsoft Outlook or IBM's Lotus Notes software.

Figure 7-16 shows a request for time off in the Workflow inbox of the manager's Business Workplace. From this screen, the manager can either approve or deny the request. If the request is approved, the employee receives notification of the approval by email. If the request is denied, the manager can include a note explaining the rationale. The rejected request will be sent to the employee's Workflow inbox, where that person can either modify the request or cancel it.

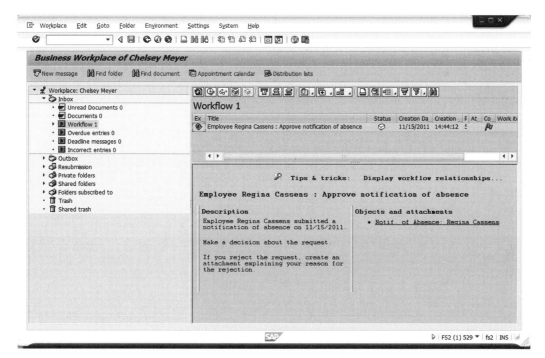

Source Line: SAP AG.

FIGURE 7-16   Manager's Business Workplace with workflow task

SAP's workflow tool provides a number of useful features. Employees can track the progress of workflow tasks they have an interest in, reviewing their status at any time. The system can be programmed to send reminders to the employee(s) responsible for a task after a predetermined period of time. Managers can also build flexibility into workflow tasks in terms of who can perform the task. For example, suppose that the Accounts Receivable (A/R) Department has three employees who can set credit limits. The A/R manager could create a workflow task to set a new customer's credit limit and send it to the Workflow inbox of all three A/R employees. When one of the employees completes the task, the system removes it from all three Workflow inboxes. The manager could also generate statistics on the number of workflow tasks handled by each employee and the average time taken to complete the tasks, resulting in better staffing decisions.

For regular, day-to-day business processes, workflow tools are not required. But for sporadic processes—those that are repeated frequently enough to justify the development costs—workflow tools are a powerful way to improve process efficiency and effectiveness.

IMPLEMENTING ERP SYSTEMS

In Chapter 2, you learned about some of the issues and challenges in implementing ERP systems. Implementation was particularly challenging in the late 1990s, as many firms rushed to implement ERP systems to avoid the Y2K problem. The explosive growth in demand for ERP implementations at that time caused a significant shortage of experienced consultants. Since 2000, the pace of implementations has slowed considerably. Most Fortune 500 firms have implemented an ERP system. The current growth area in ERP implementations is in the small to midsized business market, and vendors have been developing products, including Microsoft Dynamics and SAP Business One, tailored to this market.

Recall that the implementation of ERP is an ongoing process, not a one-time task. ERP systems are extremely complicated, and no company ever takes full advantage of all the capabilities in a system. Because of the challenges in the initial implementation of an ERP system, many firms limit the scope of the implementation projects to only what is absolutely necessary to operate the business, and rightly so. After the implementation is complete and the system is running smoothly, many firms seek to further improve their business processes by updating and expanding upon their original ERP system implementation. These follow-on implementation projects, while smaller than the initial ERP implementation, still require effective management.

ANOTHER LOOK

Business Process Improvement at Multi-Chem

What do you do when your organization grows so rapidly that documents start to fall through the cracks? Smart companies turn to business process management to help them get their organizations running more efficiency. Multi-Chem, an international specialty chemicals company selling to the oil and gas industry, did just that in an attempt to improve its business processes. The company is based in San Angelo, Texas, and has over 700 employees. Due to its rapid growth, the company's document approval processes had become slow and ineffective. Documents, such as vacation requests, were only trickling through an inefficient approval process and some were even languishing on workers' desks.

Before setting out to improve this inefficient business process, Multi-Chem's management established some criteria for the solution. The company wanted a program that was more than a simple email system; the solution had to be able to manage documents electronically, and it needed to be able to control the processes' workflow. Management also wanted to put the system in the user's hands, that is, they did not want a system that the IT Department would have to manage on a daily basis. In addition, the solution needed to be scalable since the company was growing fast.

The solution chosen by Multi-Chem was BP Logix's Process Director. Internally, Multi-Chem refers to the new system as eDocs. The company focused first on creating a new personnel request form, which is used for new hires and new positions. With the new system, Multi-Chem was able to design a user-friendly form that simplified the hiring process, and because the new form and process was so intuitive, it was widely accepted by employees. And through the system's use of audit trails, tracking authorizations has been simplified. Further implementation phases included the development of new documents and workflows for approving capital expenditures, training employees, and creating customer profiles.

Multi-Chem's eDocs system continues to save the company money and time. All employees are using eDocs, and the system has become a critical part of their work.

Question:

1. Think of an example of a paper-based inefficient business process, such as one you might see at a traditional doctor's office. How could an electronic document system that uses workflow improve the efficiency of that process?

ERP System Costs and Benefits

As you learned in Chapter 2, ERP implementation is expensive (with costs ranging between $10 million and $500 million, depending on company size). The costs of an ERP implementation include the following:

- *Software licensing fees*—ERP software is quite expensive, and most ERP vendors charge annual license fees based on the number of users.
- *Consulting fees*—ERP implementations require the use of consultants with the skills to configure the software to support the company's business processes. Good consultants have extensive experience in the way ERP systems function in practice, and they can help companies make decisions that avoid excessive data input, while capturing the information necessary to make managerial decisions.
- *Project team member time*—ERP projects require key people within the company to guide the implementation. These are team members who have detailed knowledge of the company's business. They work closely with the consultants to make sure the configuration of the ERP software supports the company's needs, which means these workers are frequently taken away from their daily responsibilities.
- *Employee training*—Project team members need training in the ERP software so they can work successfully with the consultants in the implementation. Those team members also frequently work with training consultants to develop and deliver company-specific training programs for all employees.
- *Productivity losses*—No matter how smoothly an ERP implementation goes, companies normally lose productivity during the first weeks and months after switching to a new ERP system.

To justify the costs associated with an ERP system, a company must identify a significant financial benefit that will be generated by the use of the software, but the only way a company can save money with an ERP system is by using it to support more efficient and effective business processes. This means that an implementation project should not just re-create the company's current processes and information systems, although that is a possibility since SAP provides the source code with its ERP package. A company could choose to alter the package through SAP's internal programming language, called Advanced Business Application Programming (ABAP)—which you first learned about in Chapter 2. With access to the SAP ERP source code, it is possible for a company to spend a significant sum of money on software code development to avoid changing a business process to the best practice process designed into the ERP software. Many companies have difficultly handling change and prefer to continue doing business as they always have—rather than adopting the best practices built into the ERP system.

As part of the implementation, a company must also manage the transfer of data from its old computer system to the new ERP system. In addition to managing master data such as materials data, customer data, vendor data, and so on, a company must also transfer transaction data, which includes sales orders and purchase orders, many of which are likely to be in various stages of processing—a challenging task.

IMPLEMENTATION AND CHANGE MANAGEMENT

How does a company ensure that its ERP investment pays off in increased profitability? The key challenge is not in managing technology, but in managing people. An ERP system changes how people work, and for the system to be effective, the change may have to be dramatic, going beyond the way employees interact with the software to the way they perform their tasks. Furthermore, business processes that are more effective require fewer people. Some employees will no longer be needed. It is no small thing to ask people to participate in a process that may not only change their day-to-day activities, but could also eliminate their current jobs.

Managing the human behavior aspects of organizational change is called **organizational change management (OCM)**. Do not underestimate the importance of this aspect of the implementation process. One of the keys to managing OCM is to realize that most people do not mind change, they mind *being* changed. If the ERP implementation is a project that is being forced on the employees, they will resist it. If employees view it as a chance to make the company more efficient and effective by improving business processes—and if these process improvements will make the company more profitable and therefore provide more job security—there is a greater likelihood that employees will support the implementation efforts. As mentioned earlier, the best way to improve a business process is to have the people most familiar with the process leverage their experience and creativity to develop process-improvement ideas. When employees have contributed to a process change, they have a sense of ownership and will be more likely to support the change.

Implementation Tools

Many tools are available to help manage implementation projects. Process mapping, described previously, is perhaps the most critical. For an ERP implementation to go smoothly and provide value, it is critical that a company understand both its *current* processes and the desired state of the processes *after* implementation.

SAP provides Solution Manager, a set of tools and information that helps companies manage the implementation of SAP ERP. In Solution Manager, the ERP implementation project is presented in an Implementation Roadmap, consisting of the following five phases:

- Project Preparation (15 to 20 days)
- Business Blueprint (25 to 40 days)
- Realization (55 to 80 days)
- Final Preparation (35 to 55 days)
- Go Live and Support (20 to 24 days)

Figure 7-17 shows an example of this roadmap. The left side of the Solution Manager screen shows a hierarchical menu structure that organizes each step in the implementation, and on the right side of the screen are the detailed items, the descriptions, documents, white papers, tools, and so on to support each step.

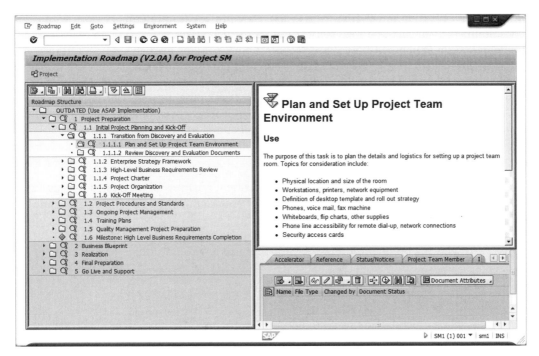

Source Line: SAP AG.

FIGURE 7-17　Implementation Roadmap in SAP's Solution Manager

The first phase of the Implementation Roadmap is Project Preparation. Some of the tasks in the Project Preparation phase include organizing the technical team, defining the system landscape (the computer servers, networking hardware, and peripherals necessary to operate the ERP system), selecting the hardware and database vendors, and most importantly, defining the project's scope—what the project is to accomplish. A common problem in ERP implementations is **scope creep**, which is the unplanned expansion of the project's goals and objectives. Scope creep causes the project to go over time and over budget and increases the risk of an unsuccessful implementation. Defining the project's scope ahead of time helps prevent this problem.

In the second phase, Business Blueprint, project team members produce detailed documentation of the business process requirements of the company. The Business Blueprint phase results in a detailed description of how the company intends to run its business with the SAP ERP system. Process mapping is critical in the Business Blueprint phase. The results of the Business Blueprint phase will guide consultants and project team members in configuring the SAP ERP system (which occurs in the third phase). During the Business Blueprint phase, technical team members determine the method of data transfer from the firm's existing computer systems (called legacy systems), which may be replaced by the ERP system or may continue to function with the ERP system through an interface.

In the Realization phase (the third phase), the project team members work with consultants to configure the ERP software in the development system. In an SAP implementation, a company uses three separate SAP systems over the course of the implementation process—a development system for configuring the SAP software to match the Business Blueprint, a test (or *quality assurance*) system for evaluating the software configuration, and a production system, on which the company runs the final software. The team also develops any necessary ABAP code or other tools (such as third-party software packages) and creates the required connections to the legacy systems.

The fourth phase, Final Preparation, is critical to the success of the implementation project. Tasks in this phase include:

- Testing the system throughput for critical business processes (determining whether it can handle the volume of transactions) in the quality assurance system
- Setting up the help desk where end users can get support
- Setting up operation of the production system and transferring data from legacy systems
- Conducting end-user training
- Setting the Go Live date

When scope creep occurs in a project, it is commonly not discovered until well into the Realization phase, when the team begins to miss deadlines, and the costs begin to exceed the budget. By the time the scope creep is discovered and its impact is understood, there is often little management can do to correct the problem, as most of the time and budget have been spent. In some cases, management chooses to shorten or omit the Final Preparation phase, which means that testing of the system and training of employees are reduced or eliminated. Unfortunately, with reduced testing, errors in configuring the system may not be discovered until it is put into use. Likewise, with reduced training, employees may not know how to use the system properly, which can create a complicated chain of problems, due to the integrated nature of the system. Any cost savings gained by shortening the Final Preparation phase are often overshadowed by productivity losses and consulting fees in the Go Live and Support phase.

In the fifth and final phase, Go Live and Support, the company begins using the new ERP system. Wise managers try to schedule the Go Live date for a period when the company is least busy. A properly staffed help desk is critical for the success of the Go Live phase because users have the most questions during the first few weeks of working with a new system. The SAP ERP project team members and consultants should be scheduled to work the help desk during the first few weeks of the Go Live period.

Although significant testing of the system and settings should have been done throughout the project, it is not possible to test all the settings and thoroughly evaluate the throughput of the system. Therefore, monitoring of the system during the Go Live and Support phase is critical so changes can be made quickly if the performance of the system is not satisfactory. Finally, it is important to set a completion date for the project. Any enhancements or extensions to the system should be managed as separate projects, not as extensions of the original implementation project.

ANOTHER LOOK

ERP Implementations Help Nonprofits

Direct Relief International, a nonprofit organization providing medical supplies and assistance to people affected by poverty, disaster, and civil unrest around the world, has used its recent implementation of an online community network to help those in need. While many nonprofits are well intentioned, they often lack the information they need to be effective. For instance, in the aftermath of the Haitian earthquake disaster in January 2010, many containers of medical supplies sat at airports, unable to reach their destination. With its online network, which is built on a foundation of SAP software, Direct Relief was able to supply victims of the earthquake with over $50 million in support—due to the organization's close attention to supply chain and logistics details.

Direct Relief initially implemented some SAP ERP modules in 2008, with a second phase in 2010. In the second stage, a new online community network interface was built using SAP's NetWeaver Portal. In addition, SAP's CRM, BusinessObjects, and Business Warehouse tools were used to create the online network, which brings donations together with need. Direct Relief's goal was to bring the efficiency of a profit-oriented company to its nonprofit organization. After users are registered and screened, they can log on to a secure portal to donate medicine and volunteer medical services. Those requesting aid can do the same to determine what supplies and services are available. The network was initially rolled out to users in the United States only; however, the new system was so successful that it has since been expanded to 70 countries.

According to Direct Relief's President and CEO, Thomas Tighe, the nonprofit has been "able to increase the flow of aid provided, help more people at a lower cost, and produce more precise reporting," all of which helps the organization match the needs of a particular group to that of a supplier of that required product or service. The new system also proved it is scalable. During the Haiti earthquake crisis, donations made through the network doubled in a two-week period, and over the course of a few days, the number of system users (donating and supplying) grew by 300 percent.

Ross Comstock, the IT director, also explains how the new system is highly user-friendly, "Because our product donors are offering products that are in many cases already in our warehouse, we decided to adapt the e-commerce functionality to have it face upstream as well—so we can take product donations through it, which I think is pretty innovative." The efficiency of running a real-time system with a single database and integrated processes has paid off in helping those in need.

Questions:

1. Do you think implementation of an ERP system into a nonprofit organization is different than in a traditional for-profit company? Why?
2. List at least three ways an ERP system can help nonprofit organizations, and support your answers using news articles that illustrate the problems that ERP would solve.

System Landscape Concept

For an ERP implementation, SAP recommends a system landscape like the one shown in Figure 7-18. In this system landscape, there are three completely separate SAP systems, designated as Development (DEV), Quality Assurance (QAS), and Production (PROD).

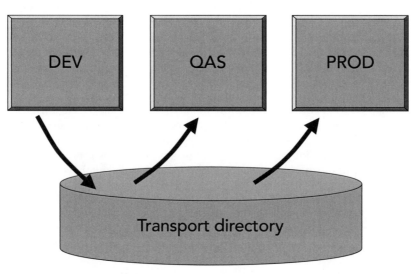

Source Line: Course Technology/Cengage Learning.

FIGURE 7-18   System landscape for SAP ERP implementation

The **Development (DEV) system** is used to develop configuration settings for the system, as well as special enhancements using ABAP code. These changes are automatically recorded in the **transport directory**, which is a special data file location on the DEV server. Changes recorded in the DEV system are imported into the **Quality Assurance (QAS) system**, where they are tested to make sure they function properly. If any corrections are needed, they are made in the DEV system and then transported again to the QAS system for testing. Once the configuration settings and ABAP programs pass testing in the QAS system, all settings, programs, and changes are transported to the **Production (PROD) system**, which is the system the company will use to run its business processes.

The use of separate systems is important during the initial implementation of an SAP ERP system, and it is even more important after the Go Live phase. All software packages have occasional updates, and having systems available to test these updates before applying them to a Production system can prevent problems. If a company wants to use features of the SAP ERP system that were not included in the initial project implementation, then the company should have a process like the one SAP provides to manage future changes to the production system in a controlled fashion.

Chapter Summary

- ERP systems provide the analysis and communication tools required to support efficient and effective business processes. Process modeling is a fundamental tool for understanding and analyzing business processes.

- Process mapping is a process-modeling tool that uses graphical representations to document business processes. Other process-modeling methodologies include hierarchical modeling, deployment flowcharting, and event process chain (EPC) diagramming. Value analysis is a technique that can be used to generate process-improvement ideas, and dynamic process modeling uses software to evaluate process improvements prior to implementation.

- ERP Workflow tools provide the ability to monitor and facilitate sporadic business processes so important work does not "fall through the cracks."

- Most challenges to ERP implementation involve managing personnel and their reactions to the change, rather than managing technical issues. Managing the human behavior aspects of organizational change is called organizational change management (OCM).

- SAP's Solution Manager is a set of tools and information that helps companies manage the implementation of SAP ERP software. In Solution Manager, the ERP implementation project is presented in an Implementation Roadmap, consisting of five phases.

- SAP's system landscape was introduced to show how changes to the ERP system during implementation (and beyond) are managed. In this system landscape, there are three completely separate SAP systems, designated as Development (DEV), Quality Assurance (QAS), and Production (PROD).

Key Terms

deployment flowcharting (swimlane flowcharting)

Development (DEV) system

dynamic process modeling

event process chain (EPC)

flowchart

gap analysis

hierarchical modeling

organizational change management (OCM)

process boundary

process mapping

process model

Production (PROD) system

Quality Assurance (QAS) system

scope creep

transport directory

value added

value analysis

workflow tools

workflow task

Exercises

1. Develop a process map for the following outdated course registration process in place at a local university:

    - Students first fill out forms listing their desired classes. They bring those completed forms to the academic advisement office, where, working with an advisor, they create a course selection document. Then, the student fills out a computer-readable form with the course and section number for all classes approved by the advisor. This form is submitted to the registration office where it is fed into a document reader, which electronically reads the completed forms; the data is then written to the master course schedule disk.

- At the end of the two-week registration period, data from the master course schedule disk is fed into the master scheduling program, which assigns students to courses. The scheduling program is designed to maximize the number of students who receive their requested courses while staying within class capacity limits. Once the master scheduling program has been updated for all students, the program produces three documents: (1) individual schedules for each student, (2) initial student lists for each class, and (3) the summary schedule report for the administration.

- After students receive their schedules, they are allowed to drop or add classes for a period of two weeks. To add or drop a class, a student must first obtain permission from the professor teaching the class. Once that signature is obtained on the drop/add form, the student brings the form to the computer center where the clerk enters the change into the scheduling system, which in turn updates the master course disk. The clerk then prints out a new schedule for that student.

2. Develop a swimlane process map for the online ordering process for Active Bicycle Company, shown below. Each of the following functions should be one swimlane: sales, accounting, warehouse, and shipping.

- The process begins when a customer submits an online order form to Active Bicycle via the Web. The customer supplies his or her name, address, email address, model number of the bicycle they desire, and credit card number.

- When the customer clicks on the Confirm button on the Web page, Active Bicycle's system gets approval for the transaction from the credit card company. If the credit charge is approved, the system assigns a number to the sales order, displays an order summary for the customer to print, and sends a confirmation email to the customer. If the credit charge is denied, the customer is asked to provide a different form of payment.

- The system then generates a two-part invoice, a stock release form, and a two-part packing slip form. The stock release form is sent to the Warehouse Department, and the two-part packing slip and one copy of the invoice are sent to the Shipping Department. The other copy of the invoice is maintained in a holding file in the Accounting Department to be filed later with the shipping certificate.

- In the warehouse, employees use the stock release form to pull the appropriate inventory to fill the order. Assuming there is enough stock (for the purposes of this exercise you can assume there is enough stock), the bicycle is packed into a special box for shipping, with added protection so it will not be damaged in transit. Using the stock release form, the warehouse staff inputs data into the inventory management program to update the master inventory file. The warehouse clerk also must take the information from the stock release form and manually fill out a shipping certificate, which is sent to the Accounting Department for a further check that the items are being released from the warehouse. The boxed inventory, along with the packing slip, is then sent to the Shipping Department.

- In the Shipping Department, one copy of the two-part packing slip is placed in the shipping department's file cabinet, and one is included with the goods to be sent to the customer.

- Back in the Accounting Department, the shipping certificate is matched with the copy of the invoice, and the accounting database is updated to record the completion of the order. The accounting program then submits a payment request to the credit card company, and both the shipping certificate and the invoice are filed in the accounting office.

3. Develop a process map for the following request-for-quote process:

- Your company assembles affordable washing machines from purchased parts. Your customers buy in bulk from you and then relabel the washing machines with their own brand. Customers typically want unique features for their washers, and they often submit a request for new features or other design changes, which results in a new model being created. Customers initiate the new design process by submitting a request for quotation (RFQ), which is a document that provides all the details for the new washing machine model, including the quantity to be ordered. Your company responds to the RFQ with a written quote, which details the cost for an order that would meet the requirements of the RFQ. Many different departments, as well as the manufacturers of the washing machine component parts, are involved in creating the quote. The Sales Department must work closely with the Costing Department, the Procurement Department, and the Assembly Department to provide a competitive quote to the customer. Create a swimlane flowchart to document the flow of information between departments and external partners in creating the quote, using the following information:
- The following internal departments are involved in the RFQ process:
  - Sales—Receives the customer's request for a price quote; creates the final quote and sends it to the customer.
  - Assembly—Prepares production documents that detail the labor, tools, and equipment required to produce the new washing machine.
  - Procurement—Creates RFQs for vendors for any new components needed for the new design.
  - Costing (Accounting)—Computes the final cost estimate.

- The following external parties are involved in the RFQ process:
  - Customer—Submits a request for a price quote; receives the completed RFQ.
  - Vendor—Receives the request for a quote on the cost of component parts, computes their costs, and submits a bid.

4. Develop an event process chain (EPC) diagram for the following staff-recruiting process at Yellow Brook Photography:

- The current recruitment process for Yellow Brook Photography takes approximately 90 days. It begins when a manager completes a requisition and sends it to the Human Resources Department. The Human Resources Department reviews and assigns a number to the requisition and returns it to the manager for approval. He or she approves it, obtains the required approval signatures, and then returns it to Human Resources.
- Next, Human Resources creates a job posting and announces the position internally through the company's intranet, bulletin boards, or a binder of current job openings. Human Resources collects responses internally for eight days. After that, Human Resources solicits résumés from external sources by advertising in newspapers and

online. Human Resources then prescreens the résumés and forwards information on qualified candidates to the hiring manager for review. The hiring manager tells Human Resources which candidates should be interviewed. Human Resources conducts brief phone interviews of candidates recommended by the hiring manager; if the phone interview is promising, Human Resources schedules an on-site interview. Candidates interview with the hiring manager and with a Human Resources staff member. Human Resources records the interviews in an applicant flow log.

- Once a candidate is selected for hire, Human Resources and the hiring manager prepare an offer, and a background check on the candidate is initiated. Then, the hiring manager must approve the offer and obtain the required approval signatures on a job offer approval form. Subsequently, the hiring manager extends the offer verbally to the candidate, while Human Resources sends the written offer, including an employment start date. Once the applicant accepts the offer, a drug screening is scheduled for the candidate, who must also sign the offer letter and return it to Human Resources. At that point, Human Resources notifies the hiring manager of the candidate's acceptance. Finally, if the drug test comes back negative, the new employee completes new-hire orientation on the first day of work.

For Further Study and Research

Bonneau, Lauren. "Direct Relief Brings Technology from the Commercial World to the Humanitarian World." *insiderProfiles*, 2, no. 4 (October 2011): 24–29.

Cordes, Ronald M. "Flowcharting: The Essential Tool of Quality." *Quality Digest*. January 1998. www.teamflow.com/qdjan98.html.

Coronado, Fernando. "Multi-Chem Relies on BPM Solution to Improve Operational Processes." *Business Process Trends*. February 1, 2011. http://www.bptrends.com/publicationfiles/ 02-01-11-CS-Multi-Chem-Relies%20on%20BPM-Coronado-final.pdf.

Hammer, Michael, and James Champy. *Reengineering the Corporation: A Manifesto for Business Revolution*. New York: HarperCollins. 1993.

Harmon, Paul. "Royal Pharmaceuticals Case Study." *Business Process Trends*. May 4, 2010. www.bptrends.com/publicationfiles/05-10-CS-Royal%20Pharmaceuticals-Metastorm.doc2.pdf.

Harrington, H. James. *Business Process Improvement: The Breakthrough Strategy for Total Quality, Productivity, and Competitiveness*. New York: McGraw-Hill, April 1991.

CHAPTER **8**

RFID, BUSINESS INTELLIGENCE (BI), MOBILE COMPUTING, AND THE CLOUD

LEARNING OBJECTIVES

After completing this chapter, you will be able to:

- Define RFID and its role in logistics and sales
- Define business intelligence (BI), and provide examples of its uses
- Explain how in-memory computing will change the use of BI
- Discuss the importance of mobile applications to businesses
- Describe cloud computing and why it is becoming important for ERP providers
- Explain how the service-oriented architecture (SOA) concept has changed ERP development
- Describe Web services, and outline the unique components of NetWeaver
- Define software as a service (SaaS), and identify the advantages and disadvantages of using this software delivery model

INTRODUCTION

This chapter examines advanced topics relevant to Enterprise Resource Planning (ERP) systems. As you have read in earlier chapters, an ERP system allows a company to accomplish tasks that cannot be done well, if at all, without such a system. Traditionally, ERP systems have been software applications that are run on a company's own computer systems, and the focus of ERP has been on managing business transactions. In this chapter, you will see how technologies such as radio frequency identification (RFID) are increasing the amount of data that is contained in ERP systems, how business intelligence technologies are turning this data into valuable information, and how cloud computing and mobile technologies are changing where ERP data is stored and how it is delivered.

RADIO FREQUENCY IDENTIFICATION (RFID) TECHNOLOGY

Radio frequency identification technology, known commonly as RFID, is becoming an increasingly efficient tool for tracking items through a supply chain. An RFID device, which can be attached to products, is a small package (or *tag*) made up of a microprocessor and an antenna. The location of an item with an RFID tag can be determined using an RFID reader, which emits radio waves and receives signals back from the tag. The reader is also sometimes called an interrogator because it "interrogates" the tag. Because microprocessors have continued to become more powerful and less expensive over time, the cost of RFID technology is approaching a level at which it is becoming inexpensive enough to be cost-effective for many businesses. Today, most materials are still tracked using bar codes and bar-code readers. However, bar-code labels can degrade in bad weather, and an employee must point a bar-code reader directly at a bar code to read it. RFID technology does not need this line-of-sight connection, and can withstand most environmental stresses.

Walmart has been on the leading edge of the move to integrate RFID technology into the supply chain. In 2003, Walmart announced that it would require its top 100 suppliers to begin tagging pallets and cases with RFID tags, which would allow Walmart to more efficiently track products through its logistics network. (A Walmart-sponsored report from the University of Arkansas' Information Technology Research Institute concluded that RFID reduced retail out-of-stock situations in stores by 16 percent.) However, by early 2007 reports began to surface that Walmart's RFID initiative was not progressing as planned. Although Walmart publicly denied that it was experiencing any issues with its RFID technology, by October 2007, the company announced a major change in its RFID strategy, shifting its focus to the use of RFIDs in its stores rather than in its distribution centers. Unfortunately, Walmart still faced the reality that the cost for RFID tags was still too high to put on individual items, even though that is the area from which the biggest benefit would come. The major opportunity for RFID technology to reduce out-of-stock situations is not in the supply chain between the manufacturer and the storeroom at the individual store, but between the backroom stock area and the store shelves.

Walmart initiated its third RFID initiative in July 2010, announcing that it would begin requiring suppliers to place removable RFID smart tags on individual apparel items. According to Raul Vazquez, the executive in charge of Walmart stores in the western United States, the "ability to wave the wand and have a sense of all the products that are on the floor or in the backroom in seconds is something that we feel can really transform our business." The potential return on investment of technologies that can improve inventory accuracy is particularly high in a clothing retail setting, especially in terms of avoiding out-of-stock situations. A story may have 100 pairs of blue jeans on display racks, but if there is not a pair in a customer's size, then a sale is not possible. A 2007 pilot project at American Apparel Inc. resulted in sales increases of 14.3 percent in stores that using RFID technology. Garment-level RFID tags also have the potential to reduce employee theft by making it easier to check stockroom inventory and determine what items are missing.

Pharmaceutical firms are also evaluating the use of RFID technology to comply with requirements to combat counterfeit drugs. Regulatory agencies such as the FDA are developing rules that would require companies to track pharmaceutical products down to the package level. California is leading this trend with their ePedigree law that will take effect on a staggered basis from January 1, 2015, through July 1, 2017. An ePedigree is an electronic record that contains information regarding each transaction in the supply chain that results in a change of ownership of the given prescription drug, from initial manufacturer to returns from retailers. To accomplish this, manufacturers must create a unique serial number for the smallest package size that can be sold to a consumer.

RFID technology is also being employed to track medical devices. For example, Spectrum Health's Meijer Heart Center is using RFID technology to track stents—wire mesh tubes that are implanted into weakened or narrowed cardiac arteries to keep them open. The Meijer Heart Center implants thousands of stents each year, and managing the inventory of stents is challenging. Stents are small, but can cost up to $2,000 each. In addition, stents have an expiration date. In the past, manual systems were used to manage stents, a time-consuming process that was error prone. Inventory accuracy in the old system was 95 percent accurate—a figure that might sound good at first glance, but not when you consider that if the heart center handles 2,000 stents per year (at $2,000 each), a 5 percent inventory error becomes a $200,000 problem.

With the new system, stents are stored in RFID-enabled cabinets. Attached to each stent is an RFID tag, which provides it with a unique identification number. To withdraw a stent for use, a nurse swipes his or her ID card to a device attached to the cabinet. Through the device, the nurse can then access a list of patients in the hospital database. The nurse identifies the patient requiring the stent, and the cabinet unlocks. Then all the nurse has to do is remove the required stents from the cabinet; the RFID technology tracks which stents have been removed for the patient. In addition to tracking the removal of inventory, the system sends the information on the stents used to the hospital's information system for patient billing. The system also monitors inventory levels and triggers an order for new stents when necessary. If some of the stents that were removed for a patient are not used, the nurse can return the stents to the cabinet, and the RFID device will automatically credit the patient's account. The system also tracks expiration dates so employees can make sure those stents are used before their expiration date. With the new RFID cabinet system, Spectrum's inventory accuracy for stent inventory is now nearly 100 percent.

ANOTHER LOOK

RFID and Corporate Culture

American Apparel is a unique company even by the standards of the fashion industry. The company was founded in 1989 by Dov Charney, who started out in the clothing business as a college student selling t-shirts. Eventually, Charney built American Apparel into a vertically integrated fashion company that makes its clothing in Los Angeles rather than importing it from manufacturers in low-wage countries. In addition to manufacturing its own clothes, American Apparel designs its own garments, which it sells through a network of company-owned stores. The company also creates all of its advertising and marketing materials (which are known for generating heated controversy).

However, while the American Apparel was cultivating a hip image in the world of retail, it was also developing a reputation for being soft on shoplifting. Former employees allege that managers were asked to turn a blind eye to shoplifting so the "right type of person" would be wearing American Apparel clothing. In addition, lax internal controls over shipping and delivery combined with young store employees allegedly hired more for their looks than for their management ability led to high levels of employee theft. In an initial trial of RFID tags on garments in 2007, American Apparel found that inventory "shrinkage"—a reduction in inventory due to human error, theft, or damage—was 20 percent, double the retail industry average. Employee theft was clearly a significant portion of this high level of shrinkage.

While reducing theft is an important part of American Apparel's RFID initiative, improved customer service is the primary goal. With RFID, American Apparel can use a continuous replenishment process to ensure on-shelf availability of their products. RFID also improves on-the-rack availability and inventory control at American Apparel by reducing mistaken identity. Many of American Apparel's styles look similar, and manually inputting inventory data increases inventory accuracy problems. Stores with the RFID technology now have inventory accuracy above 99 percent, and in many stores, the RFID technology has paid for itself within 6 months, based on inventory cost savings. "We measure everything, and have accountability of every item. Every item counts, and when we change that culture, employees start treating products better," says Stacey Shulman, American Apparel's vice president of technology. On February 8, 2012, American Apparel reported that it intends to equip all of its 285 stores with RFID technology.

Questions:

1. RFID technology allows a company to more accurately track employee performance—from mistakes in inventory handling to theft. How would you feel about working at a company that used RFID technology to monitor your performance? Do you think this use of technology is good for a company's culture?

2. In what other industries might RFID technology have an impact similar to that seen at American Apparel?

BUSINESS INTELLIGENCE/BUSINESS ANALYTICS

The combination of technologies such as RFID and mobile computing (described in the following section) with traditional ERP system data is providing companies with an exponential growth in business data. While this data plays a fundamental role in the day-to-day operations of a business, it also provides an opportunity for a company to perform sophisticated analyses to determine ways to improve its business. **Business intelligence (BI)**, also referred to as *business analytics*, is a term used to describe a range of different applications and technologies used to extract and analyze large amounts of data to aid in decision making. BI includes data-mining tools and querying tools, which are often interactive and visual. The growth of data-generating technologies such as RFID, combined with improvements in BI tools, has led to significant growth in the BI market. Prior to 2008, almost all of SAP's ERP business came from traditional ERP suite applications. However, in the period from 2008 to 2011, the percentage of the business that came from BI rose to 50 percent.

Figure 8-1 shows a framework for how SAP views BI.

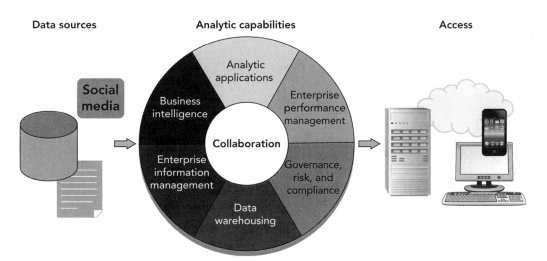

Source Line: Course Technology/Cengage Learning.

FIGURE 8-1   SAP Business Intelligence (BI) framework

On the left side of the diagram are the potential BI data sources, which are growing both in number and in the volume of data produced. For example, sources such as Facebook, Twitter, and other social media applications can provide information on consumer reaction to new products.

The center section represents the analytical capabilities of BI; it includes items such as analytic applications and business intelligence, which are similar sets of data analysis tools. In SAP's framework, analytic applications are data analysis tools applied to specific industries, such as financial services, manufacturing, consumer products, retail, and utilities or to functional areas, such as supply chain management, finance, human resources, IT, and service, sales, and marketing. SAP BI includes a set of tools for exploration, analysis, and presentation that can be applied to a wide range of business questions. Enterprise performance management is the concept of developing strategic goals for the organization and then gathering data to evaluate how the organization is performing in relation to those goals. The governance, risk, and compliance category represents a group of activities focused on ensuring an organization is functioning ethically and legally. Governance refers to the processes that ensure that top management is receiving accurate and timely data necessary to run the organization and that control mechanisms are in place to make sure that management directions and instructions are being carried out. Risk, or risk management, consists of processes to identify risks to the organization (technological, financial, information security, supply chain disruptions, and so on) and to develop plans to minimize the potential damage to these risks. Compliance means conforming to stated requirements, which could be customer specifications for goods or services, Sarbanes-Oxley reporting requirements (discussed in Chapter 5), or state and federal regulations such as those relating to product safety. Data warehousing is the technology used to store the large volumes of data used in the analysis. **Enterprise information management** is a relatively new term that describes the business and technology functions that manage information as a corporate asset.

The final section of the diagram in Figure 8-1 is titled "Access," and it describes how users will access BI. Previously, this was primarily through personal computers, but with the growth in mobile technology, an increasing variety of devices can now be used to access BI.

IN-MEMORY COMPUTING

Up until recently, BI systems have typically accessed data that was stored on data warehouse servers, which use hard disk technology to store data. Data stored in data warehouse servers usually consist of aggregated data—from an ERP system or other sources. To speed access to this data, the data in a data warehouse are structured as **multidimensional data cubes**, which allow for relationships in the data to be analyzed quickly. For example, a company might want to look at sales over time, by store, and by product. This means analyzing sales along three dimensions, and the sales data would need to be structured as a three dimensional cube. If the company was also interested in looking at these sales by geographic region, it would need a four dimensional data cube.

There are two main challenges with using a multidimensional cube structure. First, a significant level of technical expertise is needed to construct a cube, which means that an IT specialist rather than an end user usually must complete this task. In practice, the end user and an IT specialist usually have to collaborate to construct the correct multidimensional data cube, and frequently they do not speak the same language—that is, the end user thinks in terms of business problems while the IT specialist thinks in terms of database technology. Second, the multidimensional cube is a structure that necessarily restricts how the data can be analyzed.

In Chapter 2, we introduced the topic of SAP's HANA in-memory computing technology. HANA allows customers to analyze large amounts of data instantly. The key to this technology is that data is stored in computer memory rather than on hard disk servers.

The time required to access data from memory is a small fraction of the time required to access data from a hard disk. The primary performance measure for data storage systems is latency, which is the time between when a request is made for data from a storage device and when the data is delivered. For hard disk storage, typical latency is currently around 13 milliseconds. For memory, the latency is around 83 nanoseconds. To understand the significance of this speed differential, think of in-computer memory as an F-18 fighter jet that can travel at a speed of 1,190 miles per hour and disk memory as a banana slug with a top speed of 0.007 miles per hour. With such a substantial difference in speed, the obvious question is why would data warehouses use disk memory? The answer is storage capacity. Hard disk storage is now being measured in terabytes, while the maximum capacity of memory chips is still in the gigabytes—so hard disks can store one thousand times more data than memory for a comparable cost. While hard disks can store significantly more data than memory chips, the cost and capacity of in-computer memory have reached levels at which in-memory BI is becoming more feasible.

Data compression is another technology that makes in-memory BI possible. Figure 8-2 shows data for an SAP ERP data table used to store material master data. This is a typical SAP ERP table; it consists of 223 data fields, which are the column headings.

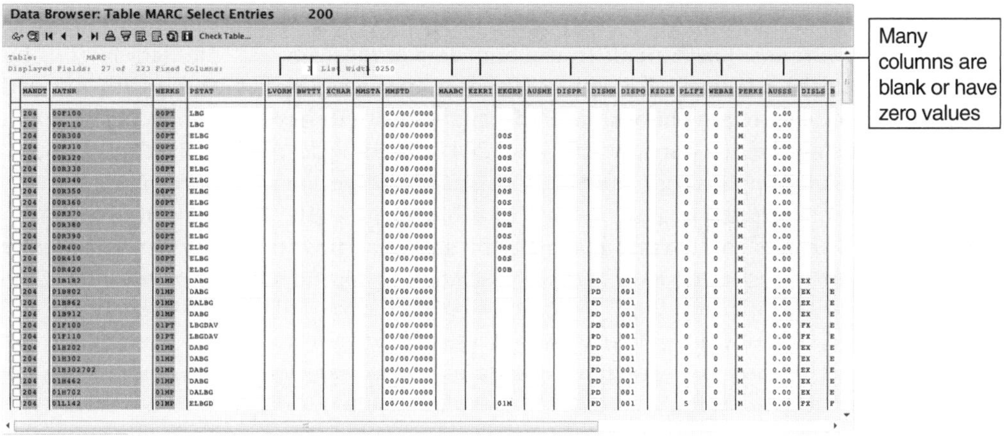

Source Line: SAP AG.

FIGURE 8-2   Material master data table

As shown in Figure 8-2, many of the fields, or columns, in the data table are blank or contain values of zero. By storing the data as columns rather than rows, in-memory systems can reduce the size of the data by eliminating the large numbers of blank or zero values by just noting their positions in the table. Essentially the system says "this entire column is zero" or "the next 100 items in this column are zero." When you look across the rows of the table, the number of zero or blank values are not as large, so the saving from noting zero or blank values are not nearly as large.

With the data compression provided by column storage, it is now feasible to store large volumes of data in memory without aggregation. This means that multidimensional cubes are not required. An end user can analyze BI data "on the fly" without needing an IT specialist to translate the data into multidimensional cubes.

SAP is not the only ERP provider with in-memory capability. In February 2012, Oracle released its in-memory solution for business analytics called Exalytics. Both SAP's and Oracle's in-memory solutions are designed to analyze what is now being termed "big data." Big data refers to the enormous amount of data that is now available for BI use from all the available sources, including ERP systems, Web sites, corporate databases, scientific research, Twitter, and other social networking applications. Big data needs fast computing to be usable, and in-memory computing allows for rapid processing. New chips designs, such as chips made from carbon rather than silicon, may be the answer to creating even faster machines. Computing's processing is moving towards memory and away from the processor, according to experts in the field such as John E. Kelly, the head of IBM research. Big data is generating a lot of interest and investments from large companies. The total investment in big data technology is in the billions of dollars, which includes investments by many companies other than SAP and Oracle, including IBM, Microsoft, and Hewlett-Packard.

Many feel that BI and its capabilities are strategic assets to an organization that can be used to enhance future growth and viability, and some experts now say that companies should be hiring a chief data officer who can link the data with the computing power and the strategy of the organization.

According to Gartner Research, in 2011, only 30 percent of employees in organizations with BI tools were actually using them. This low rate of use is due to the fact that BI software is often difficult to use and slow to perform, and the data is sometimes of limited relevance for end users. Gartner anticipates that as BI tools become easier to use, organizations with BI capabilities will have about 50 percent of their workers using the software by the year 2015. Worldwide revenue in the business intelligence, analytic applications, and performance management software market rose 16 percent to $12.2 billion in 2011 from $10.5 billion in 2010, according to a report from Gartner. SAP was the market leader in BI and analytics with a 24 percent market share. The report also showed that BI analytics was the top technology priority for CIOs in 2012.

ANOTHER LOOK

Recovery.gov

Even the federal government is getting into the BI arena. As part of the American Recovery and Reinvestment Act of 2009 (also known as the "Recovery Act"), the Recovery.gov Web site was created to serve as "the U.S. government's official website that provides easy access to data related to Recovery Act spending and allows for the reporting of potential fraud, waste, and abuse." With an interactive, user-friendly interface and a set of highly interactive BI tools, the site allows the average citizen to easily review the various destinations for tax dollars spent under the Recovery Act. The site's BI tools let users review preexisting charts and graphs or create their own. Filters are available for the data, and the results can be emailed or exported. Figure 8-3 shows a sample output of the top 10 states by funds awarded from the Recovery Act of 2009, as an example of a BI query.

(continued)

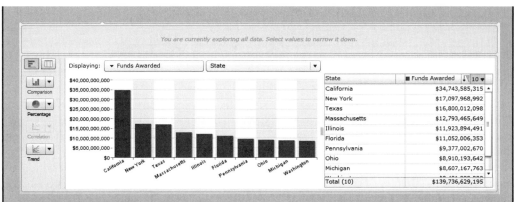

Source Line: Recovery.gov.

FIGURE 8-3   Recovery.gov's top 10 awards for states from the Recovery Act

Question:

1. Go to the Recovery.gov Web site, and run a set of analytics to compare Recovery Act spending for your state with that of a neighboring state. Determine the top three projects funded in each state, and provide a brief description of them in a memo to your instructor.

ANOTHER LOOK

Real-Time Business Intelligence (BI)

BI is now used for real-time monitoring of systems and is capable of sending out alerts based on the results of the BI. United Parcel Service (UPS) uses complex computerized event processing to monitor the transactions related to the millions of packages it ships daily around the globe. In its old system, reports would be run each evening to monitor the server loads on the computers that maintained these important transactions. If a problem occurred, UPS would find out about it the next morning. With real-time BI, which includes easy-to-understand dashboards and analytics, problems are identified immediately, and automatic emails are sent to alert employees of any problems with the company's computer systems.

Another example of the use of real-time BI is at Insurance.com, where its new IBM Cognos Now system helps the company cope with its e-commerce transactions. With Cognos Now, Insurance.com is able to monitor network performance and make any necessary changes immediately. For example, when a new call comes in to Insurance.com's call center, the business intelligence system scans for available agents and alerts the CRM software, which routes the call to one of the free agents.

Question:

1. How could real-time BI help an organization like Fitter monitor its IT systems? Be specific in your answer.

MOBILE COMPUTING

With the sale of smartphones and tablet computers exceeding that of personal computers in 2011, many organizations are facing the necessity of developing and deploying their own mobile applications. Often these efforts are driven by the expectations of young workers who—having grown up with mobile computing and a myriad of mobile apps, such as Facebook—are appalled at some companies' existing legacy systems. It is predicted that by the year 2015, there will be more than 6.7 billion smartphones in the world, and a 2011 survey conducted by *CIO* magazine found that 54 percent of the companies responding were planning to increase their spending on mobile applications. People are relying on smartphones for social networking and shopping information, with the lines of work and play often blurred. With today's smartphone—40 times more powerful than those in 2000—and cloud computing (discussed in the next section) making data available wherever a person is, it is not surprising there is pressure on companies to increase their support of mobile apps.

There are, however, many challenges to face. For example, smartphones come in a wide range of formats and operate on a variety of operating systems, and mobile applications need to be developed with that in mind. Many experts agree that to develop effective applications, companies cannot simply take computer-based applications and modify them for use on mobile devices. Rather, mobile applications need to be developed from scratch to take into account the limitations in screen size and user input capability. Companies must also set up a road map for implementation, deciding which applications may be high cost and low value (eliminate) or low cost and high value (adopt). There are many questions to answer as well: Should a company require its employees to use company-supplied devices, or should employees be allowed to supply their own smartphones? If employees are allowed to use their own smartphone, should a company limit the choice of devices or allow employees to choose the device they will use? Accenture Consulting, for example, estimates that 85,000 of its employees use smartphones, of which more than one-half are provided by the individual employee. If an employee supplies his or her own device, who will support it? Which carrier will be used? Security is always a concern, especially because most security breaches are caused by users not by technology. It has been estimated that only slightly over one-half of all smartphone users set up their password security on their phones. If a company does not directly support a device it might not be able to ensure that proper security measures are taken, which could allow for potential data breaches. Some organizations are attempting to manage mobile devices from central servers, so if a device is lost or stolen, sensitive data can be removed or the device can be wiped clean.

ERP companies have provided mobile connections in the past, but most are ramping up their offerings. For example, SAP recently acquired Sybase, a company with a platform called Sybase Unwired, which lets a company quickly develop mobile apps for almost any mobile device. Another Sybase tool, Afaria, allows IT staff to manage those mobile apps centrally and push out new applications and updates remotely. If a device is lost or stolen, the central administrator can delete the application remotely.

Although mobile device apps are typically thought of as tools to provide users with information, mobile devices can also be the source of information. For example, the increasing sophistication of smartphones is leading people to use their smartphones—rather than dedicated GPS devices—for navigation. Smartphone users can also subscribe to traffic information services that may use static sensors or traffic cameras to augment the built-in maps so users can avoid accidents and rush-hour traffic. Increasingly, this traffic information is also being provided by other smartphone users. For example, when a user of the Google Maps for mobile application chooses to enable the My Location option, which shows the user's location on the map, it sends anonymous bits of data back to Google describing how fast the user is moving. By combining the data of thousands of phones moving around a city at any given time, Google can provide an accurate picture of live traffic conditions. This traffic data is then provided to mobile users in the Google Maps traffic layers.

ANOTHER LOOK

Corporate and Military Apps

Companies are now using mobile applications (apps) in unique ways, and many companies are creating their own internal app stores. For example, the pharmaceutical company, Pfizer, has an app that helps employees who are traveling find and contact other Pfizer employees who are also traveling. Aflac, an insurance company, has an app that allows claims adjusters to see data and coordinate insurance claims on a mobile device without having to go to a computer and log onto the main enterprise system. For disaster recovery, Deloitte Consulting created an app called Bamboo, which can push emergency information out to employees' smartphones in the event of an emergency. Deloitte is implementing the app internally, and in the future, the firm plans to offer it to its customers.

The military is also a major potential user of specialized mobile devices and apps. Harris, an electronics and communications company is working on an app for tablet computers, such as Apple's iPad, to control the remote camera on an Unmanned Aerial Vehicle (UAV). While there are durability issues with using a commercial tablet in harsh environments, it could make economic sense to use a $400 tablet in a rugged case instead of a $10,000 wireless receiver. If a tablet breaks, it is much cheaper to replace. In addition, because these devices are familiar to many young soldiers from their personal experience, training costs are reduced.

In April 2011, Textron announced that the U.S. Army was beginning tests of SoldierEyes, a smartphone-based battle analysis and tracking system the company has been developing. According to Textron, this application would allow every soldier to act as a sensor. Using this application, soldiers could collect and report real-time mission critical data, incorporating photos and video, which can be linked to the geographic location of the soldier. With SoldierEyes, this information can be communicated (via the SoldierEyes Application Cloud) to existing command, control, communications, intelligence, and surveillance systems using 3G/4G cellular and Wi-Fi networks. For remote areas where these networks are not available, Textron has developed a secure mobile battlefield cellular network called FASTCOM, which can use manned and unmanned aircraft, aerostats (tethered blimps), or ground vehicles to provide cellular coverage.

Question:

1. Choose an industry in which you might eventually like to work. Think of three types of mobile apps that could be used to help you work more efficiently in that industry. Use the Internet to find out if those apps have been developed by any company. Present your findings in a one-page report to your instructor.

FROM INTERNET-ENABLED TO CLOUD COMPUTING

Cloud computing can be defined in simple terms as the delivery of a software product to a user via the Internet. The user typically accesses the cloud product through a Web browser or a lightweight (meaning small and simple) application for a computer or mobile device. Cloud computing is not a completely new concept, rather it simply represents the latest stage of the development of computing and the Internet. To better understand how cloud computing will impact ERP system development, it is useful to review the development of SAP's ERP systems with the advent of the Internet.

SAP and the Internet

In 1996, SAP introduced its joint Internet strategy with Microsoft. The core of SAP's first effort to integrate the Internet with its products was the Internet Transaction Server (ITS) a server-based software system that enabled efficient communication between an SAP ERP system and the Internet. To provide some context for the state of the Internet at this time—in 1996, Amazon.com was only one year old, and the online travel agencies Expedia and Travelocity were both just being founded. Many other Internet services we take for granted today did not exist at this time.

In May 1999, SAP announced mySAP.com, a new strategy designed to completely realign the company and its product portfolio. The goal of this initiative was to combine e-commerce solutions with SAP's existing ERP applications, using cutting-edge Web technology. In 2000, SAP began building on the mySAP.com vision by adding the capability for electronic marketplaces and corporate portals.

NetWeaver

In 2004, SAP introduced its first version of SAP NetWeaver, a collection of components that support business transactions over the Internet by providing seamless connectivity of diverse applications. By the end of the year, over 1,000 customers had acquired the product. With the introduction of NetWeaver, SAP announced that it was planning its future initiatives around the concept of enterprise **service-oriented architecture** (enterprise SOA), with a goal of making all of its business applications service based—to provide its customers with the most flexibility possible.

E-commerce needs are driving companies to connect their business applications, such as ERP systems, both internally and externally through the Internet. Software designed with an SOA can be quickly deployed and reconfigured as business conditions require changes to the applications, databases, and other infrastructure hosted in data centers owned by a company. The combination of software tools that enables an organization's various systems and applications to communicate with other applications is called **Web services**. SAP's NetWeaver is a Web services platform that allows various vendor applications to share data over the Internet.

Companies continue to warm to the idea of Web services and SOA. *Information Age*'s "Effective IT" research report found that 50 percent of enterprises have some sort of SOA strategy. One benefit of adopting SOA is the ability to quickly add new applications, making the organization more responsive. SOA also relies on open standards, allowing easier integration of software and offering the potential to reuse computer code, which can reduce the time and cost of implementing new systems. This aspect of SOA is certainly enticing, especially when compared with traditional systems that are often cumbersome and time consuming to implement. However, implementing SOA is not easy. The IT analyst group Ovum reported that one in five U.S. companies implementing SOA have experienced "unexpected complexity."

The return on an SOA investment is often difficult to determine. According to a study published by Nucleus Research, only 37 percent of 106 organizations polled claimed that their SOA projects had a positive ROI. Respondents indicated that the main benefit of SOA was the ability to reuse computer code.

NetWeaver Tools and Capabilities

SAP's NetWeaver platform is a collection of modules, including Enterprise Portal, Mobile Infrastructure, Business Intelligence, Master Data Management, and Exchange Infrastructure.

The SAP Enterprise Portal gives users complete access to all their work on a single screen, using links to connect users to all the major applications needed to perform their jobs. The Enterprise Portal acts as a central access point to a company's intranet (its secure, internal network), operating through a secure link on a browser. For example, a user in the Finance Department could set up Enterprise Portal with links to SAP ERP financial transaction processes, as well as links to financial metrics for the company, stock market indices, email, a calendar, and other information important for that person's job.

The advantage of having a personalized portal is its efficiency. A user only has to log on to one system to get all the information needed to perform his or her job. Without a portal, users often have to log on to multiple systems, such as an ERP system, email, industry exchanges, or suppliers' sites. Transferring information between systems is frequently difficult. With the Enterprise Portal, all information is available through the Web services provided by NetWeaver. All the important links are presented in one screen, and transferring data is simplified by the ability to "drag-and-relate" data from one area to another.

NetWeaver's Mobile Infrastructure module allows users to access and work with data through mobile devices such as smartphones and pagers. Mobile Infrastructure provides remote access to data within a company's SAP system and other information systems. The benefits are obvious. A salesperson could use his or her smartphone to see a customer's historical order information while in the middle of a sales call with that customer. Connecting SAP and VoiceObjects AG adds voice capability to NetWeaver, allowing users to enter data into the SAP CRM system using voice commands from their cell phones. Linking the SAP and VoiceObjects AG systems can be done without middleware or any changes to the software.

Another facet of NetWeaver is the linkage with SAP's Business Intelligence (BI) data warehouse and analytical tools. With the Enterprise Portal, BI can be delivered in a personalized fashion. It can integrate information from various sources and processes, both within and outside of the firm. BI works with any database management software and any operating system that is running NetWeaver.

Another NetWeaver module, Master Data Management, provides data consistency within a company's SAP system. NetWeaver allows a seamless Web interface to ensure proper data synchronization. While this interface simplifies the data synchronization process, it is not automatic—users with the proper knowledge and skills are still needed to manage this process.

NetWeaver's Exchange Infrastructure module allows different applications to share data. By adhering to the standard of the Exchange Infrastructure, companies can eliminate the need to write code to enable different applications to share data. For example, using Exchange Infrastructure, a business can keep its current electronic data interchange (EDI) system and seamlessly integrate that with its ERP system. SAP's Web Application Server, the development environment that is the foundation of NetWeaver, gives Exchange Infrastructure its customizability.

NetWeaver at Work for Fitter

Now we will examine how NetWeaver could help Fitter. Assume that Fitter has an SAP ERP system and that Fitter's two top salespeople, Amy Sanchez and Donald Brown, are busy selling NRG bars directly to customers and to distributors. Amy works from home, and she logs on to the SAP system with her laptop computer, using the SAP GUI. She does not know much about the SAP system, nor does she have to. She needs to know how to place customer orders and check on their status. When Amy goes on a sales call, she brings her calculator and notepad with her to determine quote prices and jot down order details. When she returns home, she plugs those numbers into the SAP system and confirms her quotes. Amy would like to have some additional information on how salespeople in other regions are doing and what mix of bars they are promoting, but she does not know how to access any of that information. She also would like to see if there are new ways to market to her customers.

Donald Brown sells Fitter's BRG bars to distributors, and he has been chosen by his manager to test SAP NetWeaver for possible implementation at Fitter. With this new capability, Donald's work day has changed dramatically. During the test, Donald logs on to his Enterprise Portal, which was tailored for his job, using his office computer. When he does so, he can see his email, sales figures from his top 10 customers, data on production and inventory, the current stock quote for Fitter on the NASDAQ exchange, the current market price for oats, wheat germ, and honey, and the local weather report. Today, Donald will make an important sales call for a regional grocery chain. He grabs his smartphone and some extra business cards, and heads out the door. During lunch with the purchasing manager for the grocery chain, Donald is able to check up-to-the-minute details on current sales orders and can confirm promises to ship additional bars to the customer next week, thanks to SAP's Mobile Infrastructure. Back at the office, Donald calls up the Business Intelligence module in NetWeaver. From there, he can run a few reports to find out which snack bars are selling best nationwide, grouped by region and time of year. He can also analyze snack bar sales using data mining, to find sales patterns that can help him plan future sales calls.

Exercise 8.1

1. Now that you have read about the features of SAP's NetWeaver and have learned how Amy Sanchez and Donald Brown perform their duties at Fitter, try to convince Fitter's CEO to implement NetWeaver across the organization. Write a memo to the CEO outlining your arguments.

2. The CEO is impressed with your work but has asked you for an ROI (return on investment) analysis. How would you begin doing that? What numbers do you need, and who are the people you would have to interview to get those numbers?

SAAS: SOFTWARE AS A SERVICE

Software as a service (SaaS) is a software delivery model in which a software product is hosted by a company—such as SAP—on its servers and is accessed by customers via a Web browser. Some people describe SaaS as a utility, similar to a telephone or electric company. It is simply a way to sell and distribute software that uses the Internet. While definitions vary, this book treats SaaS as a subset of cloud computing. For example, Amazon and Apple are promoting data storage "on the cloud," but the applications that use that data are stored on the device, updated regularly from the cloud (Internet).

A recent Forrester Research report claims that the analytics portion of SaaS will become highly important to the users of this software delivery model. Users will be also be looking for SaaS applications that can integrate social media with a company's other sources of information. According to the report, adopters of SaaS should also consider how their service providers can handle mobile apps.

SAP Business ByDesign

One example of SaaS for the ERP market is SAP's Business ByDesign. First released in 2007, Business ByDesign is a full ERP system delivered to customers via the cloud. For small to medium-sized companies, it lowers the total cost of ownership of the software and enables a rapid and smooth implementation. Customers can choose to have SAP handle the implementation of Business ByDesign, or they can manage the implementation themselves. As shown in Figure 8-4, the main screen of BBD displays easy-to-understand menu paths.

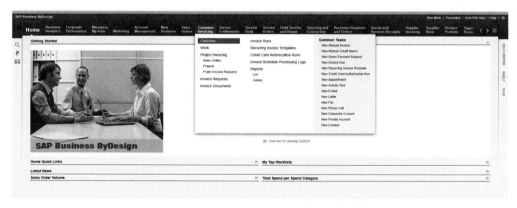

Source Line: SAP AG.

FIGURE 8-4 SAP Business ByDesign main screen

Small organizations such as PlaNet Finance, which offers microloans to customers in 30 international offices, often find that Business ByDesign is a good fit for their needs. With Business ByDesign, PlaNet was able to reduce its costs while improving reporting to donors. In terms of cost, the full Business ByDesign package will run a company about

$90 per month per user. There are different facets of Business ByDesign, which are illustrated in the Figure 8-5.

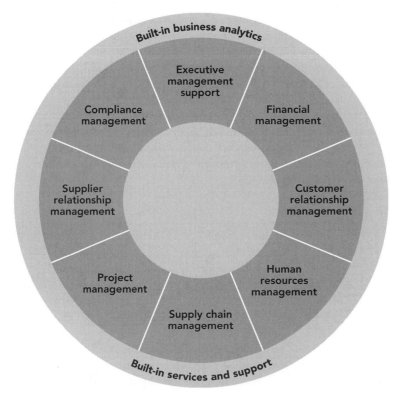

Source Line: Course Technology/Cengage Learning.

FIGURE 8-5   SAP Business ByDesign's key capabilities

Advantages of Using SaaS

Many companies find a number of advantages with using the SaaS model, including:

- *Initial affordability*—Companies that previously could not afford to purchase an ERP system—or another application—can now "lease" one on a monthly basis, avoiding the high cost of obtaining the hardware and software and hiring and training support personnel, thereby reducing their TCO (total cost of ownership). The lower cost to implement software provided through SaaS means that companies can explore whether a particular software package will work for them without a large, up-front expense.
- *Shorter implementation time*—The time required for implementation is usually shorter with the SaaS model as the user does not have to worry about the technical issues; the provider has servers, telecommunications systems,

and highly trained personnel already in place. The SaaS provider handles all the maintenance, including execution of backups, training, and customizing of the system.

- *Lower support costs and complexity*—Companies that make use of the SaaS model do not need to hire additional IT personnel to implement new systems and applications. SaaS providers can also run information systems more efficiently because they do it on a large scale; they can spread fixed costs over many users, thus achieving economies of scale that translate into a lower total cost of ownership. In addition, an SaaS provider usually has an easier time attracting, training, and retaining a talented workforce than a small manufacturing company like Fitter.

Disadvantages of Using SaaS

There are some potential downsides to using SaaS, and companies should consider these carefully before choosing an SaaS provider:

- *Security*—Companies using SaaS are turning their information systems over to a third party. They must be confident that the SaaS provider has a high level of security. An SaaS provider will typically have data from multiple clients on a single piece of hardware. Each customer's data must be shielded from other customers. Although this is a legitimate area of concern for clients looking to move to the SaaS model, the reality is that SaaS providers often have better security systems in place than many small companies do.
- *Bandwidth/response time*—The telecommunications channel from the SaaS provider to its customers must be fast enough to handle multiple users, and the SaaS must have sufficient hardware to provide the necessary computer processing capabilities.
- *Flexibility*—The SaaS provider should be flexible in working with its users and satisfying their requests for software modifications and enhancements.
- *No frills*—SaaS software providers can usually provide basic systems well, but asking for unusual configurations may cause problems, and the SaaS provider might not allow for third-party add-ons. Further, the provider might not want to develop custom software, or it may not be affordable for a small company.
- *Technical, not business focus*—An SaaS provider will understand the technical aspects of the software it is delivering, but it may not have sufficient business process knowledge, in which case the customer will need to define the business processes and make configuration decisions.

ANOTHER LOOK

Plex Systems Cloud Community

Founded in 1995, Plex Systems developed out of a project initiated at an automotive supplier. The company has expanded its customer base and develops software for a variety of manufacturing companies. In particular, Plex provides a complete, cloud-based ERP solution for manufacturing companies. Plex moved to cloud computing in 2000 and developed its cloud strategy using the multi-tenant model versus a hosted environment. In a hosted environment, a separate system is created and managed for each customer, while in a multi-tenant model, there is only one system and each customer is a tenant in the system.

Plex chose this approach because it wanted to leverage customer enhancements. Because there is only one copy of the Plex system, whenever an improvement is made to it, the update is available to all tenants. Plex makes sure enhancements are designed to add functionality that might be valuable to multiple customers, but customers are not required to adopt every update. Customers can choose whether or not to adopt a change through simple configuration settings.

While manufacturing environments are complex, Plex decided that users needed a simple interface design for the shop floor. The simple interface makes the software easy to use. In addition, the interface is configurable so individual users can organize icons and buttons and control them with user authorizations as they are provided with Plex's screen building tool. A sample Plex screen is shown in Figure 8-6.

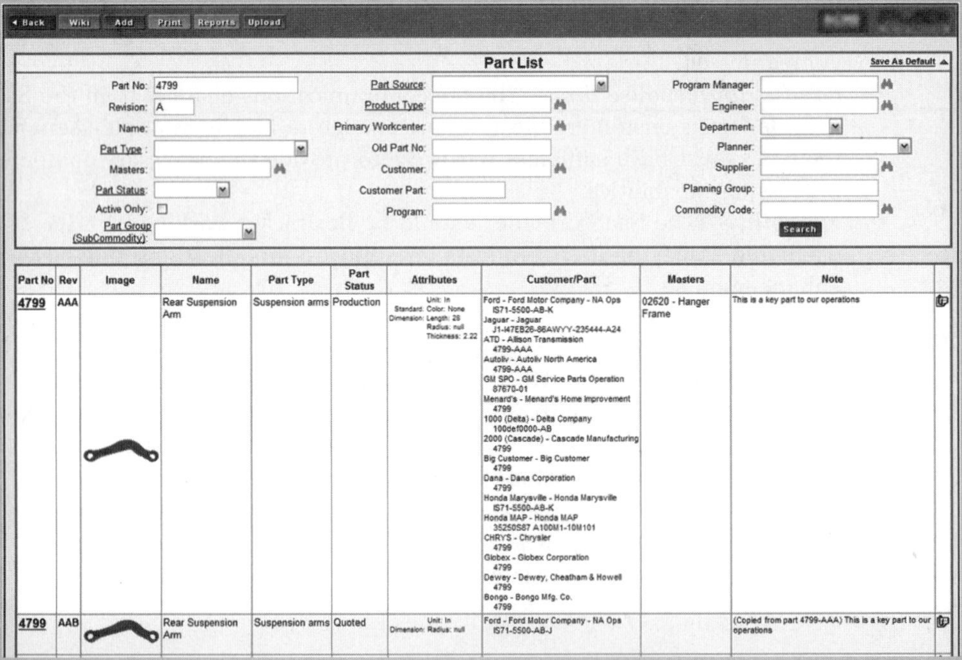

Source Line: Plex Systems.

FIGURE 8-6 Sample Plex screen

(continued)

232

Another unique feature of Plex's software is its pricing model. Many ERP companies price their software on a per-user basis. Plex saw a problem with this approach: it encouraged companies to limit the number of people who would interact with the software. Plex, however, wanted to encourage customers to use software. In addition, the company wanted to match its pricing to the real costs of transactions processed. In a seat license model, a customer may minimize users but have the same volume of transactions as a customer with many more users. Plex prices its software based on the size of the business, whether measured by company revenue or total number of employees. Plex adjusts the amount of the subscription on a yearly cycle. If a company suffers a downturn in business—and its revenue or number of employees is reduced— then its subscription is reduced. Of course, if the customer grows, so does its subscription.

Plex has observed an interesting phenomenon with its customers. At first, new customers are hesitant to use a cloud system—they are concerned about data integrity when all customers reside in a single system. But after a while, customers typically realize that other Plex customers actually form a community, and collaboration within the Plex community provides value. Rather than being a software company that is sales and marketing driven, Plex has become a company where users, and the user community, directly drive innovation, and all customers benefit.

Questions:

1. How will SaaS affect large ERP companies such as SAP and Oracle? Will their size and research capabilities allow SAP and Oracle to gain dominance of the SaaS marketplace, or will ERP systems be provided by a growing number of small companies, such as Plex, each providing specialized ERP packages specially tailored for specific industries?

2. Will Fortune 500 companies eventually leave SAP ERP for SaaS systems? Will they adopt SaaS products from smaller providers? Will they use Business ByDesign? Or will companies like SAP and Oracle migrate their current large ERP packages to an SaaS environment?

Exercise 8.2

Returning to the example company, Fitter, assume that under its newly appointed CIO, Fitter has made the decision to acquire an ERP system. Now the CIO must decide how to implement the system. After talking with various ERP software vendors, the CIO has determined that Fitter has two options for implementing ERP software:

1. Buy a license for the ERP software, purchase the hardware required to run it, and hire and train system administrators.
2. Run Fitter's ERP system over the Web through an SaaS provider, which would deliver ERP services for a monthly fee.

Both types of implementations have advantages and disadvantages, as you have already seen. For the first part of this exercise, you must write a memo to the CIO enumerating the pros and cons of each method. Use a table similar to the one shown in Figure 8-7 to organize your thoughts.

Advantages of purchasing software and computers for ERP	Advantages of using SaaS to run ERP

Source Line: Course Technology/Cengage Learning.

FIGURE 8-7   Arguments for purchasing ERP system and software versus using SaaS

After reviewing your memo, the CIO has asked you to provide some financial data to help him make a decision. He would like you to prepare a spreadsheet that analyzes the financial impact of both scenarios. You need to compare the monthly cost of using the SaaS provider with the total cost of purchasing an ERP system that would run on Fitter's servers. Weigh the pros and cons of each method, and then make a recommendation, which the CIO will present to the chief financial officer of Fitter. As you work through these calculations, keep in mind that Fitter's net income is $3.4 million (you can find more details in Chapter 5). The following sections provide you the financial details you should take into consideration.

Option 1: Buying Computers and Software Rights for an ERP System

To set up its own ERP system, Fitter must buy the following:

- *Database server*—The server would cost $70,000.
- *Application server*—Fitter needs a server to run the ERP application, which would cost about $40,000.
- *PCs*—Some of Fitter's existing PCs could be loaded with the ERP software's GUI and be used to access the system. Because more Fitter employees will be connected to the new system, however, Fitter will need 10 additional computers. Total cost for the PCs would be $15,000.
- *Computer maintenance*—Fitter needs to make sure all its PCs and servers run properly. To do this, Fitter would purchase a maintenance contract to cover all hardware. This contract would cost about $1,000 a month, or $12,000 yearly, and is in addition to any costs Fitter currently incurs to maintain its existing hardware.
- *Licensing rights*—Licensing rights to the ERP software for all users for five years would cost $500,000. The CIO does not know whether further outlays will be required after the fifth year, and therefore is limiting the analysis to the years 2013 through 2017.
- *Installation*—The ERP vendor will help install the system, but Fitter also needs to hire consultants for the six-month implementation. At $3,000 per day, the cost is estimated at $486,000.
- *User training*—Included with the purchase of the rights to the ERP software is training at a local training center for key personnel involved in the ERP implementation project. Fitter wants further training, however, for Fitter-specific business practices. The additional training will cost $2,000 per day

for two weeks. This includes a training consultant to run classes at Fitter headquarters. With travel and lodging, the total cost is $23,000.

- *Ongoing consulting*—Once the system is up and running, Fitter will need to pay for consultants to help maintain the system. Fitter believes that having consultants come in once a month should be sufficient for handling ongoing issues such as bug resolution and minor updates to the system. The consulting fees are estimated to be $3,000 per day, with a total annual cost of $36,000.
- *Network and database administrator*—Fitter would need a full-time network and database administrator to run the system. Salary, including benefits, for a skilled person is $200,000 per year.

Option 2: Using an SaaS Provider to Deliver ERP Software

The other option available to Fitter is to use an SaaS provider to deliver ERP software. Estimated costs for this option are as follows:

- *PCs*—Fitter estimates that it would still need to purchase 10 new PCs with this option because many more users will now be accessing the computer system. Each PC costs $1,500, for a total of $15,000.
- *Computer maintenance*—The maintenance contract on the additional PCs would be $600 per month, or $7,200 yearly. Because Fitter would not need to purchase additional servers, the maintenance costs are less with this option.
- *Software through the SaaS provider*—The monthly cost of delivering ERP software to Fitter over the Web is $33,333—or $400,000 yearly.
- *User training*—Training of Fitter employees is provided by the SaaS provider as part of the monthly software fee.

Calculate the NPV and Make a Recommendation

In the next part of this exercise, you will set up a spreadsheet to total all the costs of each option. In each scenario, you must deal with the net present value (NPV) of money.

NPV is a way to figure out whether an investment is profitable, or in this case, to compare outlay of funds from one method to another. NPV addresses the time value of money—that is, being paid one dollar today is worth more than being paid one dollar a year from now. Because of the time value of money, if a firm is borrowing the money for an investment, they have to pay interest on that money. If they have cash on hand to finance the investment, the company still needs to consider that the cash could be invested in other ways that would pay the firm interest. When analyzing an investment, a firm must consider the time value of money, and performing a NPV calculation is a common way to do that by adjusting future earning or expenses based on an assumed interest rate. When calculating two different investment options, the NPV calculation allows different future expenses or earnings to be calculated as an equivalent amount in the present time. For example, earning $10,000 dollars one year from now might be equivalent to having $9,345.79 today. NPV can be calculated over a number of years; in our case, we need a five-year outlay of funds for the ERP project. In an Excel spreadsheet, the syntax of the NPV calculation is =*NPV (hurdle rate percentage, range of values)*. The values in the range can be positive or negative numbers. In our case, they are all outflows, but we can work with them as positive numbers. The hurdle rate is the rate of discount over the period, and it is the minimum acceptable rate of return on a project that a company will accept. For this example, assume a hurdle rate of 20 percent.

Your spreadsheet should begin like the one shown in Figure 8-8 (with years continuing through 2017).

ERP Purchasing Options							
Option 1 - Buying computers and software outright							
Items			2013	2014	2015	2016	2017
Database server			70000				
Application server			40000				
10 PCs			15000				
Software			500000				
Consultants - initial (6 months)			486000				
Training (2 weeks)			23000				
Consultants - maintenance (1 day per month)				36000	36000	36000	36000
PC maintenance				12000	12000	12000	12000
Network administrator			200000	200000	200000	200000	200000
Total			1334000	248000	248000	248000	248000
NPV			$1,646,671.81				
Option 2 - Using SaaS							
PCs			15000				
PC maintenance				7200	7200	7200	7200
ASP cost			400000	400000	400000	400000	400000
Total			415000	407200	407200	407200	407200
NPV			$1,224,277.26				
Hurdle rate			20%				

Source Line: Course Technology/Cengage Learning.

FIGURE 8-8   Cost comparisons: buying versus SaaS

To complete this part of the exercise, perform the steps that follow:

1. Calculate the cost of the two methods of implementing an ERP system for five years. Use the spreadsheet illustrated in Figure 8-8 as your guide. Use the NPV calculations to reference the hurdle rate shown at the bottom of the spreadsheet. Vary the hurdle rate, following the directions your instructor provides.

2. Consider using different hurdle rates for each option. Why might varying hurdle rates be applicable for this decision?

3. Write a memo, with your spreadsheet attached, to the CIO. Answer this question: Which method should Fitter choose, and why? Weigh the pros and cons of each method, and make a recommendation, which the CIO will present to the chief financial officer of Fitter. Be sure to consider both the qualitative aspects and the quantitative aspects of the choice.

Your instructor might assign the following additional exercises:

1. Use the Internet or library resources to research the use of SaaS providers. Find cases of companies that have been successful in using an ERP system through an SaaS provider. Describe one success story in a report to your instructor.

2. Think about whether you would give different advice to a smaller company than you would to a medium-sized company or to a large company, regarding the use of SaaS providers. Why?

Chapter Summary

- Technologies such as radio frequency identification (RFID) and smartphones are fueling explosive growth in the amount of data available for businesses to process. This data can provide real business value, but the challenge is how to manage and evaluate this data to gain business knowledge.

- Business intelligence (BI) tools are growing in sophistication and power. Technologies such as in-memory computing will provide greater speed and flexibility to BI users and will increase the number of employees in a company that can make use of BI.

- Mobile computing technology is increasing the use of ERP and BI data by making it more convenient to access data when and where it is needed.

- Cloud computing is the delivery of a software product to a user via the Internet. The user typically accesses the cloud product through a Web browser or a lightweight (meaning small and simple) application for a computer or mobile device.

- Web services and service-oriented architecture offer a combination of software tools that enables various programs within an organization to communicate with other applications.

- SAP's Web services platform is NetWeaver, which is a collection of components that support business transactions over the Internet by providing seamless connectivity of diverse applications through the Internet. NetWeaver also includes modules such as Enterprise Portal, Mobile Infrastructure, Business Intelligence, Master Data Management, and Exchange Infrastructure.

- Software as a service (SaaS) is a software delivery model in which a software product is hosted by a company—such as SAP—on its servers and is accessed by customers via a Web browser. The SaaS model allows companies to use ERP without a large initial investment, making ERP systems available to smaller companies. SaaS solutions allow for more rapid improvements in the software through user communities. There are risks associated with using an SaaS provider, however, and the decision to buy or lease must be weighed carefully.

Key Terms

business intelligence (BI)

cloud computing

enterprise information management

multidimensional data cubes

radio frequency identification (RFID)

service-oriented architecture (SOA)

software as a service (SaaS)

Web services

Exercises

1. Assume you have just graduated and you have landed a job at Fitter as its new sales manager. The person you replaced has just retired after 35 years in the job. You are eager to put to use some of the skills you learned at school, especially the work you did on mobile computing and SaaS. Write a memo to your new boss, the vice president of Marketing and Sales, on the virtues of SaaS and mobile computing, and explain why Fitter

should develop a plan to adopt a mobile strategy for managing sales using SaaS through mobile devices.

2. Do some research on the Internet to find current opinions on the pros and cons of using SaaS. Try to find some examples of success and failure stories. Under what circumstances do you think using an SaaS makes sense?

3. List the advantages of using mobile devices from the point of view of a Fitter salesperson. Next, list the challenges of developing and supporting those mobile applications from the point of view of Fitter's IT staff. Assume the company is hosting its own ERP system. What should the company's strategy be? Why?

4. In-memory computing technology is changing the face of BI. Create a PowerPoint presentation that brings the Fitter crew up to speed on this emerging technology.

5. Research the current status of mobile applications for phones and tablets in the corporate world. Write a two-page summary of how these applications are being used, and cite specific examples. Be sure to include your references with the summary.

6. Using the library or Internet sources, write an update on the status of FDA legislation surrounding RFID packaging on drugs. Are there any privacy concerns?

For Further Study and Research

Barrett, Larry. "Who Will Win the SAP, Oracle Battle?" *Internetnews.com*. August 23, 2007. www.Internetnews.com/ent-news/article.php/3695956.

Barth, David. "The Bright Side of Sitting in Traffic: Crowdsourcing Road Congestion Data." August 25, 2009. http://googlemobile.blogspot.com/2009/08.

Bustilo, Miguel. "Wal-Mart Radio Tags to Track Clothing." *Wall Street Journal*. July 23, 2010. http://online.wsj.com/article/SB10001424052748704421304575383213061198090.html.

Eddy, Nathan. "BI, Performance Management Software Market Surpassed $12B." *eWeek.com*. April 3, 2012. www.eweek.com/c/a/IT-Management/Business-Intelligence-Performance-Management-Software-Market-Surpassed-12-Billion-in-2011.

Fox, Jason. "Bringing Order to the Chaos in Mobility." *SAP Insider*, 12, no. 4 (Oct/Nov/Dec 2011): pp. 22–24.

Giles, Martin. "Beyond the PC." *The Economist*. October 8, 2011. www.economist.com/node/21531109.

Hamblen, Matt. "iPads, Android Tablets and Smartphones Join the Military." *Computerworld*. March 16, 2011. www.computerworld.com/s/article/9214624/iPads_Android_tablets_and_smartphones_join_the_military.

Henschen, Doug. "Next-Gen BI Is Here." *InformationWeek*. August 31, 2009. pp. 21–28.

Horwitt, Elisabeth. "How to Craft a Mobile-Application Strategy." *CIO*. September 28, 2011. www.cio.com/article/690621/How_to_Craft_a_Mobile_Application_Strategy.

Kanaracus, Chris. "Forrester: As SaaS Matures, Buyers Face New Considerations." *CIO*. December 2, 2011. www.cio.com.au/article/409181/forrester_saas_matures_buyers_face_new_considerations.

Kutik, Bill. "The Hottest Trends in HR Technology." *Human Resource Executive Online*. September 16, 2011. www.hreonline.com/HRE/story.jsp?storyId=533341158.

Logan, Rebecca. "Making RFID Fashionable." July 2008. www.stores.org/stores-magazine-july-2008/making-rfid-fashionable.

Lohr, Steve. "Big Data, Speed and the Future of Computing." *New York Times*. October 31, 2011. http://bits.blogs.nytimes.com/2011/10/31/big-data-speed-and-the-future-of-computing.

McWilliams, Gary. "Wal-Mart's Radio-Tracked Inventory Hits Static." *Wall Street Journal*. February 15, 2007. http://online.wsj.com/ad/upsarticle-2-4-1.html.

Parades, Christian. "Understanding Disk I/O—When Should you be Worried?" *Scout* (blog). February 10, 2011. http://blog.scoutapp.com/articles/2011/02/10.

Roberti, Mark. "RFID Delivers Unexpected Benefits at American Apparel." *RFID Journal*. October 5, 2011. www.rfidjournal.com/article/view/8843.

SAP AG. "SAP Customer Testimonials." www.sap.com/solutions/products/sap-bydesign/customer-testimonials/index.epx.

SAP AG. "SAP Corporate History." www.sap.com/corporate-en/our-company/history.epx.

SAP AG. "SAP Solution Brief: Exchange Infrastructure." www.sap.com/netherlands/platform/netweaver/pdf/brochures/BWP_SB_ExchangeInfrastructure.pdf. 2004.

SAP AG. "SAP Solution Brief: SAP Master Data Management." www.sap.com/search/index.epx?q1=Solution%20Brief%3A%20SAP%20Master%20Data%20Management.

SAP AG. "SAP Solutions for Auto-ID and Item Serialization." www.sap.com/solutions/auto-id/index.epx.

Sauers, Jenna. "The End of an Era: American Apparel Finally Anti-Theft Tags Its Clothes." February 20, 2012. http://jezebel.com/5886604/the-end-of-an-era-american-apparel-finally-anti+theft-tags-its-clothes.

SCDigest. "Looking Back at the Wal-Mart RFID Time Line." February 23, 2009. www.scdigest.com/assets/On_Target/09-02-23-1.php.

SCDigest. "RFID News: Will WalMart Get RFID Right This Time?" July 28, 2010. www.scdigest.com/assets/On_Target/10-07-28-1.php?cid=3609.

Sullivan, Laurie. "Fast Track to Success." *InformationWeek*. June 21, 2004. www.informationweek.com/news/22100642.

Sullivan, Laurie. "IBM Takes RFID Services to Midsize Companies." *InformationWeek*. September 20, 2004.

Sullivan, Laurie. "Wal-Mart's Way." *InformationWeek*. September 27, 2004. www.informationweek.com/news/47902662.

Surowiecki, James. "EZ Does It." *New Yorker*. September 8, 2003. www.newyorker.com/archive/2003/09/08/030908ta_talk_surowiecki.

Swabey, Pete. "Most SOA Projects Bring No ROI." *Information Age*. September 6, 2007. www.information-age.com/channels/development-and-integration/news/270631/most-soa-projects-bring-no-roi.thtml.

Swabey, Pete. "Structural Hazard." *Information Age*. March 19, 2007. www.information-age.com/channels/soa-and-development/features/273511/structural-hazard.thtml.

Swedburg, Claire. "Spectrum Health's Meijer Heart Center Tracks Stents." *RFID Journal*. March 29, 2010. www.rfidjournal.com/article/view/7495.

Textron. "Press Release: U.S. Army to Test, Evaluate SoldierEyes, FASTCOM Systems." April 1, 2011. *BusinessWire*. www.businesswire.com/news/home/20110330005113/en/U.S.-Army-Test-Evaluate-SoldierEyes-FASTCOM-Systems.

VoiceObjects. "Press Release: VoiceObjects Technology to be Integrated in SAP NetWeaver Phone Application Server Technology to Enable Voice-Driven Telephone Access to SAP Applications." March 13, 2007. www.voiceobjects.com/en/news/2007/031307.html.

Wailgum, Thomas. "How Wal-Mart Lost Its Technology Edge." *CIO*. October 4, 2007. www.cio.com/article/143451/How_Wal_Mart_Lost_Its_Technology_Edge.

Weier, Mary Hayes. "Wal-Mart Rethinks RFID." *InformationWeek*. March 26, 2007. www.informationweek.com/news/198700170.

Woods, Dan, and Jeffrey Word. *SAP NetWeaver for Dummies*. Indianapolis: John Wiley & Sons, Inc. 2004.

Accounting and Finance (A/F) A functional area of business that is responsible for recording data about transactions, including sales, raw material purchases, payroll, and receipt of cash from customers.

accounts payable Accounting information that records the amount the company owes for goods it has received from a supplier.

accounts receivable Accounting information that records the amount a customer owes for goods received by the customer.

activity-based costing An advanced form of inventory cost accounting in which overhead costs are assigned to products based on the manufacturing activities that gave rise to the costs.

Advanced Business Application Programming (ABAP) The SAP ERP internal programming language.

archive Permanently stored data.

Asset Management (AM) module A module in SAP ERP that helps a company manage fixed-asset purchases (plant and machinery) and related depreciation.

audit trail A linked set of document numbers related to an order.

balance sheet A summary of a company's account balances includes cash held, amounts owed to the company by customers, the cost of inventory on hand, fixed assets such as buildings, amounts owed to vendors, amounts owed to creditors, and amounts the owners have invested in the company.

best practice The best, most efficient way of handling a certain business process.

bill of material (BOM) The "recipe" listing the materials (including quantities) needed to make a product.

business function A business activity within a functional area of operation.

business intelligence (BI), also referred to as *business analytics*, is a term used to describe a range of different applications and technologies used to extract and analyze large amounts of data to aid in decision making.

business process A collection of activities that takes one or more kinds of input and creates an output that is of value to a customer. Creating the output might involve activities from different functional areas.

capacity The amount of an item that can be produced.

cash-to-cash cycle time The time that elapses from when suppliers are paid for raw materials to cash is collected from the customer (used in supply-chain management metrics).

client-server architecture A central computer–local computer arrangement in which data stored in a central computer (a server) are downloaded to a local PC (a client of the server) where data are processed. Historically, client-server architecture replaced many companies' mainframe-based architecture.

cloud computing The delivery of a software product to a user via the Internet.

condition technique An SAP control mechanism that accommodates the various ways that companies offer price discounts.

Controlling (CO) module A module in SAP ERP that is used for internal management purposes. The software assigns a company's manufacturing costs to products and to cost centers, facilitating cost analysis.

cost variance The difference between actual costs and standard costs.

currency translation Converting financial-statement account balances expressed in one currency into balances expressed in another currency.

customer master data Permanent data about each of a company's customers; customer master data is stored in central database tables in SAP ERP. Master data are used by many SAP ERP modules.

customer relationship management (CRM) software A collection of software tools that use data from a company's ERP system to enhance the company's relationships with its customers. CRM software allows for the following activities: segmenting customers, one-to-one marketing, sales-force automation (SFA), sales-campaign management, marketing encyclopedias, and call-center automation.

data mining The statistical and logical analysis of large sets of transaction data, looking for patterns that can aid decision making and improve customer sales and customer service. Data mining is often done with data in a data warehouse.

data warehouse A database, separate from a company's operational database, that contains subsets of data from the company's ERP system. Users analyze and manipulate data in the warehouse. Thus, they do not interfere with the workings of the database that is used to record the company's transactions.

database management system (DBMS) The technology that stores database records in an organized fashion and allows for the easy retrieval of the data.

delivery In SAP, release of the documents that a warehouse uses to pick, pack, and ship orders.

deployment flowcharting (swimlane flowcharting) A method of flowcharting in which team members are depicted across the top, with each process step aligned vertically under the employee or team working on it.

Development (DEV) system In an SAP system landscape, one of three separate SAP systems; DEV is used to develop configuration settings for the system using ABAP code.

direct costs Costs of a finished product, such as labor or material costs, that can be estimated fairly accurately.

document flow The linked set of document numbers related to an order; an audit trail.

drill down In SAP, to view the details behind a summary of information by double-clicking an on-screen item.

dynamic process modeling A method of evaluating process changes before they are implemented by putting into motion a basic process flowchart using computer simulation techniques to facilitate the evaluation of proposed process changes.

electronic data interchange (EDI) A computer-to-computer transfer of standard business documents that allows companies to handle the purchasing process electronically, avoiding the cost and delays resulting from paper-based systems.

enterprise information management The business and technology functions that manage information as a corporate asset.

Enterprise Resource Planning (ERP) A system that helps a company manage business processes such as marketing, production, purchasing, and accounting in an integrated way. ERP does this by recording all transactions in a common database that is used by information systems throughout the company and by providing shared management-reporting tools.

error log A record of discrepancies that occur during a payroll run.

event process chain (EPC) A graphic model of a business process that uses only two symbols: events and functions.

Extensible Business Reporting Language (XBRL) A standards-based language for the electronic communication of business and financial data.

Extensible Markup Language (XML) An Internet programming language that uses tags that define the data contained within them.

financial accounting Accounting processes that deal with documenting the transactions of a company that have an impact on the financial state of the organization. The documented transactions form the basis for financial statements for external parties and agencies.

Financial Accounting (FI) module A module in SAP ERP that records transactions in the general ledger accounts and generates financial statements for external reporting purposes.

flowchart Any graphical representation of the movement or flow of concrete or abstract items.

functional areas of operation A broad categorization of business activities, including marketing, sales, production, and accounting.

gap analysis An assessment of the disparities between an organization's current situation and its long-term goals.

general ledger The primary accounting record of a business.

hierarchical modeling The ability to flexibly describe a business process in greater or less detail depending on the task at hand.

human capital management (HCM) Another term for human resources that describes the tasks associated with managing a company's workforce.

Human Resources (HR) A functional area of business that manages recruiting, training, evaluating, and compensating employees.

Human Resources (HR) module A module in SAP ERP that facilitates employee recruiting, hiring, training, and payroll and benefits processing.

IFRS *See* International Financial Reporting Standards.

income statement A financial statement that shows a company's revenue and expenses and profit or loss for a period of time; also called a profit and loss (P&L) statement.

indirect costs Overhead cost items that are difficult to associate with a specific product.

information system (IS) The people, procedures, software, and computers that store, organize, and deliver information.

initial fill rate The percentage of an order that the supplier provided in the first shipment.

initial order lead time The time needed for the supplier to fill an order (used in supply-chain management metrics).

integrated information system An information system that allows sharing of common data throughout an organization. ERP systems are integrated systems because all operational data are located in a central database, where they can be accessed by users throughout an organization.

intercompany transaction A transaction that occurs between a company and one of its subsidiaries.

International Financial Reporting Standards (IFRS) A set of international accounting standards.

job In SAP, a general classification of tasks that are routinely performed together.

lead time The cumulative time required for a supplier to receive and process an order, take the material out of stock, package it, load it on a truck, and deliver it to the manufacturer.

legacy system An older and often outdated information system.

lot sizing The process for determining purchase and production order quantities.

managerial accounting Accounting processes that deal with determining the costs and profitability of a company's activities.

Marketing and Sales (M/S) The functional area of business that is responsible for developing products, determining pricing, promoting products to customers, taking customers' orders, and creating sales forecasts.

master production schedule (MPS) The production plan for finished goods.

Materials Management (MM) A module in SAP ERP that manages the acquisition of raw materials from suppliers (purchasing) and the subsequent handling and storage of raw materials, work in process, and finished goods.

material master data Relatively permanent data about materials that are stored in central database tables in SAP ERP. These data are used by SD, MM, and other SAP ERP modules.

material requirements planning (MRP) A production-scheduling methodology that determines the timing and quantity of production and purchase-order releases to meet a master production schedule. This process uses the bill of material, lot-size data, and material lead times.

metrics Measurements of performance; discussed in this book in relation to the effects of supply-chain management efforts.

modules Individual programs that can be purchased, installed, and run separately, but that all extract data from the common database.

MRP record The standard way of showing the materials requirements planning (MRP) process on paper.

multidimensional data cubes The structure of data in a data warehouse that allows for relationships in the data to be analyzed quickly.

on-demand CRM CRM software and computer equipment that resides with the CRM provider rather being installed in-house.

on-time performance A measure of how often a supplier meets agreed-upon delivery dates (used in supply-chain management metrics).

open architecture Software that allows integration with third-party software. SAP ERP is an example of open-architecture software. The term can also be applied to hardware products.

organizational change management (OCM) The management of the human behavior aspects of organizational change.

organizational structure In SAP, the method used to define the relationships between organizational groups such as companies, plants, storage locations, sales divisions, and distribution channels.

overhead A company's cost of operations, such as the costs for factory utilities, general factory labor, factory management, storage, insurance, and other manufacturing-related activities. Overhead is often called an indirect cost of production.

payroll run The process of determining each employee's pay.

person In SAP, the unique individual who holds a position.

Plant Maintenance (PM) module A module in SAP ERP that allows planning for preventive maintenance of plant machinery and managing maintenance resources, so equipment breakdowns are minimized.

position In SAP, an individual employee assignment in an organization. Tasks can be assigned directly to the position, or by assigning jobs to the position.

process boundary In process mapping, a definition of those activities to be included in the process and what is considered part of the environment.

process mapping A type of flowcharting that pictorially represents the activities occurring within an existing business process.

process model Any abstract representation of a process.

product cost variant The procedure for developing a product cost analysis; many variants can be created for different planning requirements.

Production Planning (PP) module A module in SAP ERP that maintains production information; production is planned and scheduled, and actual production activities are recorded.

Production (PROD) system In an SAP system landscape, one of three separate SAP systems; the actual system that the company uses to run its business processes.

profit and loss (P&L) statement *See* income statement.

Project System (PS) module A module in SAP ERP that allows for the planning and control of new R&D, construction, and marketing projects. This module allows for costs to be collected against a project budget, and it can be used to manage the implementation of ERP itself.

qualification A skill or ability associated with a specific employee.

Quality Assurance (QAS) system In an SAP system landscape, one of three separate SAP systems; the system where testing is done.

Quality Management (QM) module A module in SAP ERP that helps companies plan and record quality-control activities, such as product inspections and material certifications.

R/3 The first integrated information system released by German software vendor SAP in 1992; now called SAP ERP. This ERP system contains the following main modules, which can be implemented as a group or selectively: Sales and Distribution (SD), Materials Management (MM), Production Planning (PP), Quality Management (QM), Plant Maintenance (PM), Human Resources (HR), Financial Accounting (FI), Controlling (CO), Asset Management (AM), Project System (PS), and Workflow (WF).

radio frequency identification (RFID) A tracking technology that uses a small package device, or tag, that includes a microprocessor and antenna that can be attached to products. The location of an item with an RFID tag can be determined using an RFID reader, which emits radio waves and receives signals back from the tag.

raw data Data on sales, manufacturing, and other operations that have not been analyzed or manipulated for presentation.

remuneration element Part of an employee's pay, such as the base pay, bonuses, gratuities, overtime, sick pay, and vacation allowances the employee has earned during the pay period.

repetitive manufacturing A manufacturing environment in which production lines are switched from one product to another similar product.

requirement A skill or ability associated with a position.

return on investment (ROI) An assessment of a project's value calculated by dividing the value of the project's benefits by the project's cost.

RFID *See* radio frequency identification.

rough-cut planning A common term in manufacturing for aggregate planning.

sales forecast An estimate of future product demand, which is the amount of a product customers will want to buy.

Sales and Distribution (SD) module A module in SAP ERP that records sales orders and scheduled deliveries.

safety stock Extra raw material and packaging kept available to help avoid stockouts.

SAP ERP ERP software produced by SAP; previous versions were known as R/3 and mySAP ERP.

scalability A characteristic of an information system that indicates the system's capacity can be extended by adding servers to the network, rather than replacing the entire system. Scalability is a characteristic of client-server networks, but usually not of mainframe-based systems.

scope creep The unplanned expansion of a project's goals and objectives, causing the project to go over time and over budget, as well as increasing the risk of an unsuccessful implementation.

service-oriented architecture (SOA) Software that enables systems to exchange data without complicated software links, also called Web services.

short list The top candidates for a position, each of whom will be interviewed.

silo An unintegrated information system configuration in which individual business functional areas each have their own hardware, software, and methods of processing data and information.

software as a service (SaaS) A software delivery model in which a software product is hosted by a company on its servers and is accessed by customers via a Web browser.

software modules *See* modules.

standard costs The expected cost of manufacturing a product during a particular period. Standard costs for a product are established by (1) studying the historical cost patterns (direct and indirect) in a company and (2) taking into account the effects of current manufacturing changes.

statutory and voluntary deduction A paycheck withholding, such as taxes (federal, state, local, Social Security, and Medicare), company loans, and benefit contributions.

stockout A manufacturing shortfall that occurs when raw materials or packaging run out.

succession planning Outlining the strategy for replacing key employees when they leave the company.

supply chain All of the activities that occur between the growing or mining of raw materials and the appearance of finished products on the store shelf.

Supply Chain Management (SCM) A functional area that includes developing production plans, ordering and receiving raw materials, manufacturing products, maintaining facilities, and shipping products.

swimlane flowcharting *See* deployment flowcharting.

task In SAP, an assigned responsibility related to a specific job.

tolerance group A range that defines limits on the transactions that an employee can process.

transport directory In an SAP system landscape, a special data file location on the DEV server that stores changes to the system landscape.

U.S. GAAP (Generally Accepted Accounting Principles) The current standard for reporting financial statements in the United States.

value added An increase in a product's or service's value, from a customer's perspective.

value analysis An analysis of each activity in a process to determine the value the activity adds to the product or service.

vertical integration The extent to which a company produces the components and assemblies used in the products it manufactures.

Web services A combination of software tools that enables various programs within an organization to communicate with other applications.

Workflow (WF) module A module in SAP ERP that can be used to automate any of the activities in SAP ERP. It can perform task-flow analysis and then prompt employees (by e-mail) if they need to take action.

workflow tasks Within the SAP ERP Workflow module, email messages that can include basic information, notes, and documents, as well as direct links to business transactions.

workflow tools Software programs that automate the execution of a business process.

XBRL *See* Extensible Business Reporting Language.

XML *See* Extensible Markup Language.

INDEX